Political Vocabularies

RHETORIC AND PUBLIC AFFAIRS SERIES

- *Eisenhower's War of Words: Rhetoric and Leadership*, Martin J. Medhurst, editor
- *The Nuclear Freeze Campaign: Rhetoric and Foreign Policy in the Telepolitical Age*, J. Michael Hogan
- *Mansfield and Vietnam: A Study in Rhetorical Adaptation*, Gregory A. Olson
- *Truman and the Hiroshima Cult*, Robert P. Newman
- *Post-Realism: The Rhetorical Turn in International Relations*, Francis A. Beer and Robert Hariman, editors
- *Rhetoric and Political Culture in Nineteenth-Century America*, Thomas W. Benson, editor
- *Frederick Douglass: Freedom's Voice, 1818–1845*, Gregory P. Lampe
- *Angelina Grimké: Rhetoric, Identity, and the Radical Imagination*, Stephen Howard Browne
- *Strategic Deception: Rhetoric, Science, and Politics in Missile Defense Advocacy*, Gordon R. Mitchell
- *Rostow, Kennedy, and the Rhetoric of Foreign Aid*, Kimber Charles Pearce
- *Visions of Poverty: Welfare Policy and Political Imagination*, Robert Asen
- *General Eisenhower: Ideology and Discourse*, Ira Chernus
- *The Reconstruction Desegregation Debate: The Politics of Equality and the Rhetoric of Place, 1870–1875*, Kirt H. Wilson
- *Shared Land/Conflicting Identity: Trajectories of Israeli and Palestinian Symbol Use*, Robert C. Rowland and David A. Frank
- *Darwinism, Design, and Public Education*, John Angus Campbell and Stephen C. Meyer, editors
- *Religious Expression and the American Constitution*, Franklyn S. Haiman
- *Christianity and the Mass Media in America: Toward a Democratic Accommodation*, Quentin J. Schultze
- *Bending Spines: The Propagandas of Nazi Germany and the German Democratic Republic*, Randall L. Bytwerk
- *Malcolm X: Inventing Radical Judgment*, Robert E. Terrill
- *Metaphorical World Politics*, Francis A. Beer and Christ'l De Landtsheer, editors
- *The Lyceum and Public Culture in the Nineteenth-Century United States*, Angela G. Ray
- *The Political Style of Conspiracy: Chase, Sumner, and Lincoln*, Michael William Pfau
- *The Character of Justice: Rhetoric, Law, and Politics in the Supreme Court Confirmation Process*, Trevor Parry-Giles
- *Rhetorical Vectors of Memory in National and International Holocaust Trials*, Marouf A. Hasian Jr.
- *Judging the Supreme Court: Constructions of Motives in* Bush *v.* Gore, Clarke Rountree
- *Everyday Subversion: From Joking to Revolting in the German Democratic Republic*, Kerry Kathleen Riley
- *In the Wake of Violence: Image and Social Reform*, Cheryl R. Jorgensen-Earp
- *Rhetoric and Democracy: Pedagogical and Political Practices*, Todd F. McDorman and David M. Timmerman, editors
- *Invoking the Invisible Hand: Social Security and the Privatization Debates*, Robert Asen
- *With Faith in the Works of Words: The Beginnings of Reconciliation in South Africa, 1985–1995*, Erik Doxtader
- *Public Address and Moral Judgment: Critical Studies in Ethical Tensions*, Shawn J. Parry-Giles and Trevor Parry-Giles, editors
- *Executing Democracy: Capital Punishment and the Making of America, 1683–1807*, Stephen John Hartnett
- *Enemyship: Democracy and Counter-Revolution in the Early Republic*, Jeremy Engels
- *Spirits of the Cold War: Contesting Worldviews in the Classical Age of American Security Strategy*, Ned O'Gorman
- *Making the Case: Advocacy and Judgment in Public Argument*, Kathryn M. Olson, Michael William Pfau, Benjamin Ponder, and Kirt H. Wilson, editors
- *Executing Democracy: Capital Punishment and the Making of America, 1835–1843*, Stephen John Hartnett
- *William James and the Art of Popular Statement*, Paul Stob
- *On the Frontier of Science: An American Rhetoric of Exploration and Exploitation*, Leah Ceccarelli
- *The Good Neighbor: Franklin D. Roosevelt and the Rhetoric of American Power*, Mary E. Stuckey
- *Creating Conservatism: Postwar Words That Made an American Movement*, Michael J. Lee
- *Intertextuality and the 24-Hour News Cycle: A Day in the Rhetorical Life of Colin Powell's U.N. Address*, John Oddo
- *Superchurch: The Rhetoric and Politics of American Fundamentalism*, Jonathan J. Edwards
- *Rethinking Rhetorical Theory, Criticism, and Pedagogy: The Living Art of Michael C. Leff*, Antonio de Velasco, John Angus Campbell, and David Henry, editors
- *Imagining China: Rhetorics of Nationalism in an Age of Globalization*, Stephen J. Hartnett, Lisa B. Keränen, and Donovan S. Conley, editors
- *Political Vocabularies: FDR, the Clergy Letters, and the Elements of Political Argument*, Mary E. Stuckey
- *To Become an American: Immigrants and Americanization Campaigns of the Early Twentieth Century*, Leslie A. Hahner
- *The Rhetorical Invention of Diversity: Supreme Court Opinions, Public Argument, and Affirmative Action*, M. Kelly Carr

Political Vocabularies

FDR, the Clergy Letters, and the Elements of Political Argument

Mary E. Stuckey

Michigan State University Press • *East Lansing*

∞ The paper used in this publication meets the minimum requirements of ANSI/NISO Z39.48-1992 (R 1997) (Permanence of Paper).

Michigan State University Press
East Lansing, Michigan 48823-5245

Printed and bound in the United States of America.

27 26 25 24 23 22 21 20 19 18 1 2 3 4 5 6 7 8 9 10

LIBRARY OF CONGRESS CATALOGING-IN-PUBLICATION DATA
Names: Stuckey, Mary E., author.
Title: Political vocabularies : FDR, the clergy letters, and the elements of political argument / Mary E. Stuckey.
Description: East Lansing : Michigan State University Press, 2018. | Series: Rhetoric and public affairs series | Includes bibliographical references and index.
Identifiers: LCCN 2017004516| ISBN 9781611862652 (pbk. : alk. paper) | ISBN 9781609175481 (pdf) | ISBN 9781628953169 (epub) | ISBN 9781628963168 (kindle) Subjects: LCSH: Roosevelt, Franklin D. (Franklin Delano), 1882-1945—Correspondence. | Rhetoric—Political aspects—United States. | Clergy letters (1935) | Clergy—Political activity—United States—History—20th century. | New Deal, 1933–1939—Public opinion. | Political culture—United States—History—20th century. | United States—Politics and government—1933–1945.
Classification: LCC E806 .S85 2018 | DDC 973.917092—dc23 LC record available at https://lccn.loc.gov/2017004516

Book design by Charlie Sharp, Sharp Des!gns, East Lansing, Michigan
Cover design by Erin Kirk New

Michigan State University Press is a member of the Green Press Initiative and is committed to developing and encouraging ecologically responsible publishing practices. For more information about the Green Press Initiative and the use of recycled paper in book publishing, please visit *www.greenpressinitiative.org*.

Visit Michigan State University Press at *www.msupress.org*

This book is gratefully dedicated,
on behalf of all the researchers you make feel so very welcome,
to Sarah Malcolm and to the archival and educational staff
at the Franklin D. Roosevelt Presidential Library.

Contents

Acknowledgments

I am always grateful for the kind assistance and generous knowledge of archivists. This book would not exist without them. Sarah L. Malcolm drew my attention to the existence of the clergy letters, and it was her affection for them that led me back to the collection, which is one of the best data sets in the world. I am also grateful to Bob Clark, whose generosity, good humor, and kindness while he was at the library honored the Roosevelts and the library itself, and made it the perfect place to do research. The archival staff is no less amazing: Supervisory Archivist Kirsten Striget Carter, Virginia H. Lewick, Matthew C. Hansen, William Baehr, and of course, Sarah Malcolm are all kind, patient, and helpful. I'm also grateful for Jeffrey S. Urbin, the library's Education Specialist, for his help in taking my research into the classroom, and to Clifford J. Laube, who runs an amazing public education program.

This project started out, as projects tend to do, as something very different. I'm very grateful to those who helped me develop and refine my ideas: Joseph Rhodes and David Cheshier were especially helpful as the project evolved. I'm also in debt to Jim Jasinski, Tom Goodnight, Robin Rowland, and Debbie Hawhee for their wisdom and encouragement. Bryan Blankfield was kind enough to send along a helpful essay, and Kyle Jensen provided very helpful comments on myth. Kirt Wilson and David Zarefsky provided enormous help in improving the project. I'm also appreciative of the members of the 2015 RSA Institute Workshop on Political Campaign Communication, who helped me think through a number of the issues regarding the connections between regimes and rhetoric. Tim Barouch read chapters with sympathy for the project and a ruthless attention to its flaws. It is not his fault that some of those remain; he eliminated many more. Thanks also go to my advisees, who never fail to impress and inspire me: Zoë Hess-Carney, Matthew Klingbell, Phil Kostka, and John Russell. And while I will never actually admit defeat, conversations with Rob Mills and Stephen Heidt always make me smarter. My most special thanks go to Milene Ortega Riberio, who provided considerable help with the most thankless of tasks.

I took some lovely breaks while working on the project and am grateful to my companions on various adventures: Pamela and Tim Thompson, Pat Stuckey, Brandon Inabinet, Meredith Neville-Shepard and Ryan Neville-Shephard, Lisa Corrigan, and Leslie Harris. I was ever so happy to get to spend time with Jennifer Beese, Brave Heart Sanchez and Victoria Sanchez, Bill Balthrop and Carole Blair, Karla Stevenson Mastracchio, and Chuck and Linda McCarty. I'm no less grateful to David Cheshier, Sergio Gallo, Tonia Edwards, Rasha Ramzy, Holley Wilkin, and most especially to Beth Gylys for the smaller but no less important respites from writing and for their friendship. I am grateful to my family: Steve, Carolee, Amanda, Robert, Philip, Pam, Tim, and my mom. They not only always let me in, they always make me feel welcome, too.

The folks at MSU Press are great to work with, and I appreciate all they do: Julie Reaume, Anastasia Wraight, Kristine M. Blakeslee, and Annette Tanner. Last but never least I am unendingly grateful for the support and wisdom provided by Marty Medhurst. As an editor, he is unequalled; as an inspiration and model, he is greatly valued.

Author's Note

A note about the clergy letters: The letters are archived at the Franklin D. Roosevelt Presidential Library in Hyde Park, New York, collected as PPF 21. There are thirty-four boxes of letters, filed by state. They are cited throughout the book only by author, city and state, and date (when this information is all available, which is not always the case), because they may be shifted from one box or folder to another as archival needs dictate. I have reproduced the spelling and syntax of the originals largely without correction—I made occasional interventions into matters of spacing and capitalization. I believe that the full flavor of the letters can only be captured in the originals, however, and the letters themselves are a captivating collection, well worth your time.

Sample Letter to the Clergy

THE WHITE HOUSE
WASHINGTON
September 24, 1935

My Dear Rabbi.

As a clergyman you come into daily contact not only with your own parishioners but with people generally in your community. I am sure you have a sound understanding and knowledge of their problems.

The grave responsibilities of my office require that I have the service of unbiased and unselfish men throughout the nation. I am sure that no group is better qualified to advise and assist me than are the Churchmen.

I am very anxious that the new Social Security Legislation, providing for old age pensions, shall be carried out in keeping with the high purposes with which the law was enacted. It is also vitally important that the Works Program shall be administered to provide employment at useful work, and that our unemployed as well as the nation as a whole may derive the greatest possible benefits.

I shall deem it a favor if you will write me about conditions in your community. Tell me where you feel our government can better serve our people.

The improvement of the social, economic and spiritual condition of our people can be accomplished if we will all cooperate in a sincere and devoted effort.

I will appreciate your help and your advice. I am leaving on a short vacation but will be back in Washington in a few weeks, and I will be grateful if you will write to me.

Very Sincerely Yours,

[signed by President Franklin D. Roosevelt]

Introduction

American politics are generally quite stable—except when they are not. Political change in the United States, whether understood as marked by a critical election, a change in regime, or cultural changes in our shared "structures of feeling," brings with it corresponding changes in political coalitions that form around different sets of issue cleavages and initiate new kinds of political organization.[1] These changes also require new ways of understanding and articulating politics and our national identity and are structured by different sets of what I call political vocabularies. Those vocabularies are the subject of this book.

Scholars of national identity tend to focus on its consensual aspects, reading it through presidential and thus largely majoritarian texts.[2] In doing so, we are able to distinguish the broad parameters of our shared identity and map its changes over time, but this focus also neglects the ways in which that identity is always contested. There is a national imaginary of course—an ideological space strangers inhabit that facilitates common action[3]—but that space is never entirely acceded to by all citizens. At any given time, there are at least two competing versions of the national imaginary: the dominant one favored by and articulated through the majority party, and the one that opposes it, often articulated by members of the other party.[4] Because it is possible to locate these imaginaries in partisan discourse, that discourse also reveals the ways in which these imaginaries are themselves tied to political processes and institutions. That is to say that although political language orders reality, and while it does so in generally stable ways, political life is not static and neither are the political imaginaries created through rhetoric.

Political scientists understand both stability and change through the theories associated with partisan realignment, moments when the demographic composition, issue orientations, and administrative structures associated with the major parties alter.[5] This set of processes is profoundly rhetorical because these new partisan alignments are talked into being, new issues are delineated through argument, and new administrative structures must be justified and defended. This project, which focuses on one set of arguments during the New Deal realignment, aims to understand both that moment in time and, through it, the linguistic components of stable sets of political debate, which I call political vocabularies. Political vocabularies are thus rhetorical markers of what might be understood as a political paradigm shift, acting on our civic life in ways that evoke Thomas Kuhn's notions of scientific paradigms.[6] As the parameters of political understanding shift, so do the ways we talk and act in common. The elements of political vocabularies eventually coalesce reasonably coherently, as they are used to order political imaginaries. But as one regime fails and another begins to form, the elements are more or less free-floating; political life is temporarily chaotic, and our shared political language reflects that confusion.

Americans generally share strong commitments to a set of unifying values—freedom, equality, justice—but the interpretation of those values varies across time and is valenced at every point in time by the differing interests of the political parties. So while there is a broadly accepted narrative of the national political imaginary that attaches citizens to the nation as a whole, there are also smaller iterations of that imaginary, attaching citizens to regions, to ideologies, and to political parties. I call these sets of smaller iterations political vocabularies. In completing this investigation, I rely on letters the U.S. clergy wrote to Franklin D. Roosevelt in 1935.[7] I use this set of texts from a group of nonparty elites because I am interested not just in the completed, stable articulations of these vocabularies, but also in the ways that they form and circulate among the mass public. These letters represent a middle range of discourse, capturing both elite rhetoric and the language of those with less power, for in these texts the clergy are writing for their congregations to the president and use both the language of their congregations and language that they believed would influence the chief executive. In doing so, they necessarily wielded the shifting political vocabularies of their time. The clergy were in a position to shift from one set of political vocabularies to another. They had expertise that allowed them to negotiate between the concerns of their local communities and the burgeoning administrative state; they were able to envision the national and the local; and they were intimately involved in all of the various dislocations—ideological, geographical, and political—that led to increased demands on the state. They are a key node in the circulation of the 1930s political vocabularies.

Political vocabularies are the indexical markers of our political imaginaries. They exist always in tension with one another, undergirding the stable political tensions of any given partisan epoch. They are both stable and porous, never fully complete, and always in motion even as they inscribe political stability. One of them will always be the dominant national narrative while others comprise imaginaries that counter or run parallel to that narrative, expressing different understandings of our national identity and national purpose. Undoubtedly, multiple alternatives always exist. In general, however, the most important variants are associated with political parties, and we can analyze them through partisan lenses.[8] In other words, when it comes to our national identity and national purpose, there is always conflict, and historically that conflict has been structured—institutionally by political parties, rhetorically by political vocabularies.

Partisan realignment isn't merely a matter of a minority imaginary overtaking a previously majoritarian one. Instead, at times of such change, the entire system is broken and reset. Some elements (federal versus state power) have great longevity across eras. Other elements (slavery, a national bank) extend across more than one party system but eventually fade. Still others are subjected to constant reinterpretation and adaption (the myths of American Exceptionalism and the American Dream). But every system of partisan disputation is also a system of stable disagreement between political vocabularies. Because political vocabularies structure systems of political disagreement, they provide an analytic through which we can understand their corresponding political imaginaries. They are complex rhetorical compilations that undergird those imaginaries and that offer different modes of political judgment. They are comprised of at least five interlocking elements, all of which circulate differently, are evident in a variety of texts, and are made especially clear in these letters.

First, they involve rhetorical authority. New regimes locate political authority in new places: it moves as part of the new administrative arrangements associated with regime change. And so political authority is very much a site of dispute between differing political vocabularies at any moment in time. Second, opposing political vocabularies are grounded in opposing characterizations of the specific political moment, its central issues, and its citizens, for we cannot imagine a political community without populating it and giving it purpose. Third, these issues and people are hierarchically ordered, which provides the imaginary with a sense of internal cohesion and which is also a central point of disputation between competing vocabularies in a specific epoch. Fourth, each vocabulary is grounded in political tradition, read through our national myths that authorize the visions of national identity and purpose. Finally, each political vocabulary contains significant deliberative aspects, for each vision of the nation impels distinct policy imperatives. They are, in fact, our political priorities in action.

Political vocabularies are not just the languages of governance. They are also the languages through which citizens inhabit, share, and participate in the entirety of their political life. They facilitate (and impede) citizen action and attach citizens to politics (or fail to do so). They can best be understood in their specific iterations at given points in time, for they change and adapt as our politics change. All of these entangled elements are part of every change in our political vocabularies over time. Each element is entangled with the others in a reasonably coherent and cohesive way. Each filters around and through the polity, but they do so via different routes. Authority, for example, must be negotiated. As presidents reach for more power, as presidents tend to do, other elites either accede to or resist such grasping. But authority is generally negotiated primarily among elites, and those negotiations filter down to and then among members of the mass public. Characterizing and ordering the polity, on the other hand, primarily circulate from the vernacular to the national. The presidency, as I have noted elsewhere, is a conservative institution, and it reflects our political culture more than it moves it.[9] The opposition to dominant characterizations and the prevailing hierarchies among citizens are also more likely to come from below than above. Broad reinterpretations of myths are used to justify new arrangements of political authority, but smaller adaptations of those myths work from the vernacular to the national. Similarly, some policies begin at the national level and filter downward, while other policies begin with localities and states, and other policy preferences and innovations circulate primarily in niche networks. The elements of political vocabularies are always a product of negotiation between national and local elites, between sources of cultural and political power, and between the governed and those who govern.

In order to detail the workings of political vocabularies in general, I rely here on one extended example. By focusing on one moment of political change, this book illuminates the elements of our political vocabularies more generally. I take as my text the 1935 clergy letters, written to FDR at his request in the midst of the Great Depression. Written over a period of a few months by over eight thousand members of the clergy from every state and comprising a broad swath of demographic variety, these letters give us access into one moment of political change and the emerging set of political vocabularies that sought to capture and describe it. Because we know the shape of the New Deal set of political vocabularies as they eventually coalesced, these letters allow insight into the process of political change as these authors used elements of both the old and the emerging political order. The letters thus also illuminate the creation and circulation of political vocabularies in general.

In making this case, I continue the introduction by providing historical and analytic context for the argument that follows. I start with a brief discussion of political realignment and its relationship to political language. I follow that with material on the clergy letters. In arguing that these letters represent a particular kind of political intervention, I place them both within the American political culture and within the wider tradition of political letters more generally. In doing so, I contend that they are an especially good site for the analysis of the elements of the New Deal set of political vocabularies and thus also of political vocabularies more generally. The introduction concludes with an overview of the rest of the book, with each chapter focusing on one element of political vocabularies, providing an eye toward both the specific case and the more general possibilities of the potential of political vocabularies to illuminate moments of institutional political change.

Political Realignment and Political Argument

Scholars are divided on the nature, history, and extent of political realignments, but there is widespread agreement that the New Deal does, in fact, represent the kind of seismic political shift associated with realignment.[10] Immediately prior to the 1930s realignment, there was a relatively stable partisan division, stemming roughly from 1896. For its part, the Republican Party was comprised largely of the white middle class, Midwestern and Northern white Protestants, and saw itself as the party of business.[11] Republicans did not see significant differences in the interests of capitalists and workers. They favored laissez-faire trade policies but also advocated improved working conditions, collective bargaining rights, and trust busting. Their political vocabulary located authority primarily in the private sector. Their conception of citizenship was, for its time, reasonably inclusive, especially on issues of class and women's suffrage, but it also depicted the nation as ordered by a clear and immutable set of hierarchies, stratified by ascriptive characteristics, especially race. They relied specifically on the myth of the American Dream and articulated clearly the ethos of the self-made man (I use the noun intentionally). Strong believers in the importance of self-reliance, they argued for a minimal role for government, supported women's suffrage, and defended anti-interventionist foreign policies. They were specifically suspicious of European entanglements, supported protective tariffs, and were avowedly cautious on immigration.

So it is not surprising that the 1928 Republican platform stressed the importance of character as a prerequisite of stability and prosperity.[12] For Republicans, virtue and "sound principles" were the most reliable guarantee of a prosperous and contented nation. Their standard bearer, Herbert Hoover, underlined these themes in the context of American Exceptionalism, arguing that the distinctive "American system," which had "decentralized local responsibility [as] the very base," was characterized by "ordered liberty, freedom, and equal opportunity to the individual." Hoover argued that the government should serve as "an umpire instead of a player in the economic game." The more active the role of the federal government, the more deleterious the effects. For Hoover, the government's job was to regulate business and the economy in order to ensure fair practices—and then to let the outcome be determined by the talents of the individual players. This, he argued, allows for the kind of "freedom of initiative and enterprise" that brought the nation ever "nearer to the abolition of poverty, to the abolition of fear of want, than humanity has ever reached before." The "American system," then, rested on an "adherence to the principles of decentralized self-government, ordered liberty, equal opportunity, and freedom to the individual," and resulted in a virtuous and prosperous polity.[13]

In this imaginary, authority rested with the private sector, which was the seat of innovation and constituted the main driver of national life. The nation's citizens were free individuals, whose private enterprise and hard work entitled them to increasing prosperity and security. The nation relied on "ordered liberty," however, which created a specific kind of hierarchy measured by both work and its visible rewards. In a world governed by equality of opportunity, failure to achieve was individual, not structural. This imaginary is rooted in the myth of the America Dream and is supported by a demand for local government and minimal federal regulation of the economy. This imaginary, powerful in the 1920s, was seriously undermined by the stock market crash and the economic calamity it triggered. Faced with a crisis of political authority, what was left of the Republican Party clung to some elements of this imaginary while adapting others. Many of its previous adherents forsook that party for an equally reshaped Democratic imaginary, what would become the New Deal coalition.

The pre–New Deal Democratic imaginary was even more strongly dedicated to diffusing the power of the federal government, and the 1928 Democratic platform criticized the Republicans for their "centralization . . . and destructive tendencies" while in office.[14] Democrats during this era were largely rural, Southern, and agrarian. They endorsed both William Jennings Bryan's populism and Woodrow Wilson's moralism.[15] They did not support unions or collective bargaining and were, in general, more exclusionary than were the Republicans, especially on matters of race. The Democrats argued that "the constitutional rights and powers of the states" needed to "be preserved in their full vigor and virtue," which meant both local control of economic matters and the protection of Jim Crow and racial hierarchies. Democrats were very profarmer and advocated tariffs that protected farmers and farm relief programs. In the interwar period, they too were anti-interventionist and opposed unilateral presidential power in the making of international agreements.[16] Reflecting their strong moralistic and religious ethos, Democrats advocated Prohibition.

In what has been considered a preliminary movement toward the New Deal coalition, Democrats in 1928 nominated New York governor Al Smith, who was Catholic, urban, and in many ways the antithesis of previous Democratic candidate, John W. Davis.[17] The 1924 convention that nominated Davis took a record 103 ballots to do so and was characterized by conflict between Davis and his main rival, William McAdoo. It was the first national party convention to have a woman's name placed in nomination (Lena Springs, nominated for the vice presidency) and was infamous for the prominence of the Ku Klux Klan (the convention was called a "Klanbake"). Davis was soundly defeated by Coolidge, and the Democrats began to reshape their politics, giving them first Smith and then Roosevelt.

So it is not surprising that in 1928 Smith called upon the ghost of Wilson rather than that of Davis and argued for a more "progressive" Democratic party.[18] In accordance with Democratic principles and the party's platform, he argued for tariffs that were less punitive to farmers and underlined his support for the Eighteenth Amendment and for the primacy of the Monroe Doctrine as the cornerstone of U.S. foreign policy. Accepting the Democratic nomination, he declared his commitment to "the fearless application of Jeffersonian principles. Jefferson and his followers foresaw the complex activities of this great, widespread country. They knew that in rural, sparsely settled districts people would develop different desires and customs from those in densely populated sections and that if we were to be a nation united on truly national matters, there had to be a differentiation in local laws to allow for different local habits."[19] Smith articulated the Democratic imaginary as a polity grounded in the bucolic virtues of the Jeffersonian republic and sustained by the authority of local governments. The citizens were virtuous because of their agricultural roots and were ordered along the lines predicated by those virtues. Good citizens were understood as hard-working, independent, and dedicated to the precepts of common sense. The myth evoked in this imaginary is a nostalgic one, connected to American Exceptionalism as read through an idealized past. National policy for Democrats should be aimed at protecting that past while giving it a progressive edge.

Smith thus represents a kind of way station between the old Democratic Party and the emerging New Deal political imaginary, as Hoover articulated the passing dominant Republican imaginary. There are elements of the old and the emergent in both 1928 platforms and candidates; realignments are associated with elections but are more complex and lengthy processes than can be captured in a single campaign.[20] But while it was not apparent at the time, by 1935 the new alignment was largely in place, driven by the long-term effects of industrialization and the devastation wrought by the Depression and comprised by a new ideological divide centering on the proper role of government in the polity.[21] The Republicans had become the minority party, restricted largely to the Northeast and upper Midwest. The Democrats, on the other hand, were strongest in the white, "solid" South, but had majorities among working-class ethnic urban Protestants, Jews, and Catholics as well. African Americans shifted allegiance to the Democrats.[22]

Along with these shifts in demographic constituencies came a shift in the composition of the political imaginaries associated with the parties. Republicans resisted the authority of the national government and especially the growth of presidential power. Their conception of the citizenry narrowed as they expressed considerable suspicion of immigrants and the contagions that they were presumed to bring with them. The hierarchies ordering their imaginary became more explicitly class-based and more rigidly defined. Their conception of the American Dream was one that presumed a level playing field and that resisted policies aimed at redistributing wealth. They remained anti-interventionist in foreign affairs until the onset of the Second World War.

Democrats occupied a different imaginary, increasingly committed to a strong federal government and a strong president at its head. For Democrats outside the South, political authority was invested in the national government. For those within the South and into the border regions, national power was legitimate so long as it was restricted to the economy and did not touch local institutions or hierarchies such as those that characterized Jim Crow. With the important exception of race, Democrats in general argued for leveling the nation's hierarchies, which they increasingly understood as interest- rather than as acriptively based. They supported policies like Social Security and the elimination of child labor, as well as favoring redistributive economic policies, and saw the federal government as a welcome agent of economic equity.

There is, of course, overlap between these two partisan articulations, for both participated in the larger, national imaginary. Prior to the New Deal, authority resided in localities and in the private sector; the federal government was assigned a supervisory but not an active role. Citizens were understood as self-motivated and self-sustaining. They were also connected politically through their economic priorities: workers and capitalists shared goals, although they had different interests. Citizens in the national polity were hierarchically ranked, by both ideology and ascriptive characteristics. A version of the American Dream governed the national ideology, as politicians from both major parties argued that the United States was a land of opportunity and promise. Foreign policy, of limited interest to both parties, was understood through the myth of American Exceptionalism, in that the United States was thought to offer a moral example for the world, and that example was best illustrated through attention to our own hemisphere and a refusal to be entangled in the affairs of the Old World. Neither imaginary had a vision of the world that extended further than Europe and the Americas. Citizens in general agreed that the nation's policies should be managed with an eye toward improvements at home. This national imaginary was largely agreed to by a majority of those invested and able to participate in national politics. The parties offered variations on this theme.

It is thus possible to see the ways that elites articulated these imaginaries, but it is not just the elites who inhabited them or who transmitted them through the contemporaneous political vocabularies. These vocabularies circulated through the polity as a whole, sometimes in fragmentary ways, but also over time in ways that coalesced into coherent variations of the national imaginary. One place that we can find these emerging articulations is in the collected clergy letters.

The Clergy Letters

Long before the United States engaged European dictatorships on the battlefield in World War II it engaged them philosophically in an ideological contest over the nature and form of modern governance. Equally opposed to the militaristic rule of the Nazis in Germany and the imperial government in Japan, and suspicious of the Soviets' totalitarian model, Franklin D. Roosevelt also had reservations about the colonial model exemplified primarily by Great Britain, and to a lesser extent by other European democracies. In proposing his "Good Neighbor Policy," Roosevelt was also proposing a model for democratic governance in a globalized world. Roosevelt's arguments had domestic as well as international implications, for the rules by which he argued governments should abide had applications for the U.S. government's treatment of its own people. Roosevelt himself realized this and argued that he had a definitive model for the future of American as well as global democracy.[23]

Roosevelt was not, however, the only one making arguments about the future of American democracy. In fact, the 1930s were a cacophony of such arguments, which ranged from the bitter fulminations of Father Charles Coughlin and the fascist arguments of William Dudley Pelley on the Right to Huey Long's exhortations and Upton Sinclair's and Norman Thomas's various proscriptions for a more socialist nation on the Left. The 1930s were, in fact, awash in arguments about the best way to move the nation forward in the aftermath of the Great Depression's various dislocations.[24] Capturing the range of this argumentation can tell us a great deal not only about the historical era but about both the form and content of our contemporary political landscape, for just as the world that FDR crafted is in many ways still with us, so too are the political vocabularies engendered by his decisions in crafting that world. It was a moment of political realignment, in which older political vocabularies were losing ground to a new way of conceiving politics.[25]

In 1935, Roosevelt made it possible for us to get some insight into the alternatives that were so clearly before the public during these years. In advance of his reelection campaign, he sent a letter to every member of the mainstream American clergy, requesting their help and advice on national policy. The White House reported sending 121,700 letters, of which approximately 120,000 were delivered. By October 17, 1935, they received 8,294 replies, which they believed represented the views of "about 100,000 people."[26] It was a poor return for the effort, and members of the White House considered the attempt to assess clerical opinion a mistake.[27] But the letters are well suited for my purposes. Because of both their number and the range of criticism directed at the president, they reveal a great deal about the scope and nature of political argument in the 1930s.

The letters were compiled in the executive office, and opinions on issues like repeal of Prohibition, neutrality, and "the dole" were tabulated for the president's attention. They thus create what Gerard Hauser called an "epistolary public sphere" that both reflected and allowed the president to connect to public opinion.[28] These members of the clergy explicitly addressed the president, his understanding of politics, and his policies. They delved into political theory and offered their thoughts on the new science of public administration. They discussed the changing American political culture and worried over the various fissures they saw developing within it. They wrote also from a specific vantage point, one that exploited the space between an official discourse and a vernacular one. Considering them private, sometimes even intimate, the clergy nonetheless also wrote as if they were public.

As indeed a number of them were. Many of these letters were also published in parish and local newspapers as well as being sent directly to the president.[29] A number of the clergy solicited the views of their parishioners before crafting their final epistles to the White House, and others argued in those letters that they were doing their best to represent the views of their congregations. Their writing can be treated as exercises in public rhetoric, for they sought to persuade the president to their point of view regarding matters of local and national political import and were meant to contribute to public debate. One analyst notes that "judging by the length, tone, and content of their letters, most thought their advice would be taken very seriously."[30] These letters are examples of the ways in which citizenship itself is a discursive phenomenon, for the clergy were acting both as pastors concerned with the spiritual health of their communities and as civic leaders acting on a secular level and concerned with more material matters.[31]

This book takes both levels of concern seriously, as exemplifying particular kinds of political opinions on specific issues and as language that uses certain kinds of rhetorical tools in order to further those arguments. These letters illuminate the implicit connections between values and policy and the ways in which those connections are articulated. The clergy, operating in a space that involves elite and official languages as well as more citizen-based public ones, provide insight into both kinds of discourses as well as into the places where they meet. They offer us the elements of political vocabularies in readily accessible form.

In what follows, I first locate the clergy vis-à-vis the government by providing a brief overview of the role of religion in American politics with specific attention to the 1930s. I then situate these letters through a discussion of letter writing as an act of public citizenship. Next, I connect these two broad discussions through what I call political vocabularies, which establish political authority, rely on depiction as a way of describing current political reality, naturalize a particular social order, depend on reformations of foundational myths, and delimit the means and ends of public deliberation. Together, these interwoven elements eventually created a coherent pair of disputing political vocabularies out of an era's political confusion. Traces of the New Deal's political vocabularies are still with us, although their ability to define our contemporary moment and provide compelling guides for national action is very much open to question.

A Divinely Inspired Nation

The relationship between organized religion and the American national state is long and complex. Scholars have, of course, addressed the rhetoric of specific religious figures and those who adopt religious language.[32] The religious element in national politics is not always easily accommodated, for the relationship between church and state is fraught with difficulty, paradox, and complication. Arguments and political practices based in religious traditions can, on the one hand, provide a moral and human rights–centered orientation for public action but can also provide a basis for exclusionary, destructive, and even inhumane policy.[33] Religion is different from other kinds of political warrants and rationales because of its grounding in transcendent truth, and in at least the Judeo-Christian tradition, the connection between political action and the afterlife renders palpable stakes for political choice. Those arguing from religious warrants therefore, on both the Right and the Left, often find in those warrants justification for offering dichotomous choices, treating compromise as akin to anathema, and advocating exclusionist policies as divinely inspired. When the soul of the nation is at stake, extreme measures are generally deemed appropriate in response.

This has been true since prior to the nation's founding. Specific religious traditions influenced and guided the early colonies, and the nation was founded with a strong sense that political independence and spiritual authority went hand in hand.[34] Fleeing religious persecution on the one hand, many colonists exhibited no compunction about establishing communities that demanded adherence to strict religious codes on the other. They condemned dissidents like Anne Hutchison and Roger Williams, conducted genocidal wars against indigenous peoples, and provided both religious sanctuary and religious oppression in the New World. These conflicting impulses run throughout the colonies and into the new republic.[35]

As Patrick Deneen, in his study of the role of religion in democratic theory writes, the U.S. political system presents a paradox, requiring inquiry into "how a political system designed to minimize claims of faith itself rests on faith, how a regime embraced for its modesty may be immodest in that embrace, how the rejection of truth in politics has led to the creation of a guiding truth in politics, and how that most anti-utopian regime may become the most dangerously utopian at the moment it congratulates itself loudest for its defeat of utopianism in politics."[36] Sacred warrants provide a position from which governmental actions and policies can be critiqued but also potentially threaten national stability by providing a transcendent value to which citizens may feel primarily loyal.[37]

Throughout U.S. history, then, the national sense of a divinely inspired communal mission has led to a strain of immense certainty in the rightness of national actions and at the same time has provided warrants for challenging those actions and that certainty. The voices proclaiming that Manifest Destiny was God's will, for instance, were countered by other voices proclaiming the opposite. All manner of political positions have found justification in the word of God. The realignment under consideration here is a prime example of that tendency.

A Clerical Intervention into Depression-Era Politics

In 1935, the nation still suffered from the Depression, which lingered in the United States longer and with more intensity than in many other countries.[38] Because there was no national safety net, and because the need quickly overwhelmed state and local relief organizations, economic dislocations quickly led to physical ones as well, destabilizing communities across the nation.[39] These dislocations reached deep into the middle class, causing concern over the consequences for national political stability as the national economy foundered.[40]

The Roosevelt administration acted both quickly and comprehensively, but the policies of the first hundred days and the first New Deal had little immediate impact, and in 1935 the nation was still well short of recovery. As a consequence, opposition to the president and his programs, always strong on the Right, began to rise on the Left as well.[41] By 1935, even the formerly friendly national press corps was increasingly willing to criticize the president and his policies.[42] At issue were disagreements over specific policies, widespread concern over increasing the power of the federal government, and worries about the growing power of the presidency. The rise of dictatorships in Europe fueled fears about the viability of republican forms of government in the United States, and many saw

FDR as emblematic of threats to both the American way of life and the form of government on which it was presumed to rest.[43] The various fears increased as the nation's economic and social woes continued and even seemed to deepen and as the early promise of Roosevelt's administration seemed elusive.[44]

There was no shortage of proposed alternative solutions to the nation's problems. There were, Russell L. Hanson argues, four competing views of democracy during the era: the reformist impulse represented in the New Deal; socialism; what he calls "Depression Demagogues"; and the conservative, small-state views of the Republicans.[45] There were a plethora of other views as well, and there was actually very little consensus among many of those he calls demagogues. He also ignores the potential strength of the American Far Right.[46] Many of the voices advocating solutions to the nation's problems did so through explicit or implicit references to divine warrants.[47] But these warrants weren't confined to FDR's critics. Roosevelt, for example, who relied heavily on advisors like Cardinal George Mundelein and Father John A. Ryan, advocated policies like Social Security through specifically Christian imagery.[48] Aide Robert Jackson argued that this was at least part of the reason for FDR's oratorical success.[49] Roosevelt famously defined his political identity as that of "a Christian and a Democrat." It was axiomatic that he didn't see much difference between the two.[50] It is notable that at least in his rhetorical practice, he combined both Christianity and party politics into a seamless whole.[51] Using religious language himself, Roosevelt, who claimed to have "wanted to be a preaching president like his cousin," has also been credited with "encouraging a revival of religious sentiment" nationally.[52] His own moderate faith notwithstanding, many Americans hailed his administration as divinely inspired and likened him to both Jesus and Moses, perhaps reflecting the redemptive elements in his rhetoric.[53] In part, the use of divine warrants across the political spectrum reveals the extent to which secular authority was rendered precarious. Advocates for new forms of political organization in the context of ruptured political authority relied on transcendent justifications for their policy preferences.

The Depression brought with it a resurgence of radicals on both the Right and the Left. Religion infused the very different kinds of claims offered by Dorothy Day, Saul Alinsky, and Reinhold Niebuhr.[54] On the

Right, interlocutors often explicitly relied on ominous and biblically informed rhetoric, so much so, in fact, that both literal and metaphorical evocations of the apocalypse were commonplace.[55] Anti-Semitism was also rife, and rhetors like Henry Ford and Father Coughlin argued for policies based on religiously endorsed exclusion and fear.[56] Others, like Huey Long, often called demagogues, also grounded their political appeals in Christian imagery.[57]

Religious language was possible across the political spectrum because of a broad cultural consensus on the Judeo-Christian (understood as Protestant) underpinnings of the nation. In framing arguments through biblical warrants, interlocutors were relying on two distinct understandings of the way religion operates in the American context. First, they could depend on the fact that the vast majority of citizens shared a common, largely Protestant, culture. So those attempting to intervene in the public realm could shape arguments and policies around this shared understanding of how communities ought to be formed and how they ought to behave.[58] This broad use of religion, however, was increasingly giving way to a second understanding and produced arguments that depended upon very specific uses of the Bible to endorse equally specific policies in the name of religion.[59] So while almost every orator of the period and certainly FDR himself relied on broad claims to what Roosevelt would later call "the Christian ideal" in articulating their positions, it was also increasingly common for them to argue in a more specific way for very narrow policies.[60] In the clergy letters, then, the president was asked to call the nation to prayer, to stop holding cabinet meetings on Sundays, to restrain his wife and their children from encouraging the consumption of alcohol and participating in social scourges like divorce, and to craft all manner of policies that would govern the moral life of the nation. Bringing the Kingdom of God to earth was increasingly understood as a uniquely American endeavor and an increasingly sectarian one as well.[61]

The kinds of religious language political actors employ reveal cultural orientations toward both religion and politics. By the mid-1930s both the degree of faith and the kinds of political actions and leadership endorsed by the faithful seemed, at least to FDR's clerical respondents, to be changing. To the extent that publics exist as a matter of shared judgments, these letters gave the president and his advisors access to an important kind of national public and a kind of national public opinion.[62] Although Roosevelt never seriously considered actions like reintroducing Prohibition, his continued use of religious warrants for his reforms would have found approval among much of this clerical audience, at least to the extent that they considered this use sincere.

This would have been important to him not least because the clergy represent a specific kind of rhetorical authority, and authority was very much a matter of debate during these years. Realignment is a peculiarly moral process in that new definitions of the purpose and mechanism of government are very much at issue. As relatively educated and privileged participants in the public sphere, the clergy had at their disposal the resources available to all civic leaders. As religious leaders, they also spoke with transcendent authority. They operated in a realm that allowed for a certain kind of "speaking for," in which they were both elite and public, and able to speak to the nation as a whole but also focused in these letters on the local.[63] They were also members of local communities and wrote in the vernaculars of those communities. These letters thus represent a multilayered view of American politics in which the local informs the national, the sacred provides warrants for secular action, and private communication advocates public action. They are a wonderful example of rhetoric understood as practical collective reason expressed through public discourse.[64]

This clerical intervention in national politics came at a time in which scientific principles of management and secular values were becoming increasingly central in national life. Religion itself was subject to such secularization. John Dewey, for example, writing in 1934, a year before Roosevelt sent his letter to the nation's clergy, argued that religion could be stripped of its association with what he termed "the supernatural" and be treated as "the religious." For Dewey, "the religious" was a pragmatic devotion to the common good that relied on human intelligence rather than a superstitious devotion to the divine. He wrote, "I cannot understand how any realization of the democratic ideal as a vital moral and spiritual ideal in human affairs is possible without surrender of the conception of the basic division to which supernatural Christianity is committed. Whether or not we are, in some metaphorical sense, all brothers, we are traversing the same turbulent ocean. The potential religious significance of this fact is infinite."[65] Dewey and others like him wanted to keep the stress on humane values and the common good that they found inherent in religious faith but also wanted to distance themselves and their political preferences from what they considered the superstitious elements they associated with religion.[66] Dewey, of course, represents only one of the increasingly secular views of the common good circulating at the time. The clergy were fighting a cultural battle in defense of religious faith and for the political influence of the faithful. In their letters it is clear that they hoped to enlist the president in this battle. It was less clear to many of them which side he would ultimately take.

Since the 1930s, the increased secularization of the Left has created no small number of problems for the Democratic Party, but in the 1930s, Roosevelt was more than willing to use the common understanding of the nation as grounded in and operating through Judeo-Christian precepts to justify his policies and his leadership. He was, however, less inclined to endorse specific policies favored by many of these clergy. However, as rhetors like Roosevelt enacted policies that were explicitly based on this understanding of social Christianity, its precepts were also increasingly articulated in world-historical terms. The liberal reform agenda of the Democrats, justified through reliance on universal values, came to dominate the national stage. As those policies devolved into a kind of corporate or interest-group liberalism, however, the power of sacred warrants dissipated, leaving the policies themselves unmoored to a broadly shared vision of the public good.[67] He thus considers the New Deal as a moment in which policy was both strongly linked to and also subverted Progressive values as grounded in religion.[68]

In sum, the tension between a common Judeo-Christian heritage understood in broad, cultural terms and an increasingly sectarian impulse toward specific policy mandates understood in narrow, denominational terms marks an important shift in the ways religion has come to influence our national politics.[69] Christianity is less useful now as a foundation for our political vocabularies. The additional complication of an increasingly secularized version of social life added to the rich mix of voices that infused the period.[70] The clergy letters were written in the midst of that cacophony and represent important examples of all of the contributing voices. The clergy were often at odds with one another and with the president as well.

Even those who endorsed some of his programs were not reluctant to criticize others, and they often deplored the president's social policies and personal behavior as well. In this way, these letters also provide a useful corrective to much of the literature on the presidency by reminding us that the president's power to authorize specific notions of national identity is always contested, sometimes vehemently.[71] In this case, that contestation occurred in the rhetorical form of the quasi-public letter.

The Clergy Letters as Political Action

Letter writing, as Samuel McCormick so nicely illustrates, has been a form of public rhetoric since at least the Roman Empire.[72] As a rhetorical form, letters can be used to challenge power, to contend with those in authority, and to insinuate the public into an implicitly private discourse.[73] McCormick's analysis is especially helpful here, for it is clear that the clergy writing to Roosevelt understood their letters to be both public and private. They often articulated both elements, on the one hand treating the letters as private, even intimate, messages between close friends, and on the other hand making claims about the public nature of and consequences of this interaction. Many of the clergy published their letters and/or shared them with their congregations and communities. In many instances, the clergy explicitly refer to the ways the public and private were blurred and met in the executive institution they addressed as they sought to encourage the president to act as a kind of institutional exemplar, leading the nation into a more thoroughly Christian and moral understanding of itself.[74]

Critical analysis of letters in general can provide insight into the writer's education, circumstances, and contemporaneous events, as well as providing information concerning the writer's relationship to the addressee and to the world at large.[75] They can serve as a substitute for the idea of meeting, establishing an author's presence as part of a dialogue.[76] In so doing, letter writers create both their audience and themselves as dialogic partners.[77] Letters like the ones the clergy wrote in reply to Roosevelt can be profitably understood as a form of political action in their own right, a "self-narration" that allows writers to demonstrate their agency and to make demands on the political system.[78] These letters, written from varying political perspectives, from places that ranged from small, rural, and impoverished communities to prosperous urban centers (and from prosperous small towns to financially stressed cities), indicate both the ways that they have a clear representative character and provide insight into the depth of national need in the mid-1930s and the complexities inherent in trying to address that need.

Given their education, the clergy would certainly have been aware of how letters functioned within their various traditions. For Christians, of course, the Pauline letters provided an important example of the sermonic uses of letters, which could be used to exhort, educate, and correct members of their audience.[79] The letters in many ways exemplify a kind of epistolary jeremiad in which the audience—in this case the president and the public—is condemned for its sins, punishment is promised and sometimes seen in the national devastation wrought by the Depression, and hope is held up for national salvation if the country returns to God.[80] For many of the responding clergy, the Depression was best understood as something of a visitation, and they did not hesitate to offer their views on the nature of national sin and the need for equally national repentance and atonement in the hope of national redemption.[81] The letters are thus full of both anger and hope. Their authors express enormous belief in the capacities of national action, whether for good or ill.

These letters illuminate the large issues of the day—the character of democracy and how it ought to be practiced, the nature and limits of political authority and its relationship to transcendent values, the proper management of the United States' growing international role, and its corresponding relationship to the prevention of war and the provision of peace—articulated in a particularly significant vernacular. In a world awash in religious imagery and biblical justifications for every conceivable policy, the American clergy wielded an important authority over religious texts and the warrants that stemmed from them.

The letters also illumine the operative social and political hierarchies in the 1930s.[82] In their salutations, their form, and even their content, letters in general make both implicit and explicit use of social norms and conventions.[83] The clergy addressed Roosevelt in terms as widely divergent as "Your Excellency" and "Frank," addresses that reveal their awe of the man and the institution he occupied as well as the familiar nature of the leadership he was crafting with the national public.[84] The letters themselves are written on embossed stationary, on paper torn from exercise books, on notepaper, on scraps of other kinds of paper, and on the backs of Roosevelt's original letter. They thus reveal the resources available to their authors and place themselves, although not cleanly, along a socioeconomic hierarchy.

They highlight the politics associated with that hierarchy and with the ways it was becoming less stable because letters also, of course, serve a clear instrumental goal.[85] At the most basic level, the clergy sought to influence the president and his actions with reference to the specifics of their personal experience illustrated through their parishioners. These letters thus offer an example of the use of practical reason in public deliberation.[86] The clerical respondents argued from the condition of their communities to that of the nation and offered the president their best ideas on how the wisdom gained in experiencing the local could help ameliorate national problems. Many of the clergy acknowledged some progress in the nation's economic plight, although most feared it was and might remain incomplete. Many also articulated a strong sense of connection between national values and the nation's economic woes and the impossibility, for them, of strengthening the second without addressing the first.

Letters entail a circulation of meaning, because they follow one another and are understood not as a singular, individual act, but as part of an ongoing conversation. Letters, in fact, "imply one another," and thus also always evoke another to whom they are addressed, and in this case a public whom they also implicate.[87] The clergy, then, often understood themselves as joining a national conversation in which their communities, the national government, and often God himself were joined. To all appearances, they understood that conversation as consequential, as a result of which the United States would either stand or fall, politically, economically, and morally. Because of their particular place within the social world of the 1930s, the clergy are well suited as windows into the negotiated creation of competing sets of political vocabularies. As culturally authoritative speakers themselves, they sit at the intersection of elite rhetors like the president and the everyday citizens of their communities.

These letters reflect a wide range of views expressed in a variety of vernaculars, but in articulating their political imaginaries, they rely on common ideas and rhetorical tools, what I am calling the elements of political vocabularies.

The clergy toggled between articulating their understanding of God's will and their responsibility to represent their parishes to a growing national government. They specifically noted the requirement that government—in the person of its president—listen both to God and to their flock and that they had a uniquely important position as mediators between the transcendent values and the real needs of the lowliest among the nation's people. Just as letters themselves mediate between interlocutors and between the present and the future, these letters sought to mediate between God, the government, and the people, making clear to the government the requirements of the one and the needs of the other. In a nation where the local was being rapidly replaced by the national and as visions of the common good were being lost to negotiations among more narrowly conceived interests, the clergy were endeavoring to bring a sense of common good and higher purpose to the public arena.[88] They were also, of course, advancing their own sense of the common good.[89]

These letters thus offer an important view into the ways public opinion was understood and articulated.[90] As Susan Herbst points out, the way political actors measure public opinion at any given time affects the uses that voters, legislators, and journalists make of it.[91] She identifies 1936 as a pivotal year, during which polling began to assume an increasingly important place in American politics.[92] These letters, then, represent an important example of the kinds of interventions at least some members of the mass public might make when given the opportunity to formulate their own unprompted ideas about what kinds of issues and questions ought to animate the national agenda.

These letters provided FDR with information on the nature of public opinion at a national, regional, and local level and also on the opinions of members of specific demographic groups. This was both useful to him electorally and provided him with an important rhetorical resource as he was able to invoke public opinion with some confidence.[93] Given FDR's fondness for authorizing his policies through religious warrants, these letters were potentially of very real importance to him.[94] All political vocabularies both rest on and assert specific visions of political authority. The New Deal political vocabulary authorized an increase in presidential power; the clergy participated in and resisted this increase while at the same time they defended their own locally based authority.

The clerical respondents were thus also enacting a kind of democratic citizenship characterized by active engagement rather than spectatorship.[95] This is especially significant because the Roosevelt administration marks a pivot between one kind of national citizenship and another. As the national government took on more responsibility and accrued more power, more citizens were both encouraged to participate in politics and paradoxically disempowered by the processes associated with centralizing government functions and comprehending an increasingly diverse national public.[96] The clergy, by responding to Roosevelt's request for their help and advice, contributed both to the public acceptance of his leadership and to the president's ability to exercise that leadership through access to public opinion.[97] But they were doing so in an active way, framing their responses to his general question in specific terms they determined, engaging in acts of democratic deliberation by representing their communities, to the best of their abilities, to nationally powerful actors. The clergy resisted and embraced the New Deal, with its reliance on national and executive power, and thus indicate for us the role of political authority in the era's competing political imaginaries.

These letters don't merely serve to represent, however. They also demand a kind of political acknowledgement. They explicitly seek to make the government accountable both to God and to the nation's people, and they express differing ideas about who those people were. The clergy letters thus are also a form of witnessing, which always has to do with the need to make something present; it involves both seeing and saying.[98] Witnessing is an act of engagement. The clergy sometimes feared, as did Paul A. Lomax, that the president intended to disregard "our answers entirely, and the letter was really to flatter us into political patronage."[99] Others were even more acerbic. Ralph Supplee, for instance, wrote, "As this letter will only be tabulated by a clerk, I will mention only a few items which I believe are unsound in your Administration policies."[100] His avowed belief that only a clerk would read the letter didn't stop him from including several things he appeared to want the president to hear.

As in this example, their very insistence on writing to the White House despite this asserted belief was also a demand on the president and on the government as a whole.

For leadership in a democracy to be understood as legitimate, the clergy argued, it has to acknowledge both God's will and that of the American people. Relying on the first, it must educate the second. The clergy thus positioned themselves through the president as the mediating agent between God and the people and weighed in on the contemporaneous negotiation of how "democracy" (always a contested term) was to be understood. They would speak for both God and his people and would make sure that government listened to both. This positioning reflects the fact that these letters were written by members of the clergy, of course. But it also reflects the long-standing role of religion in American politics. And more to the point for this analysis, it also reflects the ways in which a crisis in political structures puts authority in play rhetorically and facilitates a search for alternative means of authorizing communal action. By depicting their communities to the national administration, the clergy were describing differing perspectives on the political world and helping to negotiate a set of institutions, processes, and discourses appropriate to that world. In offering this perspective, the clergy exemplify the way in which some aspects of political vocabularies circulate from the public to those in positions of political power.

As witnesses, the clergy relied on certain givens as a means of understanding and interpreting that which they witnessed. The clergy thus offered justifications and challenges to the social order. Depictions as an element of political vocabularies report on the world. Hierarchies proscribe the political action required as a response to those depictions. The clergy naturalized the appropriate ordering of collective life. Each of the developing political imaginaries of these years had different senses of who "the people" were and also competing ideas about how they were best to be collectively organized.

The creation of a new partisan alignment, a new regime, also requires the creation of a new set of political vocabularies. For new sets of political vocabularies to become established, they must not only rest on credible authority, respond to perceived political realities, and appropriately order the world, they must also provide an element of stability, which circulates from the elites downward. Those elites must present the new social and political organization in familiar terms and must prove consonant with national myths, demonstrating that any changes bring us collectively closer to the instantiation of our national ideals. And so we can see in the clergy letters the use of specific elements of those myths in making their cases to the president, defining and redefining individualism, community, and the other mythic elements that connect them. In doing so, they authorize both different mechanisms of making political judgments and different kinds of judgments as well. As the dominant politics of the New Deal became less local and more national, less sectionally driven and more based on economic interests that crossed regional boundaries, different kinds of political processes—and an increased number of them—were subjected to political debate. Those debates run through the clergy letters.

Political vocabularies help us define the nation and help us delimit policy choices and the rules of deliberative judgments about policy. By uniting elements of national identity, national myth, and policy, the clergy presented to Roosevelt versions of the plethora of arguments that characterized the era. They thus represent the range of arguments circulating at the time and allow access to the prevailing political imaginaries. Like other national interlocutors, the clergy provide evidence of how the shards of a previously shattered vocabulary can be reassembled into a new interpretive prism, reordering the national narrative into a different reflective apparatus, one better suited to the nation as it emerged into a new context.

Political vocabularies are how we make sense out of politics. They depend upon and reinforce relevant issue cleavages, animate political coalitions, and authorize administrative arrangements. I argue that these vocabularies are associated with political regimes, in that as regimes rise and fade, political vocabularies adapt and change. The clergy letters allow us insight into the various entangled elements of one political vocabulary as it is in the process of developing. The following chapters take these elements one at a time.

Political Vocabularies

The evidence for a political vocabulary is found in its circulation, both by those with institutional power, like the president, and those with cultural power, like the 1930s American clergy. The clergy wrote to the president at a time when political authority was very much in flux. Power, as I have argued elsewhere, was moving from the states to the federal government, and within the government, from Congress to the presidency.[101] Cultural and economic changes were sending people from rural to urban areas and were undermining the power of local authorities. While it has been argued that all speech is sermonic, in this chapter I am trying to evoke something akin to the notion of "by benefit of clergy."[102] Chapter 1, "By Benefit of Clergy: Authoritative Political Vocabularies," thus examines the changing nature of authority and the rhetorical means through which the clergy invoked it. I also interrogate the question of whether that authority can best be understood as institutional and what that might mean for the ways in which their rhetorical authority came to be construed.[103] I note here that in the 1930s some members of the clergy, like other Americans, ceded considerable interpretive authority to the president. They thus authorized a new kind of political power. Others resisted that power, maintaining a different view of authority consistent with their political imaginary.

Political vocabularies not only authoritatively circulate and thus reinforce and challenge authority, they must also evoke a sense of correspondence with lived political reality. The clergy worked hard to depict their communities to the president, invoking a sense of place and of circumstance to make the case for their political preferences. They did so, as chapter 2, "Witnessing Politics: The Depictive Element of Political Vocabularies," makes clear, by reporting facts, using metaphors, telling stories, and offering analogies. These elements facilitate a shared understanding and action that are based in description, contain arguments about causes and consequences, involve an element of personification, and render judgments. I chart some of the ways those tactics were used in that context, and thus how they helped to create specific kinds of warrants for political action. For a political vocabulary to operate, it must render the polity somehow visible to its government and its citizens. As depictions of the nation become standard, mutually agreed upon views of who we are, they provide the basis for political hierarchies and political action.

The lived political reality articulated and circulated through political vocabularies justifies specific choices about the shared social order. Democracy is a contested term; its meaning changes as our political vocabularies and the contexts within which they are embedded change. Multiple versions of democracy circulated in the 1930s, providing a rich set of inventional resources for members of the clergy as well as for national political elites. As chapter 3, "Revelations: Naturalizing Hierarchies in Political Vocabularies," indicates, the clergy relied on various techniques in advocating their various understandings of American democracy. They also wielded specific kinds of cultural premises related to the "obvious" traits of women, African Americans, and other minorities, justifying their places in the political hierarchy or serving as warrants to advocate change. Relying on these sets of givens as their texts, the clergy supported and challenged social and political hierarchies through reference to a divinely ordained order.

When political arguments resonate across a culture they activate elements of foundational myths. While myths may remain relatively stable over long periods of time the meaning of specific elements of those myths change. So while the frontier myth, for example, has been important to every pivotal moment in U.S. history, the weight given to each element of that myth has changed, and so have the ways in which we have defined its constituent parts.[104] In chapter 4, "The American Eden: Mythic Elements of Political Vocabularies," I look both at the overall national myths and the ways in which those parts were mobilized as part of the competing sets of the 1930s political vocabularies. The ways the clergy used mythic elements to make political arguments reveal the constitutive functions of political arguments and also illuminate the ways in which myth stabilizes changes in our political vocabularies.

Different political moments bring with them changes in relevant issue cleavages and institutional responses to those cleavages. Political vocabularies both entail the rules for making collective judgments in a given political moment and also determine the kinds of policies that will be understood as relevant at that point in time. Rhetoric fuses the symbolic and the material. Political arguments have both symbolic and material consequences. Symbolically, they pertain to authoritative hierarchies of national identity. Materially, they justify specific kinds of policy. Chapter 5, "Making a City on a Hill: Political Vocabularies and National Policy," examines the ways the clergy used deliberative rhetoric and articulated specific policy preferences. The clergy letters thus reveal the kinds of issue cleavages that formed and were formed by the New Deal political vocabulary as well as the ways in which political arguments can be said to be deliberative in both context and content.

The nation is always a collectivity, always based on inclusions and exclusions, authorized by institutional arrangements, political processes, and the discourses that stitch them together. Over time, whether as a result of slow erosion or sudden crisis, a prevailing political paradigm will lose its ability to describe the political world and guide action in it. It will then give way to new institutional forms and new political vocabularies. The conclusion reviews this process of change and re-creation as seen through the clergy letters and uses them as a way to reflect on the operation of the New Deal political vocabulary in our current time.

CHAPTER ONE

By Benefit of Clergy: Authoritative Political Vocabularies

Scholars associate realignments with single elections, but realignments are better understood as processes rather than as events.[1] Of the many things that characterize realignments as processes, one of the clearest is that that by unsettling the previously stable system of interparty conflict, they cause a crisis in political authority. Political institutions, operations, and discourses all shift, resettling only when a new set of political vocabularies has coalesced and is understood as both capturing shared political reality and providing a guide to collective action within that reality. We can see this occurring in the context of the clergy letters, for the New Deal era, like the letters, was preoccupied with issues of authority.

Authority is integral to political imaginaries and the political vocabularies that order them. Political authority must reside somewhere. Prior to the New Deal, it was primarily placed in the private sector by

Republicans and in local governments by the Democrats. Both parties shared a sense that a limited federal government was preferable, but to the extent that it had authority, that authority resided in Congress. So before the Roosevelt administration, neither of the dominant political imaginaries included a powerful federal government or a powerful president, although Republicans were marginally more willing to grant some regulatory power to Congress. The New Deal brought a reconfiguration of authority, granting power to the federal government and the president at the expense of the private sector, local government, and Congress. This change was embraced by Democrats and resisted by Republicans. Elite voices dominated this debate, of course, as the element of authority is contested at the elite level and travels through the polity from there, but it also took place in local vernaculars as it circulated and filtered through the polity. The contours of the contestation can be seen throughout the clergy letters.

Federal Power and the New Deal

The massive increase in federal power in domestic affairs is an important aspect of the Roosevelt presidency. Prior to the New Deal, the federal government managed a fairly small amount of the nation's business. Foreign policy, of course, fell under the national government's domain, as did the bigger umbrella policies concerning the national economy, and so on. But there was no national safety net, no system by which the nation could protect its most vulnerable citizens in times of economic difficulty. Most of the nation's charitable burden was managed by either states or local governments; a great deal of it fell outside of government's purview altogether and was administered by private civic and religious organizations.[2] This was consistent with both national ideology and long-standing political practice.

Ideologically, national belief in a relatively weak federal structure supported and was supported by the traditional American suspicion of centralized power.[3] Both the rise of the Soviets in Russia and the Great War fueled that fear. The Soviet model, understood as destructive of individual liberty and strongly centralized, was something of a bogeyman for Americans even as early as the 1920s.[4] The Great War, which many citizens regarded as perpetrated by the national government in cooperation with the arms merchants, increased U.S. isolationism and worked against the establishment of federal power.[5] Fearing with the authors of *The Federalist* that a too-strong national government tended toward monarchism and threatened individual liberty, federal action was regarded with suspicion.

Practically, prior to the 1930s the United States was a decentralized federal system, preferring political structures that allowed for local control, provided consistency with local mores and customs, and facilitated policy innovations that could then be adopted by other states and localities as they proved workable.[6] This also meant, of course, that there was great variation among and between these states and localities. Prior to the New Deal, Democrats were content to locate political power here, as it allowed for the perpetuation of such local practices as Jim Crow.[7] Republicans, equally willing to locate power in the states, also saw a need for some national regulation and viewed the private sector, with support from the federal government, as the best mechanism of that regulation.

When the stock market crashed, it took with it the authority of the private sector as a regulator of collective action. It also overwhelmed the capacity of state and local governments to manage the crisis. This combination created a real problem for Republicans and Democrats alike. Republicans, who had previously located authority primarily in the private sector, searched for ways to restore its authority as a guide for collective action and generally began to reassert the need for unfettered business as the best path to national economic recovery. They called for minimal government involvement in economic matters. As the Democrats began to argue for federal power, Republicans became its adamant opponents. Democrats, on the other hand, on matters other than Jim Crow, increasingly argued for both federal and executive power as correctives to what they considered the untrammeled and unhealthy power of the private sector. This argument evolved over time to encompass both a strong national state and strong president. In 1935, as positions on both sides of the partisan aisle were in flux, they centered as much on the person of the president as on theories of government.

Authority in Crisis

One way to understand the Great Depression is through the dislocations it caused. Individual businesses and entire industries foundered, reshaping the national economy.[8] Lacking work, people left their homes, their communities, and often their families, as they searched for employment.[9] Politically, the coalitions associated with the two main political parties shattered. As new mainstream political configurations developed, the nation was inundated with other possibilities as movements like Bundism and fascism vied with more narrow programs like Share the Wealth and the Townsend Plan for the people's attention. As the Depression stretched out, old verities of all kinds loosened their hold, taking with them the easy belief in existing structures and logics of authority.[10] Under FDR, the national government attempted a plethora of programs designed to rationalize and control—and thus hopefully to improve—the national economy. Federally administered programs like the National Industrial Relief Administration were attempts to manage business and industry from the national level, causing no small amount of acrimony among urban dwellers.[11] Other national programs, like the Agricultural Adjustment Administration (AAA), did the same for farming, creating resentment as the government mandated the destruction of livestock and crops in an effort to reduce supply and thus increase prices. The destruction of food amid the real starvation and suffering in the nation was appalling, even to those who understood the intent, helping to undermine belief in the beneficence of the New Deal.[12] This was a particular problem for Roosevelt, as the president, who had sought, obtained, and exercised unprecedented power in his first term, was increasingly accused of abusing the power he had and seeking dictatorial power as well as he headed into his second.[13]

In this context, those who exercised social, political, or economic power had to find new warrants for that power. Regime change, as Stephen Skowronek notes, is both organizational and ideological.[14] It is also rhetorical. As new structures develop, new warrants for those structures are required. Political vocabularies require and legitimate political authority. In making sweeping organizational changes, FDR also had to forge ideological understandings that made those changes possible and craft new arguments in their defense.[15] In this case, that meant a national debate over the nature of power and how it could best be organized in the American system. The 1930s were, in the terms separately used by Ed Schiappa and Lynn Clarke, a moment of "definitional rupture," in which the authority tied to a specific definitional structure was undermined as that structured weakened.[16] Ruptures were evident in partisan shifts, as African Americans, for instance, as well as members of other ethnic and religious groups, deserted the Republicans for the Democratic Party, and the New Deal coalition redefined American politics.[17] Ruptures were visible in the changing structures of political administration that accompanied New Deal reforms.[18] They were evident in the various ideological options pervading the nation. And finally, they were evident in the nation's public rhetoric. All of this fluctuation meant that political decisions had to be authorized in new ways or that the old ways had to be rearticulated to fit the new context.

Roosevelt was a master of integrating new authorizations with repurposed and rearticulated authorizations for his new policies and forms of governance. His political speech is laced, for example, with visual metaphors that captured a new way of understanding the nation and its new forms of governance in explicitly democratic terms.[19] He also engaged in a variety of other rhetorical techniques designed to reassure, unite, and motivate the nation.[20] Of these techniques, his use of biblical imagery and religious warrants is of most interest to a discussion of authority, for when secular, human-made structures prove vulnerable, authorizing new forms of collective action with reference to transcendent values is a natural step, especially in a political culture infused with religious references. Such warrants spread widely and deeply in Roosevelt's public speech and opened a particular rhetorical space for the clerical voices we hear in these letters.

Political institutions were not the only ones in flux during the 1930s. Social institutions and mores also altered. Many of Roosevelt's clerical interlocutors expressed concern, for example, over the social changes that they understood as fueled by the Depression, repeal, the machine age and the dislocations it brought, and the resulting breakdown in religiously based social organization. They wrote of their fear that they were losing influence among their parishioners and in their communities and looked to the president to help them reestablish their authority even as they supported and challenged his. In both attacking and supporting the president's claim to authority, the clergy also defended their understanding of the nature and limits of political authority in general. In defining political authority, the clergy buttressed their own authority and reaffirmed their understanding of the role of the sacred in secular affairs.[21]

Political vocabularies entail the allocation of authority. When the president grounded his claim to power in religious warrants, he empowered the clergy as able to offer judgment on his use of that power. When the clergy responded with judgment, they authorized and challenged Roosevelt—and more importantly, the presidency itself—as a legitimate locus of interpretive power.[22] The presidency, then, for a variety of reasons, found itself at the center of contestation over the role of the federal and executive power. One emergent political imaginary included the endorsement of such power; the other increasingly determined to oppose it. The clergy letters allow a window into how those imaginaries were being developed, articulated, and circulated among members of the public.

Clerical Claims to Authority

For obvious reasons, no matter how the individual clergy located themselves within the competing political imaginaries, for them, the role of religion was central. But they were not always willing to assume that this role should be centralized as a matter of public policy. So while many of the clergy avowed themselves humbled and honored by the president's invitation to correspond with him, and others were aggravated that he hadn't consulted them sooner, some rebuked Roosevelt for blurring lines between secular and sacred authority. Still others, in their silence on the matter, appear to have assumed that the president was reasonable in asking for their advice and help, and they could reasonably oblige his request. And many of them, in declining to respond to the president's letter, left their reasoning undeclared. In the case of those who did choose to respond, the clergy were, while ostensibly commenting on the president's authority, also establishing grounds for their own.[23] Some of these grounds widened clerical authority; some of them limited it. But in every case, simply by making claims about their ability to weigh in on the state of the nation to this particular audience, the clergy were also assuming that they had the standing to make such judgments.[24] For my purposes, also lurking in their discourse is a locally authoritative articulation of the emerging set of New Deal political vocabularies.

As Martin J. Medhurst notes in a different context, clerical rhetors who assume political roles often wield arguments from circumstance and consequences, and the assumption of a prophetic role entails making arguments from causality. Medhurst associates the priestly role, on the other hand, with arguments from authority.[25] Whether they were rabbis, priests, or pastors of some other kind, Roosevelt's clerical respondents were mindful of their roles as mediators between the government, God, and their congregations. They used language they believed resonated with those audiences. They wrote in the vernacular of their time, revealing relics of the previous alignment and the emerging language of the new. In keeping with the president's request to them, the clergy offered him arguments about policy based on their capacity to observe and to understand their own communities. These observations were taken through a very specific lens. Their reports to the president were thus infused with arguments about the ways in which the president's policies, their local conditions, and the will of God reflected upon one another.[26] For the clergy, their letters were authorized by the president; their observations were authorized by their standing in their local communities; and their judgments were authorized by God. They thus transferred sacredly based social capital into secular political capital.[27]

Authority is always about hierarchy.[28] For these clerics, the hierarchies in which they operated were clear. Their primary obedience was to the Deity. Their secondary responsibility was to their local community. Their judgments, both positive and negative, about the national administration were a direct result of their understanding of that obedience and responsibility. In making the political dependent on divine mandate as revealed in local conditions, however, the clergy were also establishing themselves atop a hierarchy of their own. As mediators between God and the political world, the clergy had a particular claim to authority over that political world and particular rhetorical authority over the development and circulation of political vocabularies.[29]

The clergy thus explicitly connected their authority to religious values, which they construed as consistent with national values.[30] The values these clergy associated with the nation are congruent with their understanding of God's will. There is, of course, variation among them in how they interpreted those values and which ones they saw as foundational. Each political imaginary lines these elements up differently. But in general, when the clergy made the connection between God's purpose and national goals, they also tied their own political authority as judges of policies intended to enact national values to their sacred authority as arbiters of the will of God.

Relying on sacred warrants on the one hand, the clergy also relied on arguments that marshaled conventional wisdom in which their interpretations of national values, and thus national policy, were embedded. For these members of the clergy, forging the connections between abstract values and concrete consequences was accomplished through a kind of practical reason. They criticized, for instance, Roosevelt's overreliance on "academics" or "theorists," like the Brain Trust, as lacking such practical wisdom and experience in the "real world."[31] They preferred to rely on a locally oriented, commonsensical approach to social analysis.[32] This is especially interesting in the light of the changes in political authority I associate with political realignment and regime change. By arguing for practical rather than theoretical sources of authority, these clerics were negotiating a specific path through the perils of transitional politics, one that was grounded in an empirical, lived political reality.

In relying on the local, they spoke for their communities in important ways. Grounding their arguments in their description of their localities, they marshaled geography and a sense of place in both the local and the national to warrant their own authority.[33] But authority is generated through rhetoric as much as it is grounded in institutional position, and rhetors both mark and exert their authority through rhetoric that reflects and enacts their place in the social hierarchy.[34] Reflecting the political imaginaries they inhabited, some members of the clergy argued that existing social hierarchies clearly reflected the proper ordering of the world in accordance with biblical strictures and ought not to be disturbed. Others, occupying a different imaginary, saw those hierarchies as equally obviously maintained despite those strictures. Their argumentative reasoning was a product of their institutional position as spiritual and social leaders of their communities, and they generally interpreted abstract principles in accordance with their lived experiences in those roles. The connection between political imaginaries and lived experience is critical. Political vocabularies order those imaginaries in ways that resonate with and order collective lives. The significance of the local in these clerical claims to authority cannot be overstated. Authority is a "grounded entitlement to offer a perspective on appearances based on some claim to a constituency."[35] For the clergy, their perspective was grounded in their religious training and standing, in their ability to connect the abstract to the vernacular, and in their ability to speak for the members of their parishes and communities.

The exercise of authority, however grounded, also depends upon the creation of a relationship between the rhetor and the audience. In the Western tradition, the more powerful the rhetoric is perceived as being, the more it is understood to have dominated the audience.[36] Thus, we think of eloquent rhetoric as "captivating" its audience, rendering it "spellbound," somehow immobilized. When addressing an audience like the president, whose social or political position is higher than that of the rhetor, however, the goal is to command attention rather than to appear to command more generally. The clergy assume a variety of postures, then, from the overtly resentful and angry to the obedient and humble as they seek to establish their authority to advise the occupant of the nation's highest office on secular matters. Some clergy, whether by answering the president's letter or refusing to do so, specifically decline to exercise that authority. Sometimes they argue that they do so because they lack authority themselves; sometimes because they consider the president as having exceeded his authority by requesting their service. In either case, they voluntarily limit their authority in the secular realm of politics. When they do choose to exercise their ability to advise the president, they extend their authority from the local to the national and, at the same time, extend the president's from the national into the local. The differences among these letters reveal the ways political vocabularies operate in tension with one another across the dimension of authority. The clerics who advocated presidential authority generally were advocating this power in the service of specific policy goals and a more egalitarian view of the public good.

Those who resisted federal and executive authority had different policy preferences and preferred a more hierarchically based nation.

Negotiating Shifting Authority during Regime Change

Clerics, of course, have considerable authority by virtue of their positions within their various religious organizations. As rabbis, ministers, priests, imams, and pastors, they are also de facto community leaders, wielding both ecclesiastical and secular authority, although their capacities are obviously greater in the first than in the second instance. And yet there is a paradox here, for in the American context at least, while clerics are accorded significant religious and social power, their intercession in the political realm is trickier. On the one hand, there is a constitutionally mandated separation between church and state and a suspicion of church power having too heavy a hand in state affairs, and for these clerics, the controversy over Democratic presidential candidate Al Smith's Catholicism was a recent memory. On the other hand, there is also a tradition of clerical interventions in politics; the role of some churches in the abolition movement, for instance, would have been equally well remembered.[37] So these clerics would have been aware of the cases both for and against the president's request for their political advice, and in many cases, they included defenses of their position on this issue as part of their replies to him.

ARTICULATING CLERICAL AUTHORITY

The case for clerical authority was, in a number of these letters at least, grounded in a notion of pastoral care: many of Roosevelt's clerical respondents noted that they were motivated by their concern for the communities under their charge. Their arguments in defense of their authority to make political judgments were, unsurprisingly, based in sacred texts. In a charming example of such argument, Martin P. Simon of Eugene, Oregon, informed Roosevelt that "I am glad you asked me for advice. Pharaoh had his Joseph, Darius had his Daniel, and you have me."[38] For this cleric, there was a biblically endorsed tradition of advisors to the powerful, and he was willing to maintain that tradition. The implication of his framing, of course, is that he well understood the distance between his abilities and those of Joseph and Daniel. He may also have been noting the distinctions between Pharaoh, Darius, and the president.

While few of the clerics brought such wry humor to their letters, many of them were equally sensible of their humble place in the historical arc of advisors and made their awareness of that clear. Paul P. Meiser, for instance, reported smiling when he received the president's letter, because "of the patent fact that a good fisherman goes fishing in all waters; and I understand that you have the honor of being known as a real fisherman. . . . Well, I'm going to nibble at the bait, even though I know that you will never be allowed to see what I am writing."[39] Here, Meiser not only notes his own place in the hierarchy—he is fish, not fisherman—he also implicitly associates Roosevelt with Jesus, the preeminent biblical fisherman. Interestingly, however, once having established Roosevelt atop the hierarchy, he then also places him under the control of his own staff, noting not that he will not choose to see the clerical letters but that he will not be allowed to do so. Roosevelt's capacities are limited, as are Meiser's, and both of them were at once leaders and subordinates. As Sam McCormick has pointed out in his study of Seneca's letters, there is a certain power (and thus authority) to be had in the carefully wielded claim to the absence of such power.[40] Clerical authority, like political authority, was bound to its institutional limitations.

But for the clergy as for the president, institutional position was more of a resource than a constraint. Roosevelt's interlocutors were not shy about asserting their role as interpreters of divine revelation, and sometimes coupled that with the idea that the nation enjoyed a divinely appointed mission. This combination meant that the clergy were in a unique position as arbiters of both God's will and national history and thus maintained a kind of authority over both. O. B. Sarber, for example, wrote, "After making all due allowance for the human selfishness, inconsistencies, and mistakes of our early history, it is still clearly patent that this nation was founded by God-fearing, God-honoring men, and upon the principles of the Bible. And certainly, no sincere student of American history can fail to couple the unparalleled prosperity of this country with the favor and blessing of Almighty God."[41] Sarber separated the sincere student of history from her insincere counterpart to argue that since the nation was grounded in religious principles and its adherence to them had led to its prosperity, there was but one choice for a return to prosperity, and that was a renewed dedication to Christianity. Religious authority—and thus clerical authority—was tied to national values and national prosperity. He thus also argued for an embrace of traditional authority.

The clerics also used biblical warrants to support their more specific policy preferences. In so doing, they sometimes echoed the president's words and sometimes offered their own, indicating the ways in which these arguments were circulating from the top down and then back up. George Keithley, for instance, wrote, "The racketeers should, of course, be scourged from the temple, of our economic and political life," clearly relying on FDR's famous argument about the moneychangers from his first inaugural. He also told the president, "There should, however, be no governmental 'social security' for the improvident and the dissolute. Let him be cast into the outer darkness,"[42] a phrase that appears three times in the Bible but not once in FDR's public speech. Keithley was not alone in his evocation of such warrants. W. W. Gunner asked if he might "kindly, yet frankly say that after these months of the 'New Deal,' the nation is like the woman in the Gospel of Luke, who had suffered many things of many physicians had spent all that she had, and was nothing bettered, but rather worse."[43] By couching his judgment concerning the wastefulness of New Deal programs in a biblical warrant, Gunner established his right to make such judgments by demonstrating his knowledge of the Bible and its utility as a guide to communal life. Many of the old truths were no longer dependable, but for the clergy who replied to Roosevelt's letter, biblical truth, at least, remained.

Others were equally ready to exercise their clerical authority over definitions and thus provide themselves with leverage over the political process. John Thompson, for instance, announced himself "disposed to give you credit for honesty of purpose and for making a strenuous endeavor to help the country and minister to our people, but I feel the killing of pigs and burning of cotton was a sin before God and a crime against civilization."[44] Here, rather than the indirect argument made by using biblical stories and allusions, Thompson used a more direct claim to authority, labeling the AAA's actions "sin." Using his authority over definitions to the opposite end, O. L. Prentice was equally ready to consider Roosevelt's policies "fair, just and Christian."[45] The clergy were empowered by their various religious bodies to make judgments about what was or was not "sin," and about what was and was not "Christian." They extended that authority into the secular realm (or were refusing to make a distinction between these realms) by making such judgments about political actions and political actors. The clergy considered their sacred authority as derived from a divine source; they were sure of their ground when that ground was religious. When the ground moved into the political, on the other hand, they were less obviously authorized to speak. Some of the clergy defended their ability to make political judgments while others took the time to write to the president to specifically limit that authority.

LIMITING CLERICAL AUTHORITY

Roosevelt's clerical respondents had three main ways of limiting their own authority. First, they adopted humble stances, they restricted their advice to the areas of their expertise, and they cited the constitutional or prudential reasons for their lack of involvement. Second, many of the clergy felt themselves too isolated, too uneducated, or too uninformed to speak; others simply argued that it was outside of their own knowledge and experience. Finally, others castigated the president for even asking for their input. If the authority of political language was at issue, many of the clergy wanted no part in the development of a new set of political vocabularies, clinging instead to the old one and the old forms of political organization it authorized.

Many of the clergy, like Paul R. Johnson, professed themselves honored by the president's letter. He wrote, "It is indeed an honor to be requested by a man occupying the greatest office of our land, to give one's humble opinion about affairs of national importance. I only hope I might be of some small help to you."[46] Cognizant of the president's political power, clergymen like Johnson were eager to offer what help they could, even as they declared their awareness of their limitations. The Reverend A. Davis best exemplifies the humility with which some of the clergy addressed the president:

Dear President Roosevelt,
Your Honor,

I am only a Common Laborer—preaching the Gospel and working for a living. BUT ANYTHING I CAN DO TO HELP YOU IN YOUR RELECTION FOR 1936 IN SPEAKING OR HONORING I STAND READY TO GIVE ALL THE EFFORT THAT I CAN AS A MAN 54 YEARS OLD HAVING SEEN THE STRUGGLE OF THE AMERICAN WORKING PEOPLE FROM THE OLD LOG CABIN DAYS TIL NOW. The First Campaign Song I ever heard was Hurra for Blaine and Logan I know you remember it and have never seen as good a man as you at the head of our Government nor a woman as good as your wife who visited the poor in their poverty; God Bless you both.
Please Except my Services. Resp.

Rev. A. Davis[47]

From the evidence of this letter, Davis was not the most literate of men, nor was he the most educated. But he had been politically aware since at least 1884 (the election in which James G. Blaine and John A. Logan lost to Grover Cleveland and Thomas A. Hendricks—since Roosevelt was born in 1882, it is actually unlikely that he remembered this election). Davis was willing to support FDR to the extent of his abilities. Those abilities included a capacity to speak for "working people." Having observed their struggles for many years, he was in a position to offer the fruits of his observations. But he does not do so. He simply offers his commendation to both Roosevelt and his wife and blesses them. He does not see himself as an advisor to the president but as a worker in the president's cause. He made no claim to authority himself but was happy to recognize that of the chief executive. In this, he also implicitly authorizes presidential and federal power as legitimate.

Other clergy expressed different grounds for the limits of their advisory authority, citing their lack of competence in secular matters.[48] Joseph M. Coulombe, for instance, referred to himself as "a very small pebble on the beach," while G. A. Baker wrote, "This question is too big for me to solve," and Sooner J. W. Bashore admitted that thinking about "present conditions and trends" simply "gives me a headache."[49] For these men, the problems of the national government were beyond them. Others were equally certain of their incapacities, reflecting the social and economic hierarchies of the time. R. C. Nanney, for example, wrote, "I feel my inability to write you a letter, but appesate gitting a letter from you."[50] One can only imagine the emotions with which a letter from the White House would have been received by Nanney, or with what anxious trepidation he would have struggled over his reply. Perhaps Robert Crawford felt something similar as he confessed that his reaction to receiving a letter from the White House was, "Good Lord, what have I done now?"[51] However they expressed the sentiment, these clergymen did not understand themselves as having the authority to make judgments about political matters, which they ceded to the president.

Some, like Clifford Moody, took less humble stances but still argued that the clergy had no business advising on the economy as it lay outside their expertise. For Moody, "the Christian minster is a specialist on moral and spiritual matters rather than economics" and "it would hardly be wise or consistent to heed us in matters of economic recovery."[52] Prudence, if nothing else, dictated his refusal to offer advice. Others, like A. Freeman Traverse, were equally reluctant on the basis of expertise, stating, "I do not consider myself very well qualified to advise on the matters suggested. I am neither economist nor statesman."[53] It is perhaps notable that he nonetheless offered the president some limited advice.

Many of the clergy thus found themselves honored, even excited by the president's letter. They took the time, whether out of obligation, courtesy, or some other motive, to reply to his request for their advice. But whether or not they withheld that advice they made efforts to minimize its impact and meaning. Some of them, like Reverend Davis, simply offered Roosevelt their support. Other members of the clergy took much more assertive stances. In supporting the president, they were also implicitly supporting his assertion of presidential power.

EXPANDING CLERICAL AUTHORITY

The single most common warrant for the exercise of clerical authority over politics stemmed from the clergy's pastoral role. The clergy were generally prominent members of their communities, and they were often among the most educated members of those communities. It is likely that parishioners looked to the clergy for guidance in understanding new political realities and how they could best be negotiated. The clergy were involved in the personal as well as the public lives of their congregations and were able to serve as community spokespeople, bringing the cares and concerns of their communities to the attention of those in Washington. I want to draw attention to the ways in which bringing the plight of their communities to the president's attention helped to authorize federal and presidential power. The clergy who did so were agreeing to the proposition that these had become the legitimate concerns of the federal government and of the president.

In one of many examples, W. H. Baring noted that ministers were ideally placed to observe the economic condition of their communities.[54] Other clergy reported on those observations in painfully evocative terms. Benjamin Schwartz, for instance, wrote, "Naturally, as a pastor, I am vitally related to many of the problems to which you and your administration have addressed your attention. I see them often in the stark reality of broken homes, blighted lives, and suicide. Yesterday I was called to lay away the body of a father who had taken poison because he was literally at the end of his resources. Always the last to go is Hope, but when that goes nothing remains."[55] The writer's sorrow, as well as his ability to speak to the pain of his parishioners, indicates the failure of the previous regime and the need for a new political organization—which has begun, but has so far only insufficiently addressed the dire situation of his community.

Not all those who claimed authority to judge agreed with the president, however. Samuel Andron of Poughkeepsie, New York, Roosevelt's own backyard, noted acidly, "I have lived for many years here and nearby, and yet during all my eighty years of life I have never seen such evidence of a quick degeneracy and ruin as I have witnessed since you became the misleader of our nation."[56] For Andron, his lifetime of experience and observation enabled his argument that Roosevelt, and not the Depression, led to the "quick degeneracy" of their shared neighborhood. He was implicitly arguing against the specific policies of the New Deal and also against FDR's leadership.

Others, like Henry W. Thompson, went beyond observation: "before replying to your letter," he wrote, "I took the trouble to interview many of our farm population."[57] So when he contributed his sense of their opinions, he did so with some authority. Equally authoritative were the observations of those who, like George Truman Carl, reported traveling to "study conditions carefully."[58] Alfred G. Fisk agreed, noting that

> because we clergymen are perhaps of all folk most sensitive of spirit and most idealistic of purpose, we have been pained by many aspects of your administration policies. We cannot understand your militarism, your excessive appropriations to army and navy, the provocative character of the current Pacific naval maneuvers. I say "your" because we have looked in vain for you to lift your finger against these policies, and because it is generally felt that you are back of them. . . . And it has seemed to us that you have been pathetically weak again and again when you might have been strong. . . . Indeed, we criticize not the "radicalism" of your policies, but, quite the opposite, feel that they have not gone nearly far enough.[59]

Clergymen like Fisk held the president responsible for all aspects of his administration and reported on their results as a firsthand witness to their effects. In all of these examples, the clergy were, because of their ability to observe, sensitive to and idealistic about their communities and were able to make judgments based on those attributes, making claims to authoritative arguments about government policy. Because of these observations they were in a position to judge the merits of political action and the language used to explain and justify it. Their arguments about federal and presidential power were thus rooted in the local.

In serving as channels for public opinion and spokespersons for their communities, the clergy were establishing themselves as important elements in the changing national democracy. Just as Roosevelt was arguing for national power on the grounds that the federal government was best able to see, understand, and serve the nation democratically, the clergy were assuming a similar role, representing their communities to the larger government. In claiming their own political authority, therefore, they were also making claims about the extent and limits of the president's. Many of these claims were, as we have seen, implicit. But the clergy also responded explicitly to the president's claims for institutional power.

The Clergy and Presidential Authority

As the clergy defined their authority and its limits, they also defined that of the chief executive. For Roosevelt's clerical interlocutors, executive authority was defined and defended on several bases. The presidency itself, of course, imbued its occupant with authority. That authority was related to the promises made during the election, which they understood as a contract of sorts. The terms of that contract highlighted the dependence of secular authority. To the extent that the clergy saw the president as acting in accordance with divine mandates, they were willing to grant him extensive—sometimes quite extensive—power. To the extent that they saw him as acting inconsistently with those mandates, however, they were more likely to resist his use of power. They thus were able to associate their own preferred political imaginary with divine will. It is unsurprising that the clergy assumed for themselves the ability to make judgments about the president and his relationship to the will of God.

CLERICAL DEFINITIONS OF PRESIDENTIAL AUTHORITY

The clergy endorsed FDR's exercise of presidential authority, politically a hallmark of the new institutional arrangements accompanying the New Deal realignment, with some trepidation. Some of the clergy either advocated expansion or limits on the president's power based on his willingness and ability to fulfill his promises.[60] He received praise for trying to keep promises as well as exhortations to continue doing so. In the words of Albert Gasten, "Mr. Roosevelt, in all fairness may I say that you are the most beloved of any president for years. If you will just keep in mind your campaign promises to the forgotten men and continue to carry out your promises as you have in the past you will find the country backing you and you will lead our country from doubt and despair to a new era of prosperity. Remember Jesus Christ himself began his reform with the forgotten man."[61] Should Roosevelt continue to follow in the footsteps of the savior, he too might aspire to national economic salvation.

The clergy were quick to note when they felt he was not fulfilling his promises. Samuel A. Troxell wrote, "I now share the disappointment of my community and many of my countrymen in realizing that your promises have been hollow and the 'forgotten man' is still forgotten; that desire to stay in office more concerns our executive and statesmen than true desire to render any real and lasting service."[62] For Troxell, the president valued personal political success over his duty to the nation's poor, and he was thus no longer worthy of clerical support. The clergy did not hesitate to lay responsibility for social conditions at the president's door. William Gordon, for instance, wrote, "You used the influence of your high office to repeal the 18th amendment and brought upon our fair land the greatest curse that has ever cursed the nations. That is the Legalized Liquor Traffic. Today we are producing a generation of drunkards."[63] For Gordon, the president's political authority was being used in ways that were actively destructive of divine intent. Others therefore predicted political consequences for national loss of faith in the president and his promises. Evert Leon Jones, for instance, opined, "Your prospects in this town and county are not good. The tide is running against you. Too many broken promises, Mr. President, too many platform repudiations! The people do not take your present assertions seriously."[64] The clergy and the people as a whole were capable of understanding the president's failures, and they were willing and able to respond appropriately. To the extent that the president's language couldn't be trusted, the president himself could also not be trusted. They would not accede to a new political imaginary premised on presidential power because they deemed it untrustworthy.

For the clergy, then, presidential authority was grounded in both a divine mission and public opinion. If the president failed the first, he was doomed by the second. For those who saw him succeeding in his divinely ordained mission, however, expanded presidential power seemed not only reasonable, but necessary.

CLERICAL EXPANSIONS OF PRESIDENTIAL AUTHORITY

Many of the clergy endorsed a political world in which the president had increased power over the nation's communal life. They often assigned to Roosevelt the role of national savior. James Lawson, for example, wrote, "I come to you, Mr. President, as a humble citizen, to you who have already shown you were touched by the needs and sufferings of your fellow mortals, with the earnest request that you come to the rescue."[65] For Lawson, both Roosevelt's own experience of suffering and his ability to overcome that suffering suited him for the task of national salvation.

Unsurprisingly, the theme of salvation ran through many of the clergy letters. Some of the clergy were explicit about those parallels and likened Roosevelt to specific biblical characters. Clement Saiman wrote, "I believe you are Joseph of America. As God sent Joseph into Egypt to save it, He sent you to save America. If it wasn't you who people selected as our leader, the country would now be in a revolution."[66] Agreeing with both that sentiment and the reasoning behind it, R. L. Bolton wrote simply, "I thank God for you."[67] Many of the clergy, like many Americans of the decade, considered Roosevelt's presidency divinely ordained. This authority is difficult to contest. And certainly, limiting such authority with institutional constraints seems wrongheaded at best, because for these clergy, the Depression was evidence that limits on institutional action had failed.

Sometimes it was not the presidency but the policies that were the product of divine will. In N. B. Bynam's opinion, programs like Social Security were the product of "Divine Revelation."[68] Gustav A. Papperman, for instance, approved of the president's "prophet-like rebuke of selfish greed."[69] After noting that he had a picture of the president "that I like—the picture of a serious man, not with a smile of unconcern, but with a look of a profoundly concerned thinker," Kansan M. O. Clemmons wrote, "The eyes are ever so slightly uplifted. That is symbolic for me."[70] Roosevelt was, he felt, inspired by and attentive to his God. Others found similar symbolic import in the letter itself or in other aspects of the New Deal.[71]

Other members of the clergy, like Clemmons, assumed the president had authority over the nation's spiritual and moral life. Writers like Fred Essig, for example, noted, "My community is rural. But our problems seem to be the universal ones of lowered moral and material conditions arising in great part (I think) from lowered spiritual life." Having diagnosed the problem, however contingently, Essig then assigned responsibility for its solution to the White House in a series of recommendations: "1. That the government do its best to correct the colossal mistake of selling the soul of America for a mess of liquor revenue pottage. 2. That the government officers from the president down set the Nation an example of quiet, godly living; such as the observance of Sunday as a day of rest and worship. 3. That economy and thrift be practiced and encouraged. I have yet to see a person or a nation that could borrow itself to prosperity."[72] Essig, like many of FDR's clerical correspondents, held the president responsible for both policy and example.[73] Even if Roosevelt wasn't authorized by divine will, he was still accountable to it.

Others were equally critical. Ben Bogard, for example, noted that "I am frank, but my heart burns as I write." And write he did, in great detail, of his chagrin over members of the administration who "spent the night until the small hours of the morning gambling, playing poker with a ten dollar limit and you cleaned up on the other boys."[74] Many of the clergy thought, with Bogard and G. C. Meyer, that the president's "pastoral example" could be put to much better use.[75] Even when the clergy did believe that the president's actions were misplaced, they recognized the power of his example over the nation.[76]

Seeing him as a powerful pastoral example, the clergy sometimes resented his efforts to seek their approval for his behavior and actions. Jesse Tidball's letter summarizes the remarks of many of his brethren:

> Your appeal to the clergy and religion for a solution of the difficulties of the American Government reminds me of the prayer that a would-be penitent offered for himself and others one night in the Pacific Garden Mission in Chicago. He had sipped a little too long and deep from the liquor glass and was feeling rather groggy. "Oh Lord," he prayed. "Us fellows have gotten ourselves in an awful hole. Can't you pull us out?"
>
> I am really surprised that you appeal to the clergy, for in all honesty you can scarcely expect the support of the church for your administration until you and your family show in your public and private life more sympathy and interest in the church and all it stands for.[77]

Tidball here likens the president to an inebriate who has partaken of too much alcohol and is acting with impaired judgment. In Tidball's view, Roosevelt's behavior and that of his family makes them unsuitable penitents. Because the president has failed in his own personal life, the nation will continue to suffer because his leadership must necessarily be flawed.

The president's willingness to be photographed "sitting at a table sipping beer and smoking a cigarette" enraged R. J. Lorance, as he considered that this action "started millions of our young people on the road to HELL."[78] In these comments, and in the others like them, the clergy argued that the president wasn't just accountable as the representative of the nation, acting in his official capacity. The president had authority as a person, acting in a more or less private way, doing things with his family and friends. But as president, they were arguing, he was never a private individual. He had and constantly exercised a very public kind of authority. They sometimes connected that public authority to public speech.

As Noel Parker, the Catholic bishop of Sacramento wrote, "If, in the midst of your busy life, you could arrange to give a short monthly radio broadcast, it would help greatly in building up the morale all over the country. The people like to hear from you direct, as the father of the family. Every time you speak, by your voice, your dignity, and your appeal for greater loyalty and confidence, you make friends."[79] For Parker, the president was a friendly, paternalistic figure who had significant symbolic power. Others were more concerned with the president's ability to educate the ignorant public and strongly encouraged him to do so.[80] By speaking publicly the president would be able to wield the mass media in the service of a badly needed new set of explanations describing and interpreting the world in which American citizens now found themselves. Public speech is itself central to the use of interpretive authority, and the clergy were asking the president to exert that authority more consistently.

Still others showed the same faith in the president, if less faith in the public. According to M. Theodore Hamm, for example, "Some of our fellows do not WANT to see the difference between socialism and socialized thinking and action. For those a dignified silence is the best protection. But for the sake of millions of simple minded and trusting citizens, who do not engage in the game of academic distinctions and classifications you should say a word, as Mr. Lincoln did at Gettysburg. Showing the way of true happiness thru sacrifice and co-ordinated effort of all classes of people."[81] This assumption that the president's personal attributes are as meaningful as his public policies undergirds the "new doctrine of presidential leadership" that Jeffrey Tulis sees as one of the bases for the rhetorical presidency, an extraconstitutional expansion of presidential power.[82] By relying on individual rather than limited institutional elements of the office, this aspect of Roosevelt's government encouraged fears of dictatorial power and spurred some members of the clergy to advocate limiting that power. These clerics did not share a political imaginary in which a president—especially this president—should be the locus of political authority.

CLERICAL LIMITATIONS OF PRESIDENTIAL AUTHORITY

Roosevelt's clerical respondents offered both implicit and explicit arguments for limiting the president's authority, and thus underlined their own. They argued, for instance, that he should have asked their help sooner and also that he should not have asked for it at all. They questioned his motives, and they feared his tendency to grasp for dictatorial power. And most importantly, they reminded him that both power and authority rightfully belonged to God, not to any secular entity, including the president.

The clerical respondents were sometimes quite explicit in expressing their aggravation that the president had not asked for their help sooner. Charles Alexander Richmond, for example, wrote that the request for advice on Social Security "would have come with better grace if our counsel had been asked before the legislation was enacted," while Myles Hemenway replied, "You got yourself and the country into this awful mess now get yourself and it out, if you can."[83] Others contented themselves with simple refusals to assist the president, as did M. T. Keizer, who wrote, "If your letter is onle a political gesture, God forgive you; if it is out of a heart sincere and sympathetic, which I believe it is, may you heed the voice that speaks thru this letter, and may God's blessing be upon you and his Spirit dwell in you thru the coming days of your administration."[84] By chastising and correcting the president, these members of the clergy were not only advocating limits on his authority explicitly, they were limiting it implicitly by refusing to accede to his request, and they were also using their cultural authority to help order a political imaginary in opposition to the one preferred by the Democrats.

Many of these clergy worried that he was using these letters as a lever to amass undemocratic power. Henry Sills Bradley, for example, reported being "alarmed also at your ready acceptance of almost dictatorial power."[85] Others were equally concerned, writing, as did E. J. Jarrell, that "I cannot see why your administration should want to scrap the

Constitution, concentrate power in your hands, put the Courts out of business, and turn this great Republic into a dictatorship after the pattern of Russia, Germany, or Italy."[86] It is indicative of how deeply discussion of the nature of power and its limits had permeated into the national culture that members of the clergy would assert their arguments about the nature of the proper constitutional balance between the branches of government so forcibly. It is also evidence that the assumption of political authority was contested within the polity, revealing one of the fissures between the political imaginaries and the political vocabularies that order them.

Some of them made such arguments about power on the basis of their authority as interpreters of sacred texts. One clergyman not only prophesied the apocalypse but essentially laid responsibility for it on the president. U. B. Johnson wrote: "I feel it is too late. After repealing the Eighteenth Amendment; recognizing Russia; and sitting on the International Conclave on the Sabbath Day without protest, and that the prophecies contained in the Second Psalm and Thirteenth Chapter of Revelation are about to be fulfilled and that the time of trouble mentioned in Daniel 12: 1 is imminent. Yours sincerely."[87] The tone of the letter leaves the reader in no doubt of the author's sincerity. This author was perhaps one of FDR's gloomiest correspondents, but he was not alone in his prediction. Charles B. Lewis, for instance, wrote, "Your circular letter reached me several weeks ago and I have been studying and praying over the answer. I am wondering if that letter was an earnest desire to obtain the help of the clergy in these days of depression or was it just a pretty jesture to gain the goodwill of the ministers. I will not take time to tell you, as many ministers undoubtedly have, that the only hope of our nation is getting back to God. But I would call your attention to the fact that the nation that forgets God will be turned into hell."[88] For these authors, and the many others like them, the Depression was something of a visitation and they were telling the president their only hope was an immediate return to God.

Sometimes the clergy wrote with so little deference as to have that alone constitute an argument against presidential authority. Albert Hale Plumb, for instance, addressed FDR as "Mr. 'President,'" before stating that "Never since the days of King George III has there been such an attempt to usurp the individual liberties and state rights of the American people as now."[89] Another claimed not that he was getting too big, but that he was "too small for the job."[90] And others, like Daniel S. Gage, told Roosevelt, "Personally, I regard you as a very dangerous man to be in the presidential chair. And this for many reasons. I voted for you last time but shall not do so again, no matter who the opposing candidates may be."[91] The contrast to the humble and deferential tone of other letters is both sharp and instructive. These members of the clergy had no difficulty in asserting their authority as judges of presidential conduct. They accepted the president's terms but developed out of those terms a different position on the matter at hand. Their willingness to use so sharp a tone is itself a rejection of presidential power.

They did not usually, however, let that argument remain entirely implicit. Franklin L. Graff, for example, wrote that he had quite liked the president in his first year in office before yielding to altogether different emotions:

> However, since that time, with increasing alarm and disappointment, I am compelled to record my emphatic disapproval. . . . The autocratic absorbtion into your own person of the three-fold division of our Government, and the irresponsible direction of those powers, have aroused my deep indignation. When the whim, fancy, prejudice or secret motive of the man in the White House can seriously, and often disastrously affect the freedom and life of every man, woman and child in the United States, in astounding reversal of the intention of the framers of our Constitution, not ever attempted previously in times of peace, it becomes the stern duty of every citizen to register his solemn protest.[92]

The author left no question of his capacity to make judgments; they run through every line of his letter. They are not mere opinions. They are judgments, made with reference to national history and the Constitution and with a particular political philosophy in mind. This cleric saw with alarm the development of a political imaginary with Roosevelt at its center and with equal alarm the creation of a political regime with a president at its center.

Many of the clergy agreed with Thomas Hickman and R. O. Sutton. The first wrote, "I do not believe that our Depression is economic alone. It is also moral and spiritual," which meant that the problem went well beyond the secular.[93] Sutton agreed, noting that in his opinion, "the majority of the people are following into damnation the gods of the world, rather than seeking after the Lord. It seems that our Lord has had to use many severe measures such as these to bring people to a repentant heart in times past and recorded in history. Nations have fallen and nations have been destroyed through the worship of false gods."[94] Here, God and the American people have agency; the president does not.[95] These clerics inhabited an imaginary in which the sacred trumped the secular, and they opposed one in which the president had national moral authority. For them, the president's authority ought to be limited.[96]

Just as the president was not really authorized to deal with the nation's spiritual crisis, many of the president's correspondents argued that the clergy were not prepared to deal with the nation's economic woes. Some of them, like M. E. Seltz, lectured the president on the separation of church and state. He opined, "When the government goes to the churches for politics, the devil is smiling around the corner."[97] The president, he implied, was doing the devil's work by attempting to recruit the clergy for secular purposes, providing an exemplary effort to leverage sacred authority in the service of limiting presidential authority.

For these members of the clergy, the president's duty went beyond the words of the Constitution and extended into its spirit. So John Meecham, for example, could write, "There is, I notice, much ado in the political press about your plans and policies being, as they say, out of step with the Constitution. I do not believe, however, that the American people will fail to see, and remember, that you are the first President that ever strove to give a meaning and a reality to the fundamental human thought of the Constitution—the right of every man to life, liberty and happiness."[98] There are at least two things worth noting here. First, he conflated the Constitution and the Declaration of Independence, revealing some of the confusion circling about the ways in which various political actors of the time were authorizing their policy preferences. Second, the people, according to Meecham's analysis, were a more appropriate source of presidential authority than the Constitution. The multiplicity of available warrants and the confusion among them indicates as nothing else can the transition between one set of political vocabularies and another.

The meaning of politics was shifting, and political language had not yet coalesced into forms that made consistent sense of the new political imaginaries.

Conclusion

As the 1930s wore on, Democrats were increasingly willing to accept national and presidential authority as the hinge upon which their understanding of politics hung. There were important limits on that authority, however. It was not to extend too far over other institutions: national authority would not extend over the politics and policies of Jim Crow, for example, and presidential authority was not to extend too far over that of Congress or the Supreme Court. FDR never broached civil rights and was rebuked over his efforts to purge Congress and pack the court. But Democrats were content to dwell in a political imaginary in which federal and presidential authority extended over the economy and the creation and administration of social policy. Their vision of the nation became less parochial (again with the important exception of the South) and more national. They were willing to understand the president as the progenitor and exemplar of national values.

Republicans, on the other hand, still wanted to inhabit a political imaginary in which authority over collective life was ceded to the private sector, the authority of the federal government was limited, and what power there was resided in Congress. They wanted social policy to be determined at the state and local levels and saw danger in allowing the president to wield too much social and political power. They were suspicious of federal power in general and of Roosevelt's use of it in particular.

The clergy, like the president, also exercised authority. They were empowered to make judgments on the nature of politics and its relationship to sin, on the nation's history, and on the actions of the current president. For the clergy, the authority behind these definitions was scriptural. The president had no parallel authority but transcended the need for it when the clergy assigned him the role of savior or Moses. His actions enacted scriptural requirements; the clergy's interpreted them. For those willing to inhabit an imaginary in which presidential authority was considered benign, assigning it a scriptural role makes perfect sense. They conflated the institutional with the personal and imbued trust in the president as much as they did in the presidency. Members of the clergy who resisted the growth of federal and presidential power found warrants for that belief in sacred texts.

Both the president and some members of the clergy found authority in their relationship with the public under their care. This rather paternalistic rendering accurately reflects how many of the clergy and certainly this president saw that relationship. The clergy were able to observe both the public and the more private lives of their parishioners and were able to authorize their opinions through those observations. Similarly, the president, as the recipient of these pastoral observances, was authorized to act in accordance with them. While the ultimate judge of the president's authority was for these members of the clergy always and importantly God, the more immediate judgments made by the clergy were grounded in a kind of practical reason. The clergy knew things to be true because they witnessed them. And it is therefore to a discussion of witnessing that we now turn.

CHAPTER TWO

Witnessing Politics: The Depictive Element of Political Vocabularies

As a result of the crisis of political authority caused by the onset of the Great Depression, Democrats in the 1930s were beginning to prefer a political imaginary in which political authority was centered in the federal government and in the person of the president. Republicans, on the other hand, resisted both presidential and federal power. These different views of legitimate political authority were located in different understandings of the political world—different political imaginaries, which were coming to be ordered by different political vocabularies. Just as these imaginaries offered different views of political authority, they also understood that authority as extending over different kinds of citizens and serving different kinds of functions.

For political vocabularies to be viable, they must be understood as accurately describing the political world. Old vocabularies fail because the broader political environment in which they were embedded changes. For new sets of political vocabularies to operate effectively, they must reflect this change and offer a view of the political world that is newly accurate. The depictive aspect of political vocabularies is thus especially important, for through depiction citizens and leaders come to see and develop a shared understanding of the shape of the polity. During the 1930s, the old order was shaken by the national financial crisis. The Depression changed everything: the composition of communities, their social structures, the nature of families. Finding ways to cope with these compounded crises first required understanding them. In order to understand them, they had to be seen. And that is how the depictive element of political vocabularies operates; detailing the nation makes it available for viewing and thus for understanding and acting.[1] That shared understanding and action are based in description, contain arguments about causes and consequences, involve an element of personification, and render judgments. These elements are conveyed linguistically through reportage, metaphor, narrative, and analogy; they change as regimes change and help to order the new alignment. These depictions, by necessity, circulate around the public and from the public to governmental officials. They appear in newspaper stories and other kinds of media coverage. They are the stuff of popular culture, and they are an important part of letters written to FDR by the clergy.

The pre–New Deal reliance on state and local governments to manage their affairs depended on an ideology of localism, which thrived under conditions of relative prosperity. Under the previous alignment, citizens were believed to be self-sufficient, and in a nation where economic well-being was ideologically understood to be equally available to all those who were willing to work for it, social and economic differences were not considered to require governmental intervention. Local communities could serve as laboratories of democracy, offering experiments in innovation. More prosperous communities could find ways to protect impoverished constituents without resorting to government; less prosperous communities were less able to do so, rendering those citizens' lives more precarious. Communities structured along lines of class, race, and ethnicity could protect and perpetuate those structures, which were thus naturalized, as their very perpetuation seemed to indicate that they were in fact inevitable. For better or worse, politics prior to the New Deal, especially in the area of social policy, was generally local.

Philosophically opposed to governmental management of charity and what was then known as relief, President Herbert Hoover, despite his reputation as the "Great Humanitarian," was disinclined to augment local- and state-level relief with federal dollars.[2] But the need quickly overwhelmed the capacities of the localities, and millions of Americans were thrown out of their homes and into makeshift shacks that became known as "Hoovervilles." The level and extent of the desperation and Hoover's apparent unwillingness to address it were important factors in his 1932 loss to FDR.[3]

Roosevelt himself was a reluctant supporter of relief, fearing, as did many of his time, the deleterious effects it might have on the moral fiber of the poor and its potential to undermine the nation's independent spirit.[4] But as the effects of the Depression crept upward through the lower, to the working, and into the middle classes, it became increasingly apparent that something had to be done. The New Deal, with its triple emphases on recovery, relief, and reform, included a plethora of programs designed to help those dislocated and unemployed by the Depression and to restore the nation's economic health. Chief among these programs were the National Industrial Relief Administration, the Agricultural Adjustment Administration, the Civilian Conservation Corps, the Works Progress Administration (WPA), and finally, in 1935, the president signed the iconic New Deal program, Social Security, into law.[5] Every one of these programs was federally administered. Every one of them meant an added administrative burden. And every one of them aimed at minimizing the nation's suffering either through structural reform or assistance to the needy.

But while the federal government's administrative capacity increased, suffering continued. With an election looming, it was in Roosevelt's interest to determine both the extent and nature of the nation's continuing needs and the valences of public opinion on his efforts to address those needs. If the nation was going to authorize a massive shift in power from the states and localities to the national government, it was important that the effects of the shift could be felt in positive ways. His public rhetoric, of course, was one such way. So it is unsurprising that Roosevelt specifically mentioned both Social Security and the WPA in his letter to the clergy.

His respondents did not, however, restrict themselves to Roosevelt's areas of concern. The clergy letters did important work by bringing the rich variety of the conditions and concerns of their communities to the attention of those in positions of national power. If a new political language is called for by drastically altered political conditions, that language must describe those emergent conditions in ways are widely understood as accurate.[6] The clergy themselves took this aspect of their letters very seriously, and thus participated in acts of witnessing, a kind of moral reasoning in which the rhetor seeks to influence action on behalf of justice through language. Witnessing is, as Bradford Vivian notes, a particularly democratic kind of public reason,[7] and it is this element that I want to stress here. While most of the extant rhetorical scholarship on witnessing concerns itself with public contexts such as formal testimony, I argue that it can be useful to understanding the operation of quasi-public communication such as the clergy letters as well. As examples of political vocabularies in action, these letters add an importantly explicit moral element to the consideration of public policy, and as specifically moral interlocutors, the clergy are particularly well suited to an analysis of that element of public deliberation. As the contours and content of the nation's policies were being debated, its political language was also shifting. In offering FDR their testimony, they echoed his language, contested that language, and urged upon him certain terms as central to the new competing political vocabularies. In doing so, they circulated themes preferred by the administration and added their own. Those terms made the clergy's localities present in Washington even as the act of writing and publicizing their letters brought Washington just as surely into those localities.

Those members of the clergy who inhabited a political imaginary in which federal and presidential political authority was legitimate tended to offer depictions of the polity as suffering through no fault of their own. These clergy understood their parishioners as victims of larger forces: the machine age, economic dislocation, and other broad changes in the economy. They urged the president to continue supporting these citizens, whose needs they carefully documented. The clergy who inhabited a political imaginary that preferred local and private action tended to argue for the inefficiency and waste of federal efforts and argued that the protection of the needy was more appropriately located at the local level or in the private sector. Both imaginaries were ordered in this respect by the depictive element of political vocabularies. Roosevelt's interlocutors grounded their arguments in local knowledge and conveyed it reporting facts, which enabled an argument that the depictions were based in empirical reality, relying on metaphors, which attributed causes and consequences of that reality, crafting narratives, which personified and made that reality present, and offering analogies, which facilitated judgments about the nature of the shared political reality. These devices sustain political imaginaries by offering rich senses of who citizens are and how they go about their lives. They populate the political world in lived political experience and locate political imaginaries in verisimilitude.

The Clergy as Witnesses

The act of witnessing has at least two important valences. It is an activity with certain kinds of consequences, and it operates through specific kinds of rhetorical practices, which I am collecting here under the general rubric of depiction. As a group, the clergy were situated as specific kinds of witnesses.[8] As members of the clergy, they had a particular kind of authority. That authority is employed in their service as witnesses, people with a unique ability to see and to testify about the economic, social, and political realities of their communities. In so doing, they enabled the president and their fellow citizens to see a new political reality, both calling for and peopling a new set of competing political vocabularies.

In general, the clergy held particularly important roles in their communities; this was, of course, more true of the smaller, rural sites than of larger, urban ones. But even in the cities, the clergy held positions of social power. Partly, this power was related to their roles as communitarian caretakers. Those most in need of pastoral care, whether economic or spiritual, were known to the clergy. Second, the clergy were in a position to offer judgments, an element of their position that, as I argued previously, helped support or challenge presidential power. They also offered judgments about social organization more broadly. But for the purposes of this discussion, it is important to note in the visual lexicon so popular at the time that the central position of the clergy enabled a wide-ranging vision of their communities and thus facilitated their role as witnesses able to testify to the conditions of those communities. Because their testimony appeared in epistolary form, the clergy were constituted as particular kinds of witnesses and engaged in particular kinds of depiction. They thus reveal the contours of the developing New Deal political vocabularies.

WITNESSING

John Durham Peters argued that all communication is a form of witnessing, but I use "witnessing" in a more specific sense here.[9] I want most of all to argue, following Vivian, that witnessing is an intentional activity; it is a "highly valued mode of public address" that helps sustain democratic political culture.[10] Vivian, like most of those interested in the rhetoric of witnessing, is interested in it as a kind of formal testimony, given in public with the intention of influencing public deliberation over specific acts of injustice. I extend this understanding of witnessing into quasi-public forums, retaining the idea that such testimony is a kind of "civic pedagogy."[11] In this case, rather than attempting to influence public deliberation directly through testimony, the clergy were trying to organize and distribute their understanding of civic truth for the audience in the White House, understood as the president himself and/or members of his staff. In this sense, the clergy challenged, reflected, circulated, and invented the set of political vocabularies in the 1930s.

Through their use of empirical evidence, metaphor, narrative, and analogy, the clergy sought to make their communities present, to forge between those communities and the elites in Washington an awareness of the changes that undercut the previous alignment and authorized the new one, allowing the comfortable to feel the suffering and fear as well as the hope and resilience that the clergy themselves saw.[12] This sense of presence was important, for just as Roosevelt argued for power on the basis of his ability to see, understand, and thus govern the entire nation, whether they supported or resisted his policies, the clergy took very seriously their role in facilitating the president's vision. The more accurately they could depict their communities, and the more rhetorical force they could place behind those depictions, the greater the possibility of garnering what they considered appropriate policies. The clergy thus often included photographs, histories, pamphlets, and other explanatory supplementary materials with their letters, offering visual, empirical, and historical support for their depictions.

The historical elements are especially interesting. Because, as Barbie Zelizer notes, witnessing colonizes the past to help lend credence and coherence to the present,[13] the clergy's acts of witnessing also helped organize and understand the nation's varied experiences with the Depression and its multiple efforts to ameliorate its effects. The clergy thus wielded history in at least two important senses. First, whether they preferred or opposed New Deal policies, the clergy used history as a way of situating their communities for the president and his staff. They often argued from local history, noting the closure of nearby industries or business as marking the community's descent from prosperous to impoverished, or made arguments about their parishioner's history of self-reliance and hard work as warrants for the need for governmental assistance or restraint. Among those who preferred an active government, these arguments were generally accompanied by claims that their communities included at least some who merited governmental assistance. Among those with different preferences, local history was mobilized in defense of local action.

Second, many of the clergy used history in a more generalized sense, making nostalgic arguments about the past and explicitly wishing for a return to it. They not only wanted a return to economic health, they worried a great deal about what they often perceived as a decline in public morality, and they yearned for a return to a more bucolic and thus virtuous past as well as a more prosperous one. This nostalgic tone was often used by those who opposed federal intervention, but was occasionally also present in those who were writing to the president to urge national action in support of this pastoral vision. These clerical interlocutors often evoked symbols of mechanization as summary or condensation symbols evoking the distance between the world they wanted and the one in which they actually lived.

Because all depictions are in some sense evocative, the clerical epistolary witnessing therefore isn't just the activity of the clergy, but demands participation by the audience. If a depiction is effective, it not only makes something present for the audience but actively engages the audience in the things thus evoked.[14] In bringing their communities to the president, the clergy were also bringing the president to their communities. Just as letters imply a back-and-forth relationship, including both sender and receiver in an ongoing relationship,[15] the use of depiction in these letters also implies participation by the president in the ongoing life of the community. These letters, even those that overtly argued against federal and presidential power, authorized federal power and embedded their communities within a context in which the federal government has a legitimate role in the life of local communities. Of course, by rejecting the opportunity to offer such depictions, some clergy also actively rejected the increased role of the federal government, and sometimes did so in very explicit terms.

This variation among clerical responses reminds us just how controversial New Deal reforms and policies were and how useful these letters are as a window into the ways that the political vocabularies of a particular era exist always in tension with one another. These clergy were inhabiting different political imaginaries. This is evident when we consider the letters through the lens of witnessing.

Witnessing is fragmentary; it comes in pieces and is necessarily offered from a limited perspective. Many of the clergy noted that they spoke only for themselves. Equally often, they made attempts to speak for members of their communities more broadly. Because witnessing involves a kind of reportage in which one person's testimony serves as a metonym for the experiences of many others, there is an implied relationship with public opinion.[16] So when Melford Loske Brown, for instance, reported an "ever-increasing lack of confidence in government and currency," or Philip C. Diamond reported that "the business men around the square, the old native stock, are pretty solid in opposition to the program of the present administration," that information could be compiled and collated with other sources of public opinion flowing into the White House.[17] These fragments added depth and nuance to the information available through those other sources.

But the information thus provided isn't neutral. Witnessing implies decisions about whose suffering matters. It necessarily entails selective attention to victims.[18] So first, the clergy themselves made decisions about who was worthy of their attention and that of the president. Often, those decisions relied upon and reinforced long-standing distinctions between the deserving and the undeserving poor.[19] So the clergy opposed to the New Deal would often allege various kinds of abuses of the system while those in favor of it would emphasize the virtues of those for whom more help was requested. A great many of the clergy proved ambivalent, reflecting the nation's uncertainty about the financial and moral costs of relief and their fears that it would have destructive outcomes, even as they recognized the imperatives for providing food and shelter for destitute citizens. The main line of division among the political imaginaries—the debate over the proper extent of federal involvement—was clear. The ways in which that would come to be reflected in the specific policies and the linguistic ordering of those imaginaries had yet to be fully developed.

These letters thus reveal a great deal about the various clergy's commitment to social justice and the different ways in which "justice" could be understood—the emerging issue cleavages that characterized the New Deal coalition and the new political vocabularies that accompanied them. The clergy made claims upon government on behalf of those they considered underrepresented; they criticized the government for contributing to intemperance, sloth, and any number of other social ills; and they articulated, sometimes in great depth, theories of government, citizenship, and the role they should each play in the nation's communal life. And they did so by offering testimony, based on personal experience and observation, about how the Depression and Roosevelt's policies were affecting the lives of those closest to his correspondents.

These letters thus indicate how the rhetorical practice of witnessing is closely aligned to representation. Witnessing is about the "power to reveal."[20] The clergy clearly felt, and often expressed, a sense of responsibility toward both their communities and the president, and they strove to make sure that their representation was both accurate and persuasive. In doing so, they relied on various means of depiction.

DEPICTION

Depiction is, of course, a persuasive mechanism. In Michael M. Osborn's words, it "begins with the recognition that the first, most basic function of rhetorical language—including metaphor—is to control perceptions, how we see and encounter the world in which we live."[21] Depiction involves both reason and emotion. Our perceptions of the world must match both the way in which we experience that world and the emotional valences through which we respond to those experiences—and it is not at all clear in these letters whether the reasons, ideologies, or feelings stirred in and by the clergy come first. What is clear is that they viewed their world through different political imaginaries that helped them order and understand the world about them. They sought to convey that understanding to the president and his staff.

This was all the more important given the uncertain nature of the times. The massive dislocations caused by the Depression and the resulting changes at work in the nation meant that both the government and the people as a whole were trying to envision and understand new social, political, and economic realities. By offering up these various fragments, the clergy could help the president see and understand the ways in which members of their communities thought governmental policy was—and was not—influencing those changes. That these fragments all came from the particular perspective afforded by the clergy made their amalgamation all the more coherent, expressing as they did both individual and denominational differences and a broad concern with the moral aspects of public policy. In them, there is evidence of an emergent set of contending political vocabularies.

Roosevelt's clerical correspondents worked hard to convey accurately both the material realities of their communities and the personal and spiritual consequences they associated with those realities. Osborn tells us that depiction intensifies "feelings that will power action."[22] Even as artful depiction requires correspondence with lived or imagined experience, it also evokes emotions and thus impels action. The urgency felt by the clergy in response to their experiences in the parishes and communities was translated in these letters in ways that endeavored to impel or impede national action on their behalf. This translational aspect is important, for just as when words and ideas are translated from one language to another some meaning is added while other elements of meaning are lost or obscured, when the clergy represent their communities in these letters those representations are selections of reality, put in terms that the clergy thought would make sense to those in power.

The clergy shift between their local vernaculars and the language they thought appropriate to their audience, and in doing so reveal something of their localities, their understanding of the audience, and the values that unite them. They thus reveal the ways in which depictions can exercise cultural power.[23] They are grounded in cultural practice and can authorize both arguments and social practices.[24] Depictions function as social models that influence the social imaginary.[25] They are integral to political vocabularies. When the clergy depict their communities in certain ways, they also describe the nature of those communities and the social relationships that constitute them. These definitions both reinforce and challenge social hierarchies, are justified in mythic terms, and lead to specific, natural political solutions to problems. Cultural power cannot be separated from political power, and the clergy were very clearly aware that their letters served political as well as cultural purposes. They used depictions of their local cultures in ways that they hoped would influence national politics through the language that conveys those politics. This is true whether they were advocating governmental action, working to prevent such action, or merely expressing their approval or disapproval of current action.

By tying the cultural to the political through language, the clergy were also helping to weave together a national political culture. Depictions always help create community.[26] But this leaves open the question of what kind of community is created by depiction, and Lisa Gring-Pemble reminds us that depictions can lead to both emancipatory and oppressive ends.[27] In the same way that witnessing privileges certain kinds of suffering or the suffering of certain members of the population, depiction privileges some visions of communities and tends to obscure others. Communities are created through "mythic pictures that embody common values and goals," expressing "a common history and purpose, creating a shared sense of time and cultural context."[28] The clerical depictions in these letters rely on common themes, often use similar biblical warrants, and in general are grounded in particular versions of national history. They thus reveal the political and cultural divisions that circulated through the polity and animated political vocabularies developing in the 1930s.

Clerical Depictions

Depiction serves as a kind of strategic rhetoric.[29] All depictions, conveyed through all kinds of rhetorical devices, are selective. They focus on some elements of the world and elide others; they help us make sense of events within larger contexts and create contexts through which we understand events. Different sets of political vocabularies, operating in different political eras, rely on different depictions and perhaps even wield different strategies of depiction. These depictions came in a variety of forms, but I focus here on four: reportage, metaphor, narrative, and analogy. The clergy often offered detailed descriptions of their communities, telling the president the size, demographic composition, and sometimes even the physical surroundings of their community. These descriptions were both context and argumentative content. This kind of reportage gave the depictions an aura of verisimilitude; the factual content allowed the clergy to make the claim that their arguments matched political reality. They sometimes fleshed out these descriptions with a variety of devices, such as metaphor, though which they sought to give their descriptions both life and depth. Metaphors sometimes provided explanations for the conditions the clergy sought to elucidate and sometimes were used to evoke particular elements of those conditions. Many of the clerical responses offered extended narratives. The clergy told the president the stories of their communities, sometimes offering detailed local histories and sometimes including vignettes concerning specific individuals. These stories authorized the clergy's political views and brought the local communities and their inhabitants vividly to life. Finally, the clergy offered judgments upon the realities that they depicted, quite often by offering analogies. These various forms of depiction all helped make their communities and their concerns present to those in Washington, and both made themselves present at the national level and made the federal government present in the local. They are all important elements of the 1930s set of contending political vocabularies and shed light on the workings of political vocabularies in general and their relationship to the processes of political change.

REPORTING THE FACTS

Many of the clergy included within their letters descriptions of their communities. There is a kind of humility entailed in description without embellishment, for it leaves judgments about the meaning of the information up to the reader. Yet, like other forms of depiction, such description brings events and people before one's eyes, making them present.[30] Description has an emotional component, for it involves evoking the imagination: as description sets an event before the audience's eyes, they therefore see that event; they develop a mental picture of that which is described.[31] The clergy offered factual descriptions of their communities that would help the president and his staff see both the conditions and their consequences. Because these descriptions were offered without judgment, the act of assessing conditions and consequences fell to those readers. They seemed to assume the universality of one political imaginary.

Some of these descriptions would have been helpful in presidential assessments of policy. One clerical respondent wrote, for instance, that "Chillicothe, Illinois is an industrial town. It is the division headquarters of the Santa Fe Railroad. It has a large gravel company's head offices here. Many who live here work in the industries of Peoria."[32] This information, only mildly interesting in its own right, becomes more important when it is placed alongside information about how these industries were doing in other parts of the nation or when compared to other industries in the Midwest. Such comparisons were probably useful given that the conditions the clergy reported varied widely. B. M. Collins, for instance, reported from California that "conditions are far better than in the past three years. There is more money in circulation, more, and better business, and conditions are greatly improved."[33] Mississippian C. B. Scott felt no details were necessary, as the entirety of his letter was "Waterford is in the Drouth striked section and the people need whatever aid that can be given."[34] In Maryland, however, John R. Leatherbury reported "Sir, my charge is in the hot bed of political upheaval. The entire town is OWNED by the BETHLEHIEM STEEL COMPANY."[35] All of the descriptions helped locate these communities geographically, economically, and politically.

The clergy offered social locators as well. One member of the clergy wrote, "My cure is among a plain people who work for their living . . . they are self-respectin people. The struggle has been hard this last six years, but practically none have called for relief." He then stated that "the Works Program has not accomplished much in this region yet."[36] Indeed, many of the clergy told the president that his policies were either inadequate to the need or noted that their benefits had not yet reached their localities.[37] In describing their communities they made arguments for the worthiness of their congregants and let the president know how shallowly or deeply his policies had penetrated into the needy communities around the nation.

The facts presented by the clergy concerning their communities could be remarkably detailed. William F. Cochran reported that "our farmers cry out for a lower price on farm machinery. A grain binder costs $306," while Kirk M. Dewe wrote that "there are still 95 out of the 600 families in our community who are on relief."[38] In Indiana, John W. Nicholson noted that "in this town of a population of 621 there are 13 men and women to my knowledge that are past the age of 65 years who have nothing laid in store to live on."[39] Such details allowed for assessment of the communities across a broad spectrum of variables, and each letter offered both unique and generalizable data.

Depictions that depended on factual descriptions were not necessarily dry, but could be evocative.

> The people of this district are pure-blood Navajo Indians who eke out their livelihood in a few limited ways. In the main, they support themselves by raising small flocks of sheep, a few head of cattle, and by doing a skimpy type of farming. Then too, they have a small source of pecuniary income through the weaving of rugs and the manufacture of silver trinkets. On the whole, they are a poverty-stricken people, with a limited food supply and a very questionable income. . . . Such being the conditions for the young and able-bodied, you can imagine the plight of the aged and the incompetent.[40]

This example is interesting not least because of the ways in which the author's modifiers serve to underline the description of poverty. There is a palpable sense of shrinkage in this text, conveyed through words like "limited," "small," "skimpy," and "few." In addition, they do not weave carpets, only "rugs," do not make jewelry, but only "trinkets," and their condition is described as a "plight." This language both describes local conditions and also makes an implicit argument that the shrinkage requires redress. At other cultural moments, or in other political cultures, one can imagine smallness being valorized; this clergyman, however, desired more federal help for the members of his community, and for him, "small" was something that needed correction, a marker of recovery's limits rather than its possibilities.

The news was not all about the limits of recovery, of course, but economic improvement was uneven and hard to parse by state or region. Roosevelt would undoubtedly have been relieved to hear, as he did from a number of his clerical correspondents, that "there is a distinct improvement in employment here,"[41] although some, like J. Edwin Hemphill, found conditions mixed. He wrote, "Conditions in Petersburg and its environs are improving very much among the poor and the unemployed, and the laboring people. The once wealthier class, who formerly had good salaries and incomes, are now in many cases, in real need. Many have lost all that they had and are too proud and self-respecting to ask aid."[42] Hemphill, who wanted more assistance and a stronger federal presence in his community, authorized that preference by noting the worthiness of his parishioners. He noted that poverty had reached even the "once wealthier class," implying systemic rather than individual causes, and thus requiring systemic rather than individual remedies.

Others found those systemic remedies inadequate. Joe English, for instance, wrote, "Conditions here have grown constantly worse. They are now very bad. I have never known this country is such distress before."[43] Dwight Learned reported "that as far as this little college town is concerned there appears to be no benefit whatever from the New Deal."[44] As much as the descriptions could help the White House uncover patterns and determine policy, they could also impede these efforts through the sheer number of disparate responses. As witnesses, the clergy were offering data that could serve to use their understanding of the past as a guide to future action. Their views of the past and of appropriate future action were colored both by their experiences in their own communities and by the political imaginaries they inhabited.

In all these cases, the clergy offered what they considered to be the facts of the case under consideration. They reported to the White House on the local conditions they personally observed and experienced. This kind of objective reporting lent verisimilitude to the arguments the clergy made. Some of these arguments were about the causes of the Depression and the consequences of the president's policies. Those arguments can best be understood through the clergy's use of metaphor.

OFFERING PERSPECTIVE ON CAUSES AND CONSEQUENCES THROUGH METAPHOR

Metaphor is an important vehicle of depiction.[45] Metaphors are, but are not merely, an important element of style.[46] They are truncated analogies and may also enable arguments by comparison.[47] Metaphor is not just a literary device but "an event that occurs in the minds of listeners."[48] Metaphors, then, like all forms of depiction, are importantly participative, and not only bring something before an audience, but involve the audience in the evocation. Indeed, George Lakoff and Mark Johnson have argued that all humans tend to think in metaphors.[49] Kenneth Burke, of course, includes metaphor among his four master tropes and likens it to perspective, famously arguing that "metaphor is a device for seeing something in terms of something else. It brings out the thisness of a that or the thatness of a this."[50] Metaphor operates in a kind of "blended space," enabling new perspectives on even well-known things.[51] It offers, in Osborn's words, "the world in double-focus."[52] Metaphor, then, not only brings forward one element of the object or event under discussion but does so in ways that alters the audience's perspective on it.

And herein is its specific political significance. For the metaphors one chooses to elaborate on an element of an event, person, or thing selectively determine which aspect of that object will be foregrounded and which will be obscured. Such choices are necessarily political. Metaphors help to create specific kinds of warrants for political action.[53] As Robert Hariman points out, they have important ideological components.[54] Indeed, proponents of different political viewpoints tend to rely on different metaphors as they depict their understanding of political reality.[55] So we might expect people who inhabit different political imaginaries to rely on different sets of metaphors. Because political arguments always concern that which is contingent in communal life, they always depend on perspective. The choice of metaphors can determine one's understanding of the existence of a problem, its nature and extent, and therefore also their most reasonable set of possible solutions.

Because metaphors have entailments, they influence our understanding of the possible consequences of any given action or understanding.[56] And those entailments matter, for once the contours of a metaphor have been accepted, its entailments may go unnoticed or be accepted as natural. Audiences and speakers can lose sight of alternatives.[57] So as much as metaphors can open the doors of possibility by offering perspectives on the present, they can also foreclose alternative options. Once the clergy, for instance, accept the idea of the "machine age" as a world governed by the logic of technology, they tend to see the available political options as restricted to accepting those logics or returning to a more agricultural age. They do not see the ways in which attention to mechanization might limit the range of political choices, and they may be unable to perceive important contextual elements that are not amenable to being understood through mechanized metaphors.

Archetypal metaphors in particular have universal appeal and tap into basic human emotions. Such metaphors are relatively stable, draw on universal experiences, and appeal to ubiquitous human emotions.[58] By expressing transient moments in such stable ways, metaphors allow us to perceive both continuity and community. Because of their relationship to deep human experiences, these metaphors allow us to see our times in terms of a long sweep of history. If life is a tide, for instance, subject to ebbs and flows, then an economic downturn might be understood as one such ebb. The significance of any one event is minimized by attention to an ongoing pattern of like events. This understanding connects one experience in one time to a variety of such experiences and widens the context through which singular events can be understood. Because of their ability to unite people from disparate backgrounds and different experiences, such metaphors facilitate a sense of community by reminding "us of the fundamental connectedness of the universe, the unity that can bridge all separation."[59] In wielding metaphors as elements in their depictions, the clergy were both relying on their existing notions of their political communities and also integrating the president into those notions and those communities.

Lloyd C. Kelly, for example, wrote, "I cannot depict to you adequately the mental, moral, or physical condition of this vast army of underprivileged of whom none on seems to have thought. They are in the mountains by the thousands."[60] Roosevelt constituted the nation as an army in his first inaugural and premised his leadership on the image of himself at the head of such an army.[61] This kind of metaphor, used by the clergy who supported the president as well as those who did not, used the power of that metaphor to underline the limits of the New Deal. Despite the president's programs, there remained a "vast army" of underprivileged citizens who had not yet been reached and helped. For Kelly, the forgotten man appeared to remain, if not forgotten, at least unassisted.

Some of the metaphors were wonderfully mixed, as in this example from Don M. Chase, who wrote, "In conclusion, Mr. President, let me say that I am not among the despicable jackals who are yelping at your heels and decrying everything you have done or attempted. But I believe you can perform a much greater service for America than you have yet done if you close your ears to the counsels of expediency and chart a course based strictly on the greatest good to the masses of our people. . . . I plead with you to rise to your opportunity."[62] This letter, combining references to yelping jackals, voluntary deafness, and nautical and up/down orientations, still manages to convey a sense of the author's support for the president. That president, however, is depicted as under attack, under the sway of bad advice, somewhat adrift, and if not sinking, so far failing to rise. None of these images inspire one with confidence in the chief executive.

Other members of the clergy used bucolic metaphors to make arguments about the consequences of governmental action. William Maxton told the president how difficult things were in the Illinois coal country before offering this description of local conditions: "Arrangements have been made to keep the wolf from the door; and the children are being cared for; and they are attending school. The spiritual tone to be sure has suffered; and multitudes have become sour and that for no good reason."[63] For Maxton, there was some security in current conditions, the wolf was not yet at the door, but all was not well within the home, for the attitudes of its inhabitants, like old milk, had soured. Governmental assistance had helped with the community's physical well-being, but attitudinally, there were still problems, although the writer could discern "no good reason" for the continued discontent.

The clergy also used the archetypal disease metaphor to imply the weaknesses of the New Deal. Thomas Quayle, for example, wrote, "To refuse to employ the aged is a growing cancer in our body-politic, and a man is considered aged at fifty. I know in my own profession, it is an almost irretrievable calamity for a minister to be without a charge at fifty years of age. Daily, I meet men (on the streets of my own city, a suburb of Chicago) rich in experience, honorable in character, but fifty, and therefor unemployable. Some of them with children to support. Anxiety is shortening their lives."[64] For Quayle, the cancer of age discrimination threatens the nation's body politic. The nation's wealth, seen as related to individual experience, is in danger of being lost to that cancer. The implication is that Roosevelt's task, as yet unaccomplished, is to heal the nation and preserve its wealth.

Medical metaphors like that one were used fairly often.[65] One clerical respondent made his own diagnosis of the nation's economic ills: "When the spinal column is seriously effected there is not much chance for health in the balance of the body. With the farmers hobbling along, all discouraged and out of heart, we cannot hope to ever have happiness and plenty."[66] For him, the president had so far failed to restore health to the nation's agricultural sector, upon which all prosperity depended; it was the structural support of the entire body politic. When it weakened, no healthy movement was possible. This metaphor is especially interesting in its equation of mobility and prosperity. A healthy economy is one in which mobility is possible; it is active and even flexible. One that is reduced to "hobbling along" is both evidence for and productive of weakness.

Many relied on the visual language that was also prevalent during these years: James B. Dancey advised the president that "from my remote point of observation, a thousand miles from the capitol, with all the dust now being projected into the air, visibility is not the best. I find it difficult to focus the binoculars of information and misinformation, provided by the instruments of public intelligence, upon you and all the multiple activities of the national government."[67] Here Dancey both validated the president's superior vision and restricted his own ability to offer advice;

he was too far away and his vision too obscured to trust his own perception of events.

In addition to bucolic and anatomical metaphors, the clergy also used metaphors of mechanization to refer to the president's program. As one clergyman told the president, "You have brought a great machine into existence by your legislation; it is a new set of social machinery. It is, right now, not very well managed, at best."[68] The idea here, of course, is that the function of legislation was similar to that of a machine. It was cohesive and coherent, designed to execute a specific task or set of tasks, and needed only proper direction to perform that task or set of tasks. The fault did not appear to this writer as inherent in the machine but in its management. As in the case of anatomical metaphors, the ways in which metaphors work as truncated analogies are clear. Metaphors like these quickly transcend description and become arguments.

The differences between political imaginaries were illuminated in the clerical analyses of the Depression's causes. Those who wanted more federal action tended to see the causes as systemic; those who opposed it tended to find some systemic elements but also put greater emphasis on individual actions in the face of national challenges. So some of the clergy associated the nation's ills with the greater problems of modernity, which they frequently referred to under the rubric of "the machine age." Prior to the Depression, for instance, the idea of mechanization was valorized; after the crash, it became much more problematic.[69] There was some feeling that because of the new context, old policies would no longer be helpful. Making a case in support of the Townsend Plan, for example, Lawrence Radcliffe wrote, "The demand for pensions is sweeping Florida. I have not spoken to a single individual who does not object to the pauper clause in the present plan and feels that the set up is inadequate to meet the conditions of modern life."[70] Machines, according to Francis L. Baechle, were to blame for the nation's woes: "The main cause of most of our distressing conditions is the MACHINE AGE. . . . Consequently, our problems shall be permanent, not simply for a time. Machines have thrown men out of jobs. Machines have speeded up production. . . . Eventually, the producers, the machine owners, shall be obliged to SHARE more generously, the profits they reap."[71] In offering these depictions, these members of the clergy were also offering important context for their preferred policies. The cause was changing economic infrastructure, and the response therefore was often thought to be governmental innovation—changes in labor or tax policy, for example. But there was a sense conveyed in many of these letters that the events and conditions to which the clergy stood as witnesses need to forge some kind of change on national policy as well. The act of witnessing was aimed at a specifically deliberative end, for the linguistic elements of any political imaginary are entangled.

That deliberative end did not always imply adaptation to change. The more conservative clergy used the Depression as a way of advocating policies that they felt would serve to restore and reestablish American prosperity on older, rather than on new, ground. They sought comfort in the old political world and resisted the creation of a new one. By valorizing agrarian forms of social organization and elite supervision of the lower orders, such letters mobilized a fading political imaginary and its associated policies and rhetoric toward restorative ends. For them, the only possible solution to the problems inherent in modern life was a return to a more bucolic existence: B. M. Shacklette, for instance, wrote, "In this machine age with mass production, it is our opinion that it will be difficult to ever find employment for all the millions of people who are now out of employment, except to establish them on productive lands in their primitive condition there to build modest homes suited to the climate conditions and their general welfare which should be placed under proper supervision."[72] This rather peculiar solution, ignoring as it does the limited capacity of the urban unemployed to suddenly become farmers and eliding the question of how to manage such paternalistic supervision, relies on an implicit vision of an agrarian and thus prosperous and virtuous society.

Others were more directly nostalgic, recommending along with Jas. A. DeMoss, that the nation "get back to the old way of living and let prosperity return to the people."[73] For these members of the clergy, economic and political changes were to be resisted and the nation's well-being depended upon a return to previous practices, values, and the vocabularies that accompanied them. They inhabited a political imaginary that depended on an agrarian ideology; it favored citizens who exemplified "the old way of living" as central to the nation and therefore its policy making.

In all of these cases, the clergy used common metaphors—armies, animals, light, vision, bodies, disease, and machines—to convey to the president their understanding of their local communities, the relationships between those communities and the national government, and the effects of that's government's policies on those communities. These metaphors both described the clergy's perception of their communities and invited the president to share in that perception. They therefore evoked some emotional aspects of depiction. Those emotions were underlined and amplified through the kinds of personification associated with narrative.

PERSONIFICATION THROUGH NARRATIVE

To reportage and metaphor, I add narrative as an important depictive device.[74] Narratives help us understand both the contents of the world and its meaning through a kind of practical reasoning. As witnesses, the clergy offered their various stories of the Depression and of the Roosevelt administration's efforts to ameliorate its effects. The clergy used their narratives as evidence in support of a wide range of political claims. These clerical narratives both reinforced the clergy's view of the world and amplified the argumentative content through personification, which depicted the causes of the Depression and the consequences of FDR's policies on actual human lives. As the clergy told stories of unwarranted and unrelieved suffering, the case for increased relief was implicit. As they told stories of political corruption or of other kinds of abuses, the merits of the case for ending governmental relief were underlined. And in all cases, the position of the clergy as witnesses able to testify to the consequences of the New Deal was reinforced. While the White House staff counted opinions and compiled these letters as data, recording the number of those who supported Social Security or who disapproved of Repeal, the letters themselves spoke to the human side of policy and brought the actual individuals affected by policies immediately before policy makers' eyes.

These stories, like the metaphors used by the clergy, are also important because they are an indirect form of political communication. They do not make explicit arguments (although the morals are often pointed) but work indirectly, encouraging audiences to judgments about the characters and the action of the story.[75] Like the entailments that accompany metaphors, narratives imply consequences and thus courses of appropriate action. For this to work, however, it is not only important that the narrative be internally consistent, it must also match with the public understanding of events: neither metaphor nor narrative have the capacity to completely define the world; material conditions are also relevant.[76] This is especially interesting to us here because the nature of material conditions was at issue, and the political vocabularies used to describe them were thus also at issue.

It was clear, for instance, that the effects of the Depression were lingering. It was less clear why this was the case or to what extent the underlying causes were international, national, regional, or industry-based. Because of the lack of clarity, the Roosevelt administration hurled policies at Congress: there were programs for industry, for agriculture, for relief, for national control of the economy, for apparently everything. Some of these policies seemed effective, some less so, and still others seemed either internally inconsistent or likely to contradict other policies already in place. By 1935, a number of them were being considered by the U.S. Supreme Court and were of doubtful constitutionality. Like the rest of the country, the clergy had strong opinions on these policies and often expressed those opinions through narratives. These narratives came in two forms: those that told the clergy's personal stories, and those that involved members of their communities.

Personal Stories

Many members of the clergy used their epistles as a way of telling the news of their broader communities by using their own lives as metonyms for the state of the nation. Sometimes, they focused on their personal reactions to events, and sometimes they used narratives of their own condition. In both cases, their personal experiences were understood by the clergy as representative of a larger reality. They not only sought to represent their communities, they also tried to evoke in their readers the same emotional reactions that they had to events in those communities: pity for the suffering, contempt for corruption, outrage at the abuses of governmental charity. No matter what the emotional content was, it was amplified through narrative.

Often, they used their own stories as exemplary of conditions. H. H. Harris, for instance, told the president, "I am a cripple man and have been for fifteen years, part of most every year I have been down,"[77] a claim that would presumably establish identification with the president as well as grounding his claim to understand the suffering within his parish. Similarly, a pastor from Minnesota wrote, "Our eldest son graduated from High School last June. He worked his way during his senior year. We have always hoped to send him to college, but it is out of the question as my salary is only $75.00 per month, and there are seven of us in the family. He has nothing to do now, he can't find work of any kind."[78] Here, the pastor's family substituted for other worthy citizens who, despite their best efforts, were unable to find work and had "nothing to do now." This story implicitly made the argument that federal recovery efforts had not yet been sufficient to ameliorate the suffering in this man's community.

In one particularly vivid example, Walter Bump explicitly reasoned from his case to a more general social condition:

> I am an ordained Minister with twenty five years of service in that capacity. age 55 years. health good. BUT have been out of work for five years. lost my savings in the depression of 1923 to 25 and until 1930 was able to secure work. for the last five years I have been buisy applying for work and studying conditions. Living off my relations knowing that I am not wanted. Like so many other people. Who have crossed the dead line of employment. I have applied to the Board of Ministerial Relief of the Congregational Church of which I am a member. But they state I am not 65 years old so can do nothing for me. which called to my attention the fact that The Government has overlooked the FACT that from 50 year old to 70 years is the hardest years for people out of work.[79]

This letter not only heightens one's understanding of the suffering caused by the Depression but also brings into sharp focus the ways in which that suffering defied easy solutions. Relief organizations were overwhelmed and were rendered incapable of helping; the economic burdens fell hardest upon the elderly. And many people were forced into uncomfortable, unhealthy, or even unsafe living conditions. This kind of story provides important evidence for those supporting presidential policies like Social Security. Those policies were part and parcel of a political imaginary in which the government bore responsibility for the welfare of its citizens.

Some of these stories were remarkably self-revelatory, as the clergy appeared to write to the president as if he was a friend, appropriately informed of intimate details. The details heightened the letter's emotional power and, by directly appealing to Roosevelt for aid, also indicated the extent of the need in their communities:

> I will state my own case, it may be in a measure a reply to some of the needs. I am 56 years old, I have been a Minister since I was 21 years of age. My eyesight is almost gone. I now have 5% vision. As the depression closed church after church it finally hit me. I have no work for three years. I have a wife and one son, my son is in High school, we have suffered all kinds of hardships and still are suffering. It seems to me that when a man is as blind as I am there aught to be some little relief for him, but so far I am told that there has been no provision made for my class. Dear Mr. President, my case is serious and unless I can immediate help I will be forced to take my son out of school and be a tramp begging what I cn get, as many other are now doing.[80]

This story highlights many of the important elements of the lingering and, in some places, deepening Depression in 1935. Reform may have been underway, but recovery remained incomplete, and relief was inadequate. The Depression's effects, first restricted to specific classes, were creeping past the lower and working and into the professional classes like the clergy. The slightest disability or disadvantage, be it age or infirmity of any kind, was enough to disqualify a person for employment. And the margin between those able to sustain their lives and those who were in danger of being forced to give up their homes and become wandering beggars was increasingly narrow. Stories such as these provided important evidence for those who inhabited the Democratic political imaginary.

It is notable that those who rejected the New Deal did not send personal stories. The personal stories that are present in these letters, which were often accompanied by individual requests for some kind of assistance, raised the emotional stakes of the letters. They reveal one side of competing political vocabularies that included the president and the federal government in areas that had been previously local, on terms and with content that marked the connection between the president and the localities as intimate They also reveal correspondents who, through desperation or some other motive, had come to think of the president as their last hope and to whom they looked both personally and institutionally for help. The emotional amplification was strongest in these personal stories but came through also in stories the clergy told of their parishioners.

Stories Grounded in Community

More often, of course, the clergy focused on members of their communities rather than on themselves. Doing so, they often prefaced their stories by providing a sense of the overall emotional context of their communities. Ralph M. Barker, for example, wrote, "There is a widespread feeling of insecurity among all classes—producers, processers, retailers, tradesmen, professionals, and even those relatively few who live on income from investments. The prolongation of the depression and the inability of either business or government to bring definite prosperity had led directly to a feeling of great uncertainty and uneasiness."[81] Another minister noted that "there is only one word which I can use to describe the economic condition of the people of Andover—helplessness."[82] Joseph F. Panetta wrote to the president from an Italian enclave of Germantown, Pennsylvania, to tell him, "it is pathetic to see those people lamenting and not be able to help them."[83] Still another told the president that "our people suffer from a sense of futility. . . . Our people suffer from a sense of insecurity. . . . Multitudes of our people have been forced into social isolation and have lost the opportunity of realizing social recognition."[84] The individual cases these correspondents provided the president were used as individual examples that illustrated these overall emotional states. For these authors, the point that came across most clearly in their letters was less about individual policy and more about the morale they encountered in their communities. Both of these mark a political vocabulary that assumes presidential intervention and federal interest in the material and affective status of citizens.

This is especially interesting in that the president had asked them for their views on policy and on the general state of their communities. In doing so, he was undoubtedly looking for information that could be compiled and rendered somehow useful for his efforts at policy making and/or for his reelection. But this information wasn't of immediate use to either of those efforts. Yet for many of the clergy it was of obvious importance. This indicates some significant changes for those willing to accede to the New Deal political imaginary in the relationship between the people and the national government, for the clergy's sense that the president wanted to know about their parishioners' state of mind, cared about the extent to which the people suffered materially, economically, and spiritually, drove the content of many of these narratives. For those who advocated a stronger national government and a stronger president, these stories provided support for those preferences.

The individual examples themselves were sometimes quite powerful, as in this example from Joe Hulett:

> I want to say there are a lot of old folks in my community that need the pension real bad. and some doesn't need it and there are several crippled children that need medical treatment and their parents are not able to have them treated. and there are some familys that are not in the old age class that need help. For example one family of seven little girls and the Father nearly Blind can't see how to work and the relief wont help them because there is no man in the family able to work that is just one family out of dozens.[85]

Hulett used both generalization ("a lot of old folks") and specific examples ("one family of seven little girls") to make his point that the conditions he detailed extended throughout his community. For him, the problem was that relief didn't reach enough of the helpless; as with many of the clergy, his clearest examples involved children and the elderly, two groups that would benefit from Social Security legislation, although not to the extent that correspondents like Hulett felt was required. Arguments like this depend upon the ethics of care as a warrant for national authority.

Like Hulett, many of the clergy relied on the pathos connected with the suffering of children, and the letters are full of details like the ones provided by Stanley O. Whitesill:

> There is in our community a little girl. She was injured in child-birth. Her grandparents sent her to James Whitcomb Riley Hospital in Indianapolis, for treatment. Unfortunately, she was not given the kind of care her little body needed to bring her back into happy childhood-health. She was put aside to die. Her grandmother wanted her brought back to her home, and so the grandfather brought her back. Here under the tender care of those who love her she has a chance. But the grandparents are very poor. They do not have an income sufficient to enable them to provide for this little child and a little sister left with them also. If some provision could be made for those little ones by our Federal Government, Mr. President, nobody knows what a tremendous influence it might have for your program (may I say *Our Social Security Program*?).[86]

Whitesill wrote for many of the clergy here, using the same kinds of narrative tactics than run throughout the letters. The story featured the suffering of an innocent; every effort had been made to do the right thing; the people involved were worthy but unable, through no fault of their own, to solve their individual problem; other institutions had failed; government aid was thus clearly called for; the purpose of that aid was to enable people to find private solutions: to keep the child at home rather than in an institution. The language used points to both necessity and innocence: the child was "put aside" by an uncaring institution that failed to give her "the kind of care her little body needed," and her only hope lay in "the tender care of those who love her." The child becomes a narrative metonym for all the nation's citizens who, in the absence of caring local institutions, must rely on the care and concern of the federal government. The need for governmental care and concern was expressed through emotionally laden examples and mark a new kind of political vocabulary emphasizing an increased federal role aimed at an increased set of social ills.

The letters speak loudly and often of the failures of local institutions and thus of the necessity of federal help. Speaking of a local community,

Karl G. Newell of Washington, DC, wrote, "I know there, old people, two of which I have taken to Homes for the aged, and others who are strained and worried and extremely uncomfortable, some dependent on families who themselves have no financial security. I know of unemployment situations there which caused children to be underfed and people to exist rather than live."[87] As in this brief narrative, authorized by the minister's personal experience, the failures of local relief were less a matter of neglect or malign intent and more a product of the fact that the extent of the need overwhelmed local capacities.

Other members of the clergy, inhabiting a different political imaginary, used stories to an opposing end. Joseph Utschen, for example, wrote, "The serious problem is that of pauperization. Quite a number of the less ambitious have become habituated to living off the public crib and are unwilling to assume responsibility for themselves."[88] In such cases the clergy often admitted that there was an underlying structural problem behind the Depression, but also that the less ambitious among their parishioners were allowed to take advantage of the "public crib." Like livestock, they were fed by a generous hand. By extension, then, the continuation of those programs would lead to a continued failure of individual responsibility. Clergy making this argument noted that they had seen individuals in their communities guilty of such failures, and therefore, all individuals on the public dole were equally irresponsible.

They expressed concern over not only the weakened national moral fiber, but the material consequences that would result. T. B. Frost informed the president that "my age and experience have taught me this: We have thousands of folks, unemployed, with winter coming on, few clothes, and nothing to live on. Some are pitiful and some vicious. The pitiful class says, 'I will wait and see what the relief will do for me,' the vicious class says, 'I do not care what I do. I will kill, rob, steal. I will do anything for money.'"[89] He argued that neither class would appropriately respond to relief and therefore neither class should receive it. While some of the clergy relied on individual stories underlining the undeserved nature of poverty, others, like Frost, depended more on generalizations about classes of people and their behavior. In doing so, they drew sharp distinctions between the deserving and the undeserving poor. In this political imaginary, governmental relief programs were dangerous because they undermined the qualities necessary for the creation of productive citizenship.

All these narratives both depicted the local conditions as the clergy saw them and amplified the emotional import of those conditions. By seeing conditions through the lens of the people that they most affected, these stories also conveyed the human costs of the Depression to Roosevelt's White House. In so doing, the clergy reinforced the bonds FDR was forging between the president and the people and helped authorize the plebiscitary presidency as a legitimate form of democratic government. In looking to the federal government when local governments and charitable organizations were overwhelmed, citizens authorized an unprecedented increase in federal power. They did so by reporting to the government, through data and metaphor as well as through stories. Finally, they did so by making judgments, often through arguments from analogy and example.

ARGUMENT BY ANALOGY AND EXAMPLE

As we have seen, the clergy wrote of both the extent of the suffering in their communities and its undeserved nature. They noted the depth of despair and the courage with which their parishioners endeavored to meet impossible conditions. After telling the president about an old man "who comes to my house to play chess" and who "looks like a wraith" because "he has spent days in bed because he had no food," Edward Berger also detailed the sad story of "a young woman of unusually pleasing personality" who was "penalized for doing any work that would keep her independent," and the inspiring lesson of two "kindly folks with the Spartan courage of pioneers" who "use one pair of glasses between them." He concluded by asking the national government to give his community "tools that they may support themselves at a decent standard of living," a request that was remarkably common among the clergy.[90] Because the clergy understood the suffering as undeserved and because there was no other help available, the federal government, in the view of many clergy, had a responsibility to its citizens, sometimes in the form of direct relief, sometimes as the "tools" for self-sufficiency.

That responsibility was often made by analogizing their experiences as individuals to the correct behavior for governments. One respondent, for instance, remembered his own youth as a guide to future policy: "When I was a boy I was taught that the way to get along was to work hard, not spend what you did not have, not borrow what you could not repay, be honest; and that the boy who loafed, spent what he did not have, borrowed what he could not repay, would come to grief. I believe those principles are sound now, and that those principles are as applicable to public affairs as to private ones."[91] For this cleric, his parent's rules for their son's proper behavior were logically extendable to the proper behavior of government. It offers a political vocabulary rich in paternal imagery. This is a layered example, of course, for he is arguing both that the government should abide by these rules itself and that it should not support individuals who fail to abide by them as well.

As in this example, many clerics who did not support the New Deal in general or relief programs specifically relied on analogic reasoning. Self-identified "biologist and minister" Robert C. Rhodes, for instance, argued that "a great many of the underprivileged people are really like submarginal land, not fit for cultivation. No program for the underprivileged can be justified which does not in wisdom and justice to all concerned seek to discriminate between individuals and families which are able though underprivileged, and those who are submarginal and inferior."[92] Rhodes of course relied on an extended metaphor that became an analogy to make his case that government should only invest its energies in productive areas; presumably nonproductive members of society would be left fallow.

Another clergyman used an example to point out the failings of New Deal programs: "Last week I conducted the funeral of a woman 74 yrs of age, who had been bed fast for more than six months. She was living with her sister, who had been in bed with a broken hip for more than a year. Her age is near 70. Her husband is about 65 yrs of age and is paralyzed, having to use a crutch. They have received $3 per week from relief and neighbors have carried the rest of the load. A sample of relief administration."[93] This correspondent toggled between the one case he narrated and the operation of governmental policies in general. The example worked less as emotional support for his claim and more as an argument in which the one example was understood to serve as a placeholder for a whole series of governmental failures.

As with the other examples of depiction, these analogies and examples helped the clergy make their cases for and against the president's policies in ways that relied upon the human element of governmental policy. Their reporting techniques helped bring the rich variety of the nation to the fore. These highlighted the immediate human costs and consequences of the New Deal. And they provided evidence for the verisimilitude of the competing political imaginaries.

Conclusion

Clerical depictions of their communities had clear political import. They helped the clergy bring the president not just the contours of public reaction to the New Deal but also the context of that reaction. They made judgments about the efficacy of the government's programs based upon their judgments of the nature of citizenship and how it was to be understood in the modern context. They looked to the past with a sense of nostalgia and to the future with both hope and fear. And they told story after story, provided example after example, and put human faces on the Depression. In making their communities present, the clergy also offered their own perspective on the Depression and the Roosevelt administration's efforts to deal with its causes and effects. They sometimes did so using language that indirectly warranted an increased presidential presence on local policy by directly asking for federal help and by relying on affective appeals that made emotional connections between the American people and the federal government. Clergy who opposed extensions of federal power sometimes did so by using the president's preferred terms and sometimes by resorting to the previous political vocabulary. That perspective was conveyed through reportage, metaphors, narratives, analogies, and examples of their personal experiences and those of their parishioners.

The clergy were inhabiting—or beginning to inhabit—two different political imaginaries. In one, federal and presidential power were appropriately mobilized on behalf of the nation's weakest citizens. This argument was enabled by reports on the extent and nature of the economic dislocations, by metaphors that attributed the causes of the Depression to the national economic system rather than to individual weakness, by narratives of bravery in the face of suffering, and by examples of policy success and its limits. Those members of the clergy who inhabited a political imaginary that relied upon the resilience of the private sector and locally enacted relief policies, on the other hand, offered reports of government waste and of the ways in which government relief could be manipulated by the unworthy. They depended on metaphors that stressed the role of the individual and on narratives that indicated the prevalence of abuse of governmental largesse. Their analogies and examples offered supporting evidence for these claims.

The clergy thus united cultural power with political policy, arguing from the one to the other. The tendencies that they saw in their own parishes and communities were used by them as warrants for national political action. In making their case, they implicitly argued from history, their own and those of their localities and the nation, arguing for both the recognition of important continuities and the significance of changes. They offered ideas for both returning the nation to its previous state of economic prosperity and moral soundness and for ways to accommodate technological change while assuring moral progress.

In depicting their communities the clergy were also making decisions about whose suffering mattered and whose did not. The innocent, usually depicted as the disabled, the very young, or the very old, were employed so frequently as examples as to underline their use as vehicles for depicting the worthy poor. Similarly, hard-working, stoic, and virtuous citizens, unable to find work despite their best efforts to do so, were seen as worthy of at least some limited governmental assistance. But the clergy were often wary of the ways in which governmental largesse could be co-opted by the corrupt and programs could be abused by the venal. Relief was often understood as undermining the moral fiber of the weak and as contributing to the weakening of the nation's capacities for citizenship.

Sets of political vocabularies always exist in tension with one another; inhabitants of opposing imaginaries use the same kind of evidence but depict their political worlds with different facts, make different claims about the causes of problems and the probable consequences of policies, offer different kinds of citizens supporting their claims, and wield different examples as evidence for the rightness of their position. In some ways, the clergy occupied the same, shared political world. In other ways, they inhabited very different political realities.

Conveying those similarities and differences, of course, is the function of witnessing. Witnesses bring the past to the present and project into the future. Witnessing thus has consequences for how the present is understood. It thus contains an important element of judgment. The Depression ruptured the previously dominant national narrative as a tale of depending on the inevitability of civilization conquering the wilderness and enacting God's will on earth, instantiating a New Jerusalem. In the lingering aftermath of the financial crisis, many things that had been certain were now contingent. For the clergy, those contingencies included economics and politics; they remained sure, at least in these letters, of the certainty of God. That God was sometimes a guarantee of love and grace and sometimes a guarantee of justice. And sometimes, of course, he guaranteed both. In either case, for these clergy, the nation's fate was tied to its willingness and ability to enact his will.

CHAPTER THREE

Revelations: Naturalizing Hierarchies in Political Vocabularies

Institutional regime change also alters other elements of the political world. These alterations are reflected in, justified through, and enacted in rhetoric. The opposing sets of these reflections, justifications, and enactments are what I am calling political vocabularies. Each set of political vocabularies includes different views of the political world. Those different views entail opposing understandings of the best location of political authority. The nature and extent of political authority is explained and justified through differing depictions of the political world and those who occupy it. People who occupy different political imaginaries see the political world differently. In seeing the political world differently, they also order it along different lines.

While I separate seeing and ranking into two different chapters for analytic purposes, I am not suggesting that we see and then we judge. Following Kenneth Burke, I argue that we see, and in seeing we also rank what we see. Burke tells us that to observe is also to make judgments;

we place that which we see into a hierarchy, determining a rank order of value.[1] This process is enabled by the fact that we do not see all things equally well. Depictions of the political world serve to make its elements present, but they do not do so equally. Not only are some people and their experiences depicted while others are not, but the terms of these depictions help to make some people and their experiences more relevant and some ills more worthy of political redress than others. Political vocabularies thus have an important ideological element.

During the 1930s, for instance, the experience of poverty was so widespread as to unsettle previous beliefs about its causes. Other kinds of beliefs were less amenable to change. Southern Democrats, both before and during the New Deal realignment, were not disposed, for example, to reconsider existing racial hierarchies. Other Democrats were only slightly more willing to view racial minorities as full citizens. African American members of the clergy, and those who were sympathetic to people of color in general, struggled to offer depictions of racial minorities that would help them become more fully present to policy makers. Even when they offered such depictions, they were able to earn for their parishioners only a limited recognition. Racial ideologies determined who was seen and how they were judged. Republicans, generally better able to see and account for racial minorities as members of the polity prior to the 1930s, tended to forsake even such limited support in the face of the Depression. Their advocacy of limited federal authority and the dominance of the private sector was related to their insistence on individual rather than systemic causes of poverty. Their preference for social order was equally related to their arguments about the maintenance of political hierarchy.

This chapter, then, treats the ways in which political hierarchies are created, naturalized, and circulated as part of competing sets of political vocabularies. This element helps us see the ways in which those vocabularies operate ideologically. The depictions we saw in the previous chapter set the political world before the president's eyes and revealed the differing ways in which inhabitants of different political imaginaries viewed that world. This chapter illuminates the ways in which inhabitants of political imaginaries ordered the political world. Because power is involved, those orders are necessarily hierarchical. Because they rest on depiction and because of the inherently conservative nature of the presidency, these hierarchies are reflections of local politics and alter little as they circulate upward.

Democrats tended to view the causes of poverty and dislocation as systemic and as problems amenable to the authority of the federal government and the president. They thus tended to order their political imaginary as evolutionary, coming ever closer to exemplifying divine mandates. They relied on religious doctrine and national history as authorizing (limited) equality. Their views of class, racial, ethnic, and gender hierarchies thus skewed toward envisioning them as barriers to national destiny. Republicans, who saw these dislocations as the product of individual decisions and who preferred authority to be primarily located in the private sector with minimal government involvement, had a different view of the nation and its citizens. Grounded in a different understanding of divine intention and national history, these members of the clergy saw a nation in which natural abilities determined the national hierarchy. Governmental interference in those hierarchies meant interference in the divine plan for the nation and was to be avoided. These differing views of the nation and its natural order did not emerge easily out of the cacophony of the 1930s. Understanding that cacophony is the first step in understanding the ideological element of political vocabularies.

Ordering Politics in the 1930s

One of the startling things about the 1930s is the sheer number of political voices competing for the nation's attention. Mainstream conservatives collected themselves around a vision of politics that relied on a small national government, minimal state-level administration of politics, and robust local forms of political organization. Some of these voices were relatively calm and relatively moderate; others were more hysterical.[2] To their right, various versions of democracy were also espoused, including advocacy of hierarchically structured and elitist forms of government, promotion of military forms of political organization, and even American versions of fascism.[3] The Left was no less vocal and no more limited in the range of its ideas. Roosevelt, who tended to talk more radically than he acted, represents a fairly centrist view of the era's political possibilities.[4]

Consequently, there was no shortage of opposition on his political left: Huey Long and Francis Townsend both offered programmatic alternatives to the New Deal, for example. Midwestern Progressive voices and programs remained viable possibilities, and versions of socialism and communism circulated in eastern urban centers and in the West as well.[5]

Nearly all of these advocates argued that their vision for the nation's future was an appropriately democratic response to the changes wrought by the Depression. That is, they rested their arguments on two propositions: they argued first that modern life had changed, and second that therefore democracy had to change as well. There was widespread agreement on the first of these; the idea that the United States had entered a machine age in which technological change mandated certain kinds of political responses was generally accepted, both by the clergy and by the nation as a whole.[6] The second of these propositions, that the nation's governing structures required alteration, was much more controversial, both in the wider culture and among the authors of these letters.

Mainstream conservatives argued that the Depression did not require massive political change. Instead, they insisted that both political and economic security resided in the preservation of existing institutions and strict adherence to traditional values. Those further to the right argued for systemic changes. Many of these rhetors claimed that modern democracy required modern government and held up the fascist states of Italy and Germany as exemplars of such government.[7] The Right, defeated in the 1932 and 1934 elections, and headed for an even greater set of losses in 1936, was in 1935 united only in its opposition to FDR.[8] The Left, rendered cohesive if not coherent by their electoral success, also had a variety of responses to the idea that government should be rethought. Roosevelt himself authorized a bewildering array of programs and a massive increase in federal power on the basis that these changes were consistent with American political values and traditions.[9] This argument, which earned the contempt of the Right, was challenged on the Left largely because the New Deal was considered as not going far enough to promote the real meaning of those values and traditions.[10]

The foundation for most of these arguments was the interlocutors' definitions of American democracy and how it should best be both understood and organized. Begun as a republic, the United States increasingly thought of itself in democratic terms.[11] But the ways in which a democracy was forged out of republican political institutions was open to question. In offering their understandings of an American democracy best suited for the challenges of modern times, the clergy relied on two main texts: the Bible (or Torah) and the U.S. Constitution. The clergy, with all the authority of their institutional position behind them, depicted the nature of their own communities and then revealed to the president the relationship between those depictions and the broader context of American democracy. They did so by toggling between their understanding of their own communities and the way they felt the political life of those communities ought to be conducted, between their depictions and the nation's foundational texts. In doing so, the clergy relied on preexisting notions of how communities ought to be constructed, of how individual lives ought to be lived, and of the nature of the connection between individual lives and the communities in which they were embedded.[12] These arguments offered grounds for judgment in a changed political context and reveal the ideological elements inherent in political imaginaries and in the political vocabularies that order them.

In this chapter, then, I am specifically interested in the political hierarchies at play in the 1930s as revealed in the clergy letters. Using (sometimes) the Bible (or Torah) and (sometimes) references to the U.S. Constitution and national history as warrants, the clergy made clear and quite specific arguments about the proper organization of the national polity. In ordering political society, the clergy also aligned it hierarchically. While some of the clergy argued for strengthening or extending extant hierarchies as a defense against imminent societal breakdown, others argued for more horizontal political arrangements.

National Hierarchies

Depiction, as we have seen, makes elements of the polity present. Different political imaginaries, however, offer different depictions of the polity and thus render different elements of that polity more or less visible. The more visible an element of the polity is, the more highly it is placed in the hierarchy of a given political vocabulary, whether for good or ill. Vision is thus importantly related to judgment.[13] What we see is determined by how it is depicted; those depictions come in bundles that influence perception, disposition, and judgment.[14] This is why the number and range of political depictions are so important. They enable our vision of the polity and its population. The greater the range of depictions a group receives allows us to envision that group as diverse. The more depictions received, the more able we are to see members of that group as important. It is not a coincidence that the more marginalized members of the polity tend to have fewer depictions and those offer a narrow range of possibilities. Visibility doesn't always mean support, however. Those depicted as villains in the national imaginary may get significant attention, but as a problem requiring governmental action.

Our vision is facilitated and impeded by what Burke calls "terministic screens," or lenses through which we view the world.[15] These operate as filters determining both what we see and how we make judgments about that which is seen.[16] Those inhabiting different political imaginaries will have different terministic screens. This enables different levels of social acknowledgment among and between social groups.[17] In other words, when we see members of one group more clearly than members of another, they are granted a higher level of acknowledgment and a higher place in the communal hierarchy. To see a person through the lens of their homelessness, for example, is to see them differently and to accord them a different status than if we understood them as primarily gendered or raced.[18]

When we organize the social world we do so in terms of differential status. Social placement both orders the world and puts relative value on the components of that world.[19] That status is neither natural nor inevitable but exists by attribution.[20] Hierarchies thus established are then naturalized, rendered inevitable.[21] Different political imaginaries will establish different sets of hierarchies, grounded in and inherent in their different depictions. In the political vocabularies that sought to make sense out of the Depression, those clergy who were becoming New Deal Democrats understood the secular world as an effort to reach a divine and egalitarian order. Within limits, they sought a leveling of economic hierarchies, while also maintaining racial and gendered ones. Clerical Republicans, on the other hand, sought a divinely inspired and more rigidly ordered world in which economic, racial, and other hierarchies were maintained or altered on the basis of individual capacities, not group membership. As they inhabited different political imaginaries and wielded different political vocabularies, they also used different warrants for action, maintained different views of religious imperatives, held different views of national history, and preferred different emplacements of members of various groups in the national hierarchy.

WARRANTS FOR ACTION

One would expect that, given the nature of their expertise and the widespread knowledge of the Bible (or Torah) in the 1930s that the clergy would depend largely upon divine sources as justifications for their political ideologies. And indeed, religious warrants figure prominently in their letters. They were used to both authorize and criticize Roosevelt and the New Deal. The U.S. Constitution and examples from U.S. political history also loom large as the grounds for the clerical understandings of a political culture that naturalized for them specific kinds of political hierarchy.

Religious Warrants

The most prominent use of religious warrants traces the political genealogy of the nation itself to a divine origin. For those opposed to the New Deal, that origin meant respecting the hierarchies that were in place during the nation's founding. One of the more explicit uses of such claims came from Selsus E. Tull, who wrote, "The Republic of the United States was founded on respect for God."[22] For Tull and others like him, the nation itself was created by those who sought to honor God, and it could only prosper so long as that was still its aim. But the clergy had differing views of what that entailed. D. Earl Daniel, for example, opposed "Paternalistic Government" on the grounds that "this is a Democracy and a great Christian experiment. We pride ourselves upon our self-reliance and the ability of each to care for himself."[23] For Daniel, democracy and Christianity were identical and identified, and just as every individual soul had to find its own way to heaven, every individual citizen had to find her own economic way as well. This sentiment was frequent among the more conservative of the clerical correspondents, and it is intriguing in that it foregrounds individualism and reduces community to the background; this has important policy implications.

For many of the conservative clergy, the economic crisis was clearly related to a spiritual crisis. Some saw the Depression as the cause of moral lapse, others as exacerbating one, and still others as a kind of divine wake-up call, a moment in which citizens could, in the absence of material comforts, find themselves more meaningfully as spiritual beings. Charles C. Harris, for example, wrote, "Revival of religion is the great need," while Frank E. Wilke asserted, "And, Mr. President, we cannot solve our many problems without God."[24] Joseph E. Beal thought the nation needed to return to "a deeper spiritual consciousness," while William Hood sought "a return to God . . . a revival of religion."[25] Frank F. Walters wrote, "Selfish materialistic greed you did not invent. It has clutched at our throats for decades. Your 'Share the Wealth' program has spread materialism rather than present idealism. A moral and spiritual disease plagues us, not merely a material breakdown. Spiritual disease requires spiritual remedies."[26] For all these clerics, and for the many more these comments represent, the Depression was defined as a spiritual crisis. Its most important remedy was also spiritual. By viewing the crisis as a religious one, political solutions were disabled.

These conservative clerics worried that the president did not necessarily agree with this definition and thus would fail to take appropriate action. C. M. Grall gave voice to this fear: "We are praying for you, Mr. President, are you praying for your nation?"[27] Others were even more explicit. Victor H. Offermann, for instance, wrote of the president's letter, "I am happy that you consider spiritual leadership as one of the factors in stableizing this grand old government of so great a nation. . . . I have been hoping in my heart that you would set one day aside as a day of prayer and consecration by all denominations throughout the nation. . . . One other suggestion for your thought and that is something be done to curtail the teaching in our universities and high schools of that which breaks down faith in our God and holy word."[28] This minister chose to believe in the sincerity of the president's request for clerical advice, chose also to consider that request as pertaining to spiritual as well as material matters, and then hoped for spiritual remedies for the nation's economic woes: a national day of prayer and adjustments to the nation's educational curricula. He restricted appropriate governmental action to the support of spiritual education.

Not all of them encouraged even that limited extent of government action. C. L. Noss noted, "Personally, the writer views with alarm the Communistic and extreme Socialistic efforts to adjust the conditions of this country. Our depression has not been material alone but spiritual and social."[29] For this cleric, U.S. democracy, properly understood, excluded both communism and socialism. It also implied that governmental efforts to "adjust the conditions of this country" were also antithetical to democracy. He understood the Depression, as did writers cited earlier, as a spiritual rather than an economic event. This writer inhabited a political imaginary that conflicted with those of the ministers who sought to realign or increase governmental action. Of the myriad possibilities for federal action as a result of the economic crisis, this author and those like him wanted to see less government and more reliance on the church.

Other ministers, like L. L. Tucker, relied less on such generalizations and used very specific religious references: "In regard to the new deal (so called) that is as old as Re-ho-bo-am, who wouldn't listen to old men's council. He instead called the young men or brain trust around him and they told him to make the yoke heavy. That is what you have done. Every child that is born today has $1000.00 on it's head when it comes into the world. We are wearing a heavy yoke of taxes."[30] Tucker made detailed analogies from biblical lessons to judge the behavior of the president and his advisers. Tucker's understanding of FDR's policy depended upon his understanding of divine strictures.

Opinions on the content of those strictures spread across a wide spectrum, indicating that the terms of the realignment and of the emergent contending political vocabularies didn't capture the entire range of political possibility. Augustine Batten, for instance, felt that "Personally, as a Christian I can believe in no other system than Socialism with its distribution according to need and work."[31] For this cleric, the national government wasn't yet strong enough and needed to be even more interventionist than it was to be truly Christian. Other clerics were equally dedicated to their understanding of true faith, but thought government action should tend in different directions. Edward Williams argued that "the best way any government can best serve the people is to make it increasingly difficult for them to go to the devil," a task that he considered the president to have failed at given Repeal.[32] Others found it too late for that, arguing that "you sold you own soul and the soul of these United States" by endorsing Repeal.[33]

They did not only object to his actions on Repeal. Howard A. Gibbs thought the government's actions were antithetical to religious values:

> The Government has lately seemed to discourage the Christian religion among our Indians and to encourage the faith of the medicine man. I think this may possibly have been done with a desire to yield to the medicine man and to those that may believe in him, the liberty that we ourselves enjoy. With this spirit I am in complete accord both as an American and as a Christian. But we regret the tendency, as it seems to some of us, to lend little encouragement to the Christian Indian while the songs and ceremonies of the medicine man are encouraged. We do not feel that it is necessary to do this in order to preserve the old and worth while Navajo traditions.[34]

For these members of the clergy, Roosevelt had taken wrong action, a judgment they made based on definitions of faith, government, and the proper linkages between them.

Charles Wesley Adams, for instance, recommended that the president read ten pages of the Bible every day, hoping that this practice would properly align the teachings of the church with the actions of the state.[35] Others found them already aligned. James G. Widdlifield wrote, "Regarding the vision that is behind the programme of Social Security Legislation, I can, sir, say nothing stronger than that I believe it to be thoroughly Christian."[36] Like many members of the clergy, Widdlifield employed the word "Christian" as if its meaning was univocal and obvious; the judgments of policy actions that stemmed from that were treated as equally obvious. Also in keeping with the era's confusion, not all religious warrants seemed equally sensible. Lloyd C. Glisson, for example, told the president that "the object of this letter is the Awakening of Cosmic Memories and the Establishment of Cosmic Mindedness—which are of Supreme Importance to the People of the World—especially of America."[37] For Glisson, the president had the ability to enact spiritual values, of whatever dubious origin, through policy.

As Widdlifield's example indicates, the Democratic political imaginary, which located significant authority in the executive, did so on many bases, but religious warrants were, given that these letters were written by the clergy, prominent. Many sought to upend current hierarchies on the basis of such warrants. D. Z. Jackson, for example, wrote, "In reply to your letter I beg to advise that there is no hope for this American Government as long as human being are burned alive, lynched, and denied rights and privileges due them as human beings and citizens of this country, without a course of redress in the Local Courts or the Federal Government." He then quoted Micah 6:8: "What doth the Lord require of thee, but to do justly, and to love mercy, and to walk humbly with thy God."[38] Jackson wanted a specific policy and authorized it with a specific biblical warrant. For him, as well as for the other clerics who argued this way, the nation was authorized by God, and its policies ought to follow his will.

Having defined the nation as uniquely associated with the will of God and tending to judge its policies as either consistent or inconsistent with religious teaching, the clergy defined the form of government in similar terms. Allan Duncan, for example, argued that FDR was slipping too close to dictatorship: "many thoughtful people with whom I talk have definite misgivings about a planned and controlled economy. They fear that it may lead to government absolutism. Autocracy is a spectre in the sky, but it is not the rainbow of promise to us."[39] Duncan wrote here of his fears that the ways in which FDR was conducting his presidency might have the appearance of a divine promise (the rainbow) but that reality could well be represented by a more ominous specter.

Many of the clergy argued that such portents needed to be taken seriously. Alvah D. Griff, for instance, argued for divine retribution as a result of repeal of Prohibition: "I find myself completely out of harmony with the so called new Deal. I do not care to criticise one who occupies so high a place in American government. However the New Deal must fail. It has failed already. When you said 'From this moment the 18th Amendment is doomed,' Divine Providence stepped in, and the New Deal lies pitiful at the feet of its maker."[40] Griff argued Roosevelt had neglected his responsibilities to the will of God, and the consequences of such neglect were already evident. The only way, for Griff, to restore order to the nation was to restore policies that aligned with divine will.

Just as there were costs to neglecting divine will, there were benefits for attending to it. J. W. Hairston, for example, stressed the centrality of spiritual values in preventing radicalism among the nation's African American citizens and the role of the government in supporting those values: "the American Negro, everywhere, is dissatisfied, despair is written upon his brow, and discontent heaving from his bosom. He needs a message of hope; he needs the embracing of some mighty power for the undergirding of his moral courage and spiritual resources. The obligation of the National Government to this situation is vital, inseparable, and inescapable."[41] Peter W. Lambert Jr. also found widespread discontent and likewise attributed it to "a narrow and craped spiritual vision," which the government was asked to broaden.[42] For these clerics, existing problems could be solved or ameliorated by correctly attending to the spiritual.

In all these examples and in the many more like them, Roosevelt's clerical correspondents offered religious warrants as foundations for their political imaginaries and the hierarchies that ordered them. Those warrants, while popular with the clergy for obvious reasons, were not the only ones available to them. Equally prominent were warrants that depended upon the clergy's various interpretations of the Constitution and U.S. history.

Constitutional/Historical Warrants

Like the Bible and the Torah, the Constitution was sometimes treated by the clergy as a sacred document. Those who opposed the extension of presidential power were particularly prone to citing constitutional warrants in support of their position. Raymond B. Blakney, for example, wrote, "The prospect that the Constitution may be so amended that federal power may increase while state and individual liberties and initiatives decrease, is held to be undesirable. On this issue, you may expect intransigeant opposition from this community."[43] Similarly, C. L. Munsun argued that "above all, the Constitution must be preserved."[44] Other members of the clergy saw the country slipping into autocracy despite the president's best intentions, dissociating FDR from malign intent but describing the consequences of centralized government in negative terms. Henry Barnston, for example, wrote, "I would say that the New Deal offers a most commendable attempt to solve one of the most appalling problems which has ever been confronted by any nation. However, it largely depends upon a most dangerous assumption, that of the supremacy of the State and for that reason it was well that the Supreme Court declared the N.R.A. unconstitutional. We know full well that men like you, Mr. President, have the welfare of the underprivileged in their minds, but there is the great danger of a future President assuming the attitude of a Stalin, a Mussolini, or a Hitler."[45] Still others were less sure of or less concerned with Roosevelt's intent: "We want a man who will try to enforce the Constitution, and not try to break or change it," wrote D. S. Smith.[46] For these members of the clergy, the revealed word of the Constitution was an authoritative source of political action and political judgment.[47]

There was, of course, wide dismay and even alarm over the increase in federal power that accompanied the New Deal. C. J. Carmichael told the president, "Some express distrust at what seems a tendency to over-reach States Rights, in the course of some departments at present governmental administration. They look with concern on any loose consideration of our Great Constitution."[48] Similarly, Myron W. Adams wrote, "I wish there were far less of federal supervision and compulsion. Even if more efficient, it is far better that responsibility be widely spread. A democratic form of government is greatly helped by local discussion and action."[49] These clergymen took the Constitution as authoritative and were concerned about deviations from it. Like those who worried that the further the nation strayed from God's plan the worse national conditions would become, these writers feared that the further the nation strayed from the structures outlined by the Constitution the more distant from democracy it would be.

Others, inhabiting a different political imaginary, wanted to see the Constitution altered to bring it into line with new political imperatives. John C. Blommestein, for instance, wrote, "I must add that I disapprove of any interpretation of the constitution the New Deal calls for. I favor, however, such an amendment to the constitution as necessary to provide labor with its rights."[50] R. W. McEwan, after applauding the president's "genuine concern" for "human need in these difficult days," also worried about those who "will not be satisfied with anything less than the definite place of human rights above property rights,"[51] upending American national values.

There were clerical voices who found ways around this problem. "Your unusually keen understanding of the nat'l needs and the various problems that affect the great masses of American democracy should make you immortal in the hearts of all sincere and unprejudiced Americans," wrote J. Lawrence Connolly. He continued, "However, it does seem to me to be essential that the people generally be educated in every way possible to the fact that there is NO DANGER TO OUR CONSTITUTION, for the bally-hoo of the opposition is almost sure to turn the unwary and the unintelligent voter from the support of present legislation."[52] Connolly seemed ready to believe that Roosevelt's understanding of the "real" intent of the Constitution would create no problems as long as the people as a whole could be convinced to ignore the opposition's "bally-hoo" and brought to an understanding of political truth. These members of the clergy were more dedicated to the principles that they understood as enshrined in the Constitution than to the document itself. Joseph F. Fitzgerald, for example, wrote, "Furthermore, when Constitutionalism interferes with Justice, that Constitution should be scraped."[53] George C. Lee stated that "my idea of a *change* in our economic system is not *from* the Constitution, as some recommend, but rather *toward* the Constitution, or better still, *ahead into it*."[54] Given the extent of political change associated with the New Deal, it is unsurprising that the Constitution was mobilized as a foundational text, authorizing change and resistance to it. The Constitution and its role in the U.S. political culture was very much a part of the contestation creating the 1930s political vocabularies. And given the fact that political authority was very much at issue during these years, the circulation of various constitutional interpretations is only to be expected.

The Constitution was used to authorize a variety of distinctions. D. W. Hawkins, for instance, wrote, "My honest judgment is that conditions are improving in a business way, but they are not improving in the ways of true citizenship."[55] Ministers like Hawkins argued that citizenship and the economy were unrelated; economic improvement could, in fact, be inimical to "true" citizenship. Others were happy to disavow the Constitution altogether. John B. Reese, for example, advised the president, "Keep to the Left. You need not worry about 'Save the Constitution.' That slogan merely makes us laugh. It is an open insult to the people who have lost their homes and often their hopes. The only way to save it now is to save the people."[56] For those to the left of Roosevelt, the adherence to Constitutional precepts was inimical to the nation created by the Constitution.

While some were willing to dissociate the president and his policies from the Constitution in the interests of true democracy, others, like Loyal Y. Graham, dissociated the New Deal from American principles: "It seems foolish to suppose we can spend our way out of what has been almost, if not quite commercial, social, and domestic chaos. In what is supposed to be a land of freedom and liberty, the people have been regimented until there is, or will be if it is continued, little opportunity for individual initiatives, one of the things that hitherto we have prided ourselves on."[57] Similarly, Will A. Kelley wrote, "I think we are losing sight of one of the foundation principles of these United States which was thrift."[58] Whether advocates of the New Deal or its opponents, these clerics relied on first principles as warrants for argumentative claims that led to judgments about the contemporary political world.

Sometimes these first principles were revealed in the Constitution, and sometimes they appeared through historical analyses. Arthur L. Duncan likened, as did many of the clergy, the effects of the New Deal to the British policies leading to the American Revolution: "Certain classes of our citizens, namely ministers, teachers, etc., are excluded from its benefits, but are taxed to put it into operation. This strikes me as a violation of the same principle that produced the Boston Tea Party and the Revolutionary War."[59] Rather than accept the argument that the New Deal was going to prevent revolution, this minister and others who made similar arguments claimed it was more likely to foment one.[60]

Others relied on historical practices of citizenship. R. R. Diggs claimed, "I have not been such a delinquent student of political history, both past and present, American and universal, having studied it under Grover Cleveland; and I am constrained to say that I have not found recorded anywhere in the history of the world such inconceivably colossal benefaction, material and tangible, done or even thought of, for the citizenry of any country, as has been inaugurated, and in large measure, accomplished by the present Administration for the fortunate and unfortunate of the American people."[61] For Diggs, the New Deal was hyperbolically defined as unique in world history, which became his warrant for judgment.

Others were less sweeping and less kind in their judgments of FDR. Fred L. Hainer told FDR, "The American citizen does not take kindly to regimentation as a permanent principle, which seems to be the aim of the administration."[62] For him, and for others like him, the New Deal required individual behavior that was inconsistent with American character and American political practice. Arthur B. Papineau combined constitutional mandate with informal custom:

> I do not approve of your scheme for social security. It is too elaborate and was too hastily adopted. It also enlarges the scope and power of our national government. As in the case of national prohibition and the child labor amendment, the cure is worse than the disease. Our system of united states enables us to try experiments for social betterment in one state at a time. If a plan fails in one state it harms only a fraction of our population. If it succeeds it will be copied in other states. The increasing power of our national government, with its inevitable bureaucracy is a menace to liberty.[63]

Papineau argued against New Deal programs less because he objected to specific acts and more because of the consequences of those acts; presumably, he was not avowing support for abusive labor practices but for federalism as a principle, and for the freedom that for him meant that sometimes such practices would occur.

Leroy Allen took the opposite view: "I would advocate strengthening of the Federal government at the possible expense of states's rights. Under the present system, the spirit of sectionalism has stood in the way of promoting the welfare of the whole nation."[64] Where Papineau defined the nation's problems as the diminishment of innovation at the hands of an intrusive and overly controlling federal government, Allen defined the problem as an excess of state power to the exclusion of national welfare. The clergy used history, informal practice, and the Constitution in service of contesting political imaginaries. In so doing they both reinforced and challenged the social and political order.

DEFINING NATIONAL HIERARCHIES

Different understandings of the political world bring with them different implications for the proper ordering of that world. When these warrants depend on an authoritative text, especially religious ones, because they rely on the revealed word of God, they serve as agents of mystification.[65] They mask the choices made through human agency.[66] Theoretically unifying covenant-based appeals can be wielded to exclusionary ends, which may even be part of their appeal.[67] Like many interlocutors of the 1930s, Roosevelt's ministerial correspondents relied on foundational sacred and secular texts and imparted through their interpretations of those texts ideologically driven understandings of the political world. Those understandings often depended on a vision of virtue and had implications for racial, class, and gender hierarchies in the emerging political order.

The ministers expressed fairly broad agreement on the current state of national morality, and in general, they found it wanting. They laid the responsibility for what they saw as national moral decline on the economy, the broader political culture, and the actions of the Roosevelt administration. Often, the clergy saw the government as the chief agent of American morality. "Government has a responsibility for educating the people in self-reliance," David P. Gaines told FDR before making clear the extent to which Gaines considered the president was failing in that responsibility by promulgating relief.[68] Others offered more developed arguments. One clergyman wrote, "The thing, however, which gives me real concern in the present situation is the moral deterioration of the American people during the past few years, much of which I think must be laid to the policy of government. The unlimited extravagances and the unbalanced budget have been demoralizing in the extreme." He worried as well about "the creation of an attitude of dependence upon government rather than self-reliance and initiative."[69] A. MacAllister used child-rearing metaphors to make his case against the New Deal's effects on the nation's morality: "Paternalism will, if practiced too long, defeat its own purpose. If carried beyond the maturity of the child, it can and frequently does become irksome and ineffective. Government paternalism can and, it is the belief of many, will fall into the same error. . . . Conditions existing today are making for Communism, free love, and other disintegrating programs."[70] Some clergymen endorsed government supervision while others equated it with paternalism as they searched for language through which political practice could be made intelligible. Whatever the language chosen, it was common among the more conservative clergy to associate relief programs with increased moral degeneracy. Thomas Tyack, for instance, wrote, "The support given to the unemployed has been such that both men and women have refused to work at their former tasks and have gone on 'Relief.' They are wandering our streets, going to the movies, riding in their cars, and boasting that they do not have to work. All of this to the disgust of honest and self-respecting citizens."[71] Authors like this one divided citizens into classes and perceived a gulf between them, characterized by "disgust" for the morally objectionable by "honest and self-respecting citizens."

Many of those who inhabited a political imaginary antithetical to the New Deal argued that the able-bodied were refusing work and relying on relief. Paul E. Nelson expressed the thoughts of many of these clergy when he told the White House, "the chief criticism around this community, I think is in the failure of the laws to provide for the requiring of those who are able bodied to actually work and render a fair return for the pay they receive."[72] Ben R. Stripling referred to such people as "the worst sort of parasites" and warned, "If these parasites are allowed to increase, we will someday have a nation made up of Communists, and those who are opposed to every good and worthwhile proposition made by our leaders."[73] Inhabiting a political imaginary in which private authority was held to be superior to governmental action and individual agency was the driver of national destiny, these clergy saw the impoverished in general as parasites on the national system, unwilling rather than unable to work. That vision collapsed depiction and judgment and justified a specific set of national hierarchies in which material prosperity was held to be the product of individual accomplishment rather than systemic privilege.

Howard S. Frazer, for example, wrote, "I cannot bring myself to feel that we have to choose either the New Deal or Revolution; but I do feel strongly that the New Deal is itself working a moral, economic and spiritual revolution in our people, breeding a Nation of sycophantic, whining, dependent, spineless weaklings in place of the bold, independent race of which in the past we have been proud to call ourselves a part."[74] For Frazer, the government was eroding the national spirit in such manifold ways that it required a plethora of adjectives. Others among the clergy expressed their opinions on the nation's morality at great length and in no uncertain terms:

> Of course, we always have the lazy, shiftless, and the mentally incompetent. . . . While there is a greater need of things that are really worthwhile, there is an abundance of that which is useless and that which is absolutely harmful. The dependent class always have the cash for that which they do not need. Where this cash comes from, I do not know. . . . Our community abounds in new autos, yet I can not replace a seven year old one worn out in community service. The picture shows do a thriving business . . . the skating rinks, the cheap circuses, the beer halls, the ten pin alleys, the fould road houses do a land office business. The patrons of all these forms of entertainment owe the butcher, the baker, the clothier, the drugist, the physical, and in short, all who will credit them.[75]

Hawkins understood himself as a deserving member of the community rather than a member of "the dependent class," and his bitterness at the actions of those he deemed less deserving was palpable. He deplored the material excess available to others and denied to himself; he implied that there was in governmental policy a definite injustice.

Others, less personally inflected in their analyses, also worried about the behavior of their parishioners. John H. Nolan considered the "gambling craze is the social problem which seems to be outstanding at the moment, from my own observation."[76] Like many members of the clergy, this minister relied on his own observation of his community to make claims about the state of the nation.

They generally saved their most bitter denunciations for repeal of Prohibition, about which they were very vocal. R. R. Detweiler, for example, told the president that "Moral conditions are getting worse and worse. If these conditions continue, none of us will escape tragedy and broken hearts and homes are poor payment in exchange for taxes."[77] Harry Noble Wilson reported that he was "stirred to the depths of my heart with the present loss of morale among many of my people and growth in our city of drunkenness, gambling, and profligacy."[78] They also worried that "this, perhaps, is secondary, yet the single man and women of marriageable age, discriminated against because they do not have family responsibility, may develop another type of menace to the body politic."[79] Movies seemed to be particularly noxious to some of the conservative clergy. Charles M. Prugh even listed them as chief among the "enemies of the church."[80] For large numbers of the clergy, the Depression had either begun or exacerbated a national moral slide, and the government either contributed to or failed to arrest the progress of national moral degeneration. Their outrage at this slide and the government's participation in it was a large part of the affective and ideological orientation of their political imaginary.

This level of concern is of particular interest to a discussion of the naturalization of hierarchies because, as Ryan Skinnell reminds us, "Not to be confused with socio-economic class, moral class signifies the hierarchical classification of people by the adherences to codes of moral virtue."[81] It is, he notes, not identical to but probably aligned with socio-economic class. Appeals to moral class are appeals to the status quo and serve to realign, rather than eliminate, hierarchies.[82] When these ministers understood the nation's moral state as the central national problem they were advocating specific kinds of social and political hierarchies.

These hierarchies were clear in the letters. Carroll Hamilton offered religious warrants for his description of the intersections of race and class in Mississippi and, in the process, elaborated on the meaning of "true" ministry and "true" patriotism. He was also careful to note that he was not an extremist, and thus his views could be trusted. He wrote, "As a true minister of Christ, I know no color lines or class distinction. I have no click or group to patronize. As a true American, I believe in liberty and justice for all. I make these preliminary remarks to insure you I am no radical of any sort nor have any sympathy with the like. Please interpret my remarks as coming from as unbiased and free mind as possible."[83] Hamilton offered himself as a neutral arbiter of national identity before offering his vision of the proper social order. Members of the clergy like Hamilton defined political moderation as more credible than other positions on the political spectrum, perhaps revealing a preference for stability in chaotic times.

Others among the clergy objected to the president's implicit social hierarchies. Indictments like this one, from Richard D. Hatch, were fairly common: "I find a widespread dislike among most of the people at the leadership of college professors. The opinion prevails very generally that they are theorists and experimenters, and not sufficiently practical. The opinion also is widespread that where our government has followed their advice, failure has in almost every instance ensued."[84] For many of the clergy, the New Deal inappropriately disrupted the nation's natural hierarchies. Edgar Lucas, for example, wondered "about the social security of any of us when the government penalizes thrift, ability, and industry; and seems to place a premium on extravagance; the shiftless, the mentally, physically, and morally unfit."[85] For clergymen like Lucas, there was a natural hierarchy of merit and the New Deal was upsetting it, often at the behest of the eggheads in Washington.

Some clerical visions aligned with the changes associated with the New Deal. S. S. Pike, for example, wrote, "I am 76 years old and have been in the ministry 50 years. I have been voting the Democrat ticket for fifty four years. My observance is that we have had Democracy in all of that period but never in practice until your administration. . . . During the past we have had special privilege to the rich and burdens to the poor."[86] For Pike, the New Deal was upending economic hierarchies and aligning the nation with true democracy. Unlike those who preferred existing hierarchies, Pike inhabited a political imaginary that encouraged a shift in them.

All the clerical views of hierarchy were naturalized, of course, and some of FDR's correspondents preferred to erase the fact of political hierarchy altogether. These authors depended upon the absence of hierarchy and valorized the "average citizen." Harry Evan Owings, for instance, wrote, "Many of us feel that you have kept in mind in much of your proposed legislation the good of the average citizen and the welfare of the large majority of the people rather than any special group or class."[87] Echoing the president's insistence on his support for the average citizen, clergymen like Owings saw the Hoover administration as aberrant and the Roosevelt administration as reinstating national norms.

Robert Fred Mosley, on the other hand, relied on very specific categories in making his argument:

> The opinion prevails that only organized groups, such as a "bonus army"; a "farmer's delegation"; "Utility Groups"; so-called "brain trusts"; and "Wall Street lobbyists" have a chance to voice their wishes loud enough for the hearing of the White House. Such voices may be valuable, but there are other "voices" in this country of our and among these will be found the deep hungering desires of the great masses of un-organized peoples who feel that, in far too many instances, our Government has been more concerned with organized groups than it has with the welfare of all our citizens, regardless of class, prestige, political alignment, or position in life.[88]

He noted not the president's insistence upon the average but the New Deal's tendency to define politics by carving it up into interests. He specifically challenged this definition of national politics and the forms of administration that accompanied it. Sympathetic to the president's goals, he was unable to occupy a political imaginary in which citizens were organized into interests—a critical element of the New Deal.[89]

The Depression upended the easy acceptance of the previously dominant view that merit was central to economic well-being. In responding to the Depression, however, members of the clergy both acknowledged the change in context and relied upon old texts. In doing so, they connected cultural politics, economic dislocation, and governmental policy. These elements coalesced into very different kinds of constellations. But the elements themselves were generally the same. They clergy didn't just offer moral hierarchies, however, but extended them into race, class, and gender as well.

Race/Ethnicity

Racial questions were very much at play in the 1930s. Although there were few overt challenges to Jim Crow in the South, there was considerable pressure for action on civil rights, and an antilynching bill was a continuing if minor part of the national agenda.[90] The question of

American Indians also sounded a minor note throughout these years, and the "Indian New Deal," controversial among indigenous nations if largely unnoticed among the wider population, was passed in 1934.[91] There were also regional concerns among and concerning Latin@s, Asians, and other ethnic groups. Various kinds of racism created varying degrees of political tension, little of which rose to the president's attention. But these issues run through many of the clergy letters as they inflected many of the national political debates.

Some interlocutors, like W. H. Rourcer, noted with disdain some national priorities while taking other hierarchies for granted. "I think the principle [behind Social Security] is right. A nation that can throw away ($1,000,000) one million dollars on a prize fight can take care of its aged. . . . The white people over most of the property do not like to be taxed to pensioned negroes. Again an old negro can live on ($10.00) ten dollars per. month very handsomely while a white man needs ($30.00) thirty dollars or more. So you see the proposition is a difficult one in the South."[92] He could, on the one hand, deplore the waste and extravagance of a boxing match while assuming that the differences between white and black needs were not attributable to unreasonable consumption on the part of whites. For him, equal Social Security payments were explicitly unjust because African Americans naturally needed less than did their white counterparts. He, like many white Southerners, could accede to certain elements of the New Deal but was unwilling to endorse any change in local racial hierarchies. Those hierarchies had a strong hold in the nation and are revealed in the majority of the letters treating racial issues, sometimes in overt and sometimes in more implicit ways. In this letter, for instance, as in many others, the author doesn't capitalize the word "Negro," an indication that Eric King Watts, following W. E. B. Du Bois, sees as an overt sign of disrespect, "hateful writing," and a disposition to rank African Americans as subhuman.[93]

Others were more amenable to changing those hierarchies and had different perceptions of the relationship between hierarchy and economic recovery. A. A. Graham felt that hierarchy was in fact a critical element structuring people's lives: "Any effort to improve the condition of the people of our country must begin at the bottom and not at the top. The man furthest down must be the first to feel the uplifting effects of whatever plans are in motion by the government." He felt that "this will be especially true of the hapless Negroes in the South and in many cases in the North. The more desreving of the people therefore and the more needy, will become the most diffident, and will be left to swelter in their own ignorance and misery, while the more fortunate will grow fat on the things to which they are not entitled."[94] Similarly, H. Leonard Clark wrote, "The Negro group of this section have been neglected, and denied employment on the works alloted to help unemployed, and neither are they being helped otherwise. And in many cases they are not being considered, and they are left to do the best they can, and sometimes suffering is caused thereby."[95] There was some belief that the president would act to instantiate new hierarchies or at least mitigate the worst effects of the old ones. These ministers observed the same social conditions, judged them in very different ways, and reached very different conclusions as a result. The fact that others could argue the reverse position indicates the extent to which national understandings of race were contingent and important to the hierarchical elements of the contesting political vocabularies.

Some of the clergy essentialized entire communities. Barnabas Meyer's letter offers a good example: "My parish is composed of Pueblo Indians, Spanish Americans and Mexicans. The entire group is easily contented and the majority make their living by tilling their small farms and some caring for their small herds of cattle and sheep. Their desires are few and consequently they are satisfied with the most necessary for a living."[96] These people were not portrayed as suffering ill effects from the Depression; their inherent natures made such suffering unlikely, for they were "easily contented." Meyer defined his parishioners as outside of the government's proper concern; they were naturally outside the borders of legitimate governmental action. This kind of casual racism was fairly common and was not restricted to African Americans, Indians, or Latin@s, although they were the most frequent targets. The era's rampant anti-Semitism was expressed by Neil Ambrose, who in his description of local conditions remarked, "It has been so long since I have been able to buy any pork that I am afraid I am beginning to look like a Jew."[97] That such a comment seemed to him appropriate in a letter to the president speaks volumes about the level of acceptability such sentiments generally found in many communities. Writers like this one did not expect or endorse changes in the national hierarchies.

Others, occupying a different political imaginary, wrote about their communities in ways that made changes necessary. A. C. Smith was one such advocate, noting, "Only, the negroes are shamefully neglected in the home administration and are suffering in the midst of plenty on acct of racial discrimination of the greatest relief law ever passed."[98] Some, like Constant M. Klein, were even more explicit about the needs of their communities: "Would it be possible to better the living conditions of our Mexican laborers? Could the squalid homes of so many families be replaced by better houses? Old age pension will do a great deal to alleviate many. There should be, I believe, a stricter supervision over Mexicans in matters of education and health. Many Mexican children do not attend school, and their sick and dying often present cases, which, to say the least, are most pitiful because of lack of decent medical attention."[99] This minister highlighted the impoverished condition of his community and not its racial composition as the relevant factor, although even in so doing he made implicitly hierarchical claims, arguing Mexicans needed more supervision than their less ethnically disadvantaged fellow citizens.

Others were offended by the amount of support they saw given to minorities. R. M. Hunter's fulminations were perhaps the most explicit in this regard: "You put more stress on your African jungle friends than your white friends. In Mobile, for instance you have selected the best building for their headquarters and, they have made it an incubator for 'Communism'—'*Colored gentlemen*'? From the North are the speakers who tell their Southern proteges that they will see that white and colored schools shall be made one, and that 'Colored gentlemen'? shall marry at their will white ladies—'Not white trash.'" He unsurprisingly informed the president that "I believe in white man's supremacy in a white man's country."[100] In offering his opinions, Hunter dissociated African Americans first from the United States; rather than being equally citizens because of their birth, they were from the "African jungle." He then dissociated them from "gentlemen," marking them as inherently underserving, especially of such societal goods as "the best building" and the ability to marry "white ladies" rather than only "white trash." He warned the president that treating those who naturally belonged at the bottom of the national hierarchy as if they were equals to those who belonged at the top encouraged communism and miscegenation and was therefore also un-American.

Russell K. Smith considered Roosevelt not the progenitor of the racial problem but a possible solution to it. He wrote,

> Mr. President, if I might suggest. I am convinced that it would be well for you to send here and elsewhere, where similar conditions exist, some investigators who are not connected with any existing government organization and therefore, who have no ax to grind and no special cause or work to defend, who would investigate the matter of government help to negroes. Many of our best people speak of the fact that when they ride out through negro sections there are so many [illegible] men and women, sitting on their porches, apparently without the necessity of work, and also that it is difficult to secure servants who will work for them.[101]

This minister not only assumed that it was natural for there to be exclusively "negro sections" in his community, and that the "best people" were also white, but also that the natural place of African American workers was as servants. The race problem in this view was one of the subservient classes not understanding their proper place, a phenomenon this author hoped a federal investigation would help to ameliorate, presumably by denying relief to African Americans and thus assuring whites a plentiful supply of cheap labor.

Some blamed the conditions prevailing in their communities on race. Arthur B. Dimmick, for example, offered a history of his community in Key West, Florida, emphasizing its tendency toward "racial inbreeding," before stating, "The average mentality of the population seems to be below that of other American towns of corresponding size. Moral sense is low; promiscuous sexuality is rather more frequent than usual."[102] Roy L. Osborne was an explicit defender of Jim Crow: "Our farm tenant (Negro) situation in the South is a grave menace. I have thought that at some time it may be possible to localize the Negroes in settlements so located as to make them available for plantation work, and of such size as to make schools, churches, and a community pride and spirit possible for them."[103] This race-based essentializing was not confined to the South, of course, for there were a number of Northerners, like Clayton Grover, who told FDR that "another serious problem is the presence of a considerable group of negroes who were imported from the South within the last twenty-five years to work in a near-by steel mill which has been closed for several years and which appears to be closed permanently. There seems to be little hope that they will be self-supporting in their present location. I have often wondered if it would be a worth-while project to move this group to a locality where they could be self-supporting."[104] Not content with denying African Americans relief, this minister wanted to relocate them.

While the clergy in general worried about the effect of administration policies on the moral condition of the nation, they found some citizens more susceptible than others. Many of those deemed susceptible were people of color. Winfrid Stauble wrote for many of these clergy when he claimed,

> The Moral Aspect of the Relief Work amongst these Indians is rather discouraging. First of all, many are paid skilled laborer's wages who have not the least idea of an honest day's work. This alone tends to make the Indians lax and unappreciative. They become discontented and lazy. Most of them do not know the value of money; and they do not know what it means to save for the future. . . . On the other hand, these wage-earning Indians are being exploited and morally degraded by unscrupulous Whites wherever they come into contact with White civilization. The evil is not exactly in the Indians earning the wages but there is a lack of supervision in the expenditure of the money.[105]

In this cleric's view, while everyone was liable to lose their moral compass when offered relief, Indians, who failed to understand "the value of money," were prone to becoming "discontented and lazy." Even when they earned wages, and were thus at least potentially able to avoid that problem, they were still morally at risk because having money at all made them vulnerable to exploitation and moral degradation. The supervision of appropriate whites was the only conceivable response to the Indians' situation so defined.[106] He was not opposed to prevailing racial hierarchies and worried that New Deal policies would render them even more necessary.

But not all the clergy defined the problem as inherent to racial minorities. Many of the clergy understood the problems among these communities as systemic. These clergy occupied a different political imaginary from those trying to perpetuate extant racial hierarchies. They were often quite specific in telling the president which programs were being administered unfairly.[107] Arthur D. Gray, for example, worried about the unequal consequences of excluding "domestic servants" from Social Security, asked to "call your attention to the Wagner-Costigan Anti-Lynching Bill," and noted, "Finally, Mr. President, the TVA [Tennessee Valley Authority], the CCC [Civilian Conservation Corps] and all the other federal agencies of relief have failed to give the millions of Negroes anything like a fair chance."[108] J. L. Horace argued that "Our Government can best serve its citizens by abolishing lynching, segregation, and inequalities of opportunity everywhere. Lynching could be handled in the same manner that we handle kidnapping."[109] Charles A. Ward noted that expecting skilled African American workers "to accept the place and wages of the common laborer" was "obviously unfair."[110] Daniel Iverson was a committed advocate: "We also have another situation that is nothing more nor less than a crime. In Miami we have a negro quarter in which twenty five thousand negroes live where there ought to be not more than ten thousand. Because of an improper attitude toward the race question, politics, and other things of like nature, these negroes have not received proper consideration."[111] He here offered judgments that pertained to both attitudes and material conditions, implicitly also placing African Americans as equally entitled to government care and concern as their fellow citizens. One letter, written by the Macon Interdenominational Ministerial Alliance, was particularly pointed:

> It is to be hoped that as the plans for your "New Deal" are rapidly developed, that the "Unforgotten Tenth Man," of American civilization will not be shunted aside because of the complexion of his skin and the texture of his hair, by prejudice or racial discrimination. As we are called on to share the responsibility of protecting the Flag of our Country when the safety and security of the Government, of which we are a part

> is threatened by foreign invasion, we feel that we should be permitted to share fully in the benefits of a Nation which God has so bountifully endowed in natural resources.[112]

All of these clerics opposed existing racial hierarchies on principled grounds. It was "obviously unfair," evidence of an "improper attitude," based on politically irrelevant markers such as hair texture. These judgments were evidence of how the presence of the New Deal's political arrangements and warrants for action were fueling alternative valences in the nation's contesting political vocabularies.

As these examples indicate, race and proper race relations were a matter of more than a little anxiety in the 1930s. While FDR himself did little to upset racial hierarchies and chose to live with rather than challenge Jim Crow, the behavior of his wife and the decrees that at least some New Deal programs should be administered equitably caused concern and hope among some members of the polity. Economic dislocations and the ways in which they threatened social transformations were also a cause of both tentative hope and serious concern. The clergy though, using constitutional and religious warrants as foundational, also had judgments about the nation's proper gender hierarchies.

Gender

If racial hierarchies were threatened in the 1930s, gender hierarchies were also unstable. Women were becoming increasingly educated and increasingly likely to be working outside the home. They were often the first ones to lose their jobs during the Depression but were also likely to be the first ones hired when individual businesses began to see improvement.[113] Eleanor Roosevelt seemed to symbolize for many the ways in which women were increasingly difficult to control.[114] In addition, the president had violated tradition and caused no small amount of controversy when he appointed Frances Perkins to his cabinet, the first woman to hold such a position.[115] As a result, many among the clergy did not necessarily trust the president to maintain what they considered to be appropriate gender hierarchies. Raymond E. Brock warned, "One of your greatest handicaps is letting Mrs. Roosevelt put herself so much before the public eye and in such unfavorable light. You are the PRESIDENT, not she."[116] Like many among the general population, Brock considered that the president's private life was an important symbol of the nation's collective life. By arguing the presidency belonged to FDR and not his wife, Brock was also judging Eleanor's behavior as inappropriate, and through her he was disciplining the behavior of all women.

Walter W. Pippin Jr. also had a specific view of gender politics: "The first alphabetical relief that you inaugurated worked well in this county. It developed a beautiful romance between one of our wealthy relief workers and a relief director, which culminated in marriage. Another wealthy debutante-relief worker became inspired, and while she was unable to land her man, she succeeded in purchasing a new car."[117] For Pippin, the idea of women working for the government was laughable; they were "debutantes," not workers. They were assumed not to be serious about their jobs but seeking husbands. If that endeavor failed, they consoled themselves with material goods. Certainly, in this minister's mind, women did not need jobs nor did they find satisfaction in them. Jobs were a means to a very different kind of end.

For inhabitants of the conservative political imaginary, because women were not serious, they had no right to the jobs they had. G. M. Brassharro's letter was typical: "I now speak of another condition that is deplorable. Let me clarify this with one concrete example. One of our large stores employs more than three hundred women and men. The major number of these workers are women. Numbers of these women receive ample support from their husbands. If these women who are not dependent on their own salaries for a living, were to be forced, by law, to resign; this would give many others an opportunity for employment."[118] Similarly, Francis Jerome wrote, "Well, here is one very important matter, that would help *all of our people*. Please make a law to prevent married women holding position, when they have a Husband able to support them. They are keeping married men with families out of jobs, who are really in distress, also maiden ladies cannot get work and are merely existing."[119] In the view of these ministers, these women were not supporting themselves, nor were they contributing to their families' economic well-being in any significant way. They were taking jobs from men and spinsters and, in doing so, were also undermining the nation as a whole, working against "all of our people." The matter was so important that legislation was required to prevent it. Unwilling to authorize federal action in support of the poor, at least some members of this political imaginary were willing to advocate it in defense of the nation's gender hierarchies.

Moreover, working women were defined by these clergy as bad citizens. As Bernard Sinne argued, "For the most part, they are childless, living off the fat of the land, deriving all the benefits of the country, and giving practically nothing in return."[120] M. J. Clare was even more explicit about the role of women: "If our people are suppose to love the country they should help to populate it. Birth control should be condemned strenuously." He continued, "Children keep mothers at home, where they belong."[121] By defining women in this way, these clergy were also defining the boundaries of citizenship: good women citizens bore the nation's children and stayed home with them.

These strictures were, it should be noted, applicable to white women. A very different standard pertained to women of color. A. S. Rachal, for instance, argued, "Among the Negroes especially, a giving up of former jobs in order to report to relief as in need. If the husband can get on relief the wife promptly stops taking washing and cleaning jobs. Largely due to ignorance. To gather the relief subjects and deliver a plain lecture might be of service."[122] Women of color were as open to criticism for failing to work as their white counterparts were for working. They were ignorant and thus unable to recognize that they were making the wrong choice, a condition that might be remedied by an overt act of discipline—corralling them and giving them a lecture. By occupying domestic jobs and other low-status positions, of course, African American women were not taking jobs from men. They were instead depriving whites of domestic and menial labor. And thus, again, the members of this political imaginary were willing to use governmental power to discipline these women.

Such judgments dominated discussions of women in the letters. Few among the clergy advocated for women as others had for other minorities; their place was not to change in any political imaginary. Walter Henry MacPherson, for instance, wrote, "Women in our community are suffering more than men from lack of work. My heart aches over my own inability to help people find work. THEY WANT WORK."[123] Letters like this one indicate that there were limited options for women's work and expanding their place in the national hierarchies. While the broader society may have contained more options for working women, that wasn't reflected in many of these letters.

Given the economic chaos that characterized the era, it is no real surprise that the male-dominated clergy would adamantly oppose changes to the nation's gender hierarchies. They were collectively concerned about the nation's morality, which they saw as increasingly threatened, and policing women's bodies and women's activities was also an indirect means of policing other kinds of moral boundaries. With women in the house and in charge of child-rearing, the dangers posed by saloons, movies, automobiles, and the shiftlessness associated with too much free time would be lessened. Controlling the nation's women was a big part of controlling the nation itself. Such control is one function of hierarchy, and it is why hierarchy is integral to the formation of political vocabularies.

Conclusion

Clerical judgments and the hierarchies they authorized were a source of stability in an otherwise chaotic social world. The sheer number of competing voices in the mid-1930s is evidence for the extent of political instability during those years. Certainly, the president was a potent source of stability: he offered a set of policies, but the lack of coherence among and between his them as well as the lack of tightly structured political institutions allowed plenty of room for rhetorical competition. Presidents may have powerful political voices, but they do not exercise rhetorical monopolies. Other authoritative voices—from politics, business, and the clergy—were also influential. These judgments circulated from the local to the national and authorized a socially conservative national government. Some of these voices can be heard in the clergy letters, which express a wide range of political possibilities and do so with the specific sense that the problems of government are inherently moral problems.

The various points in this range were authorized by similar foundational texts, for in general, the clergy relied upon sacred texts or the Constitution in offering their views, and in many cases relied on both sources, conflating the wisdom of the one with the ideals of the other.

For the clergy, the United States had a responsibility to enact the will of God by instantiating democracy. Many of the clergy expressed a shared view of what that meant: a nation whose citizens were attentive to the Ten Commandments, were hard-working, and who eschewed the pleasures of the saloon, the cinema, and the dance hall to stay at home and raise their children. African Americans and other racial minorities should understand and remain in their (subordinate) place. Women should also remain subordinate. This view was expressed as both natural and necessary. By attending to the nation's moral health, its economic health could be restored. Like all judgments, these had emotional valences. This conservative view was often expressed in angry, sometimes bitter, sometimes merely sorrowful tones. The authors called the nation and its president back to God.

There is significance in this calling back. These ministers located their judgments both in foundational texts and in an idealized view of the nation that derived from them. They tended to see an American pastoral past, one that was free of conflict and populated by (generally Protestant Christian) yeomen. In the face of an unstable present, hierarchies are rooted in a vision of a stable past.

Not all of the clergy looked to the past, however. Among the other visions offered by the clergy were those that offered change. These views were less cohesive than those of the more conservative ministers and varied more widely: one minister could easily advocate more racial equality while still objecting to gender equality, for example. But for these ministers, the instability was an opportunity, often expressed as the chance to align the nation more closely to God's plan. Their tone was sometimes angry as well but more often was pleading, as they sought the help of the president to bring their vision into being. They did so by trying to persuade him that their vision of the true state of a (often Protestant Christian) democracy was the correct one.

The letters in general, focusing as they did on classifying members of the polity and fixing their place in the national hierarchies, were indications of the political and social dislocations that accompanied the economic crisis. With the nation's verities in question, the clergy turned to foundational texts as evidence for the natural state of the polity and proscriptions for how that polity ought to be managed. The political judgments that underlie our national hierarchies are thus integral to competing sets of political vocabularies. As we have seen, those sets of political vocabularies establish authority and contextualize the nation through vibrant depictions. They can be extended into frames that authorize policy choices. In order to do that, however, they need cultural authority, which they are most likely to attain when they resonate with deeply held myths.

CHAPTER FOUR

The American Eden: Mythic Elements of Political Vocabularies

Every political epoch is characterized by administrative arrangements that are created and maintained to solve particular problems. Those arrangements are made possible because one political imaginary and its way of organizing the world dominates the others; every era has competing views of the political world, the locus of its authority, the nature of its citizens, and their relationships to one another. Each imaginary justifies itself through different understandings of the nation's history and sense of purpose. These different imaginaries evolve out of previous ones and contain elements of both stability and change. Their grounding in long-standing national myths is one element that provides stability, for those myths are able to reach both into the past and the future, allowing us to change with the times without completely redefining the nation. Myths involve stable elements that are also plastic and are open to interpretation over time and across imaginaries. This plasticity is crucial, for it allows politics to adapt while maintaining a consistent belief in an enduring and timeless identity. Myths thus help organize the sets of possibilities available to various political imaginaries. They are multilayered and complex. In their broadest manifestations, they provide a sense of national cohesion, and those who participate in the national political imaginary share in these myths to at least some extent. But at any given political moment, the smaller, partisan imaginaries will be impelled and ordered by emphases on different elements of these overarching myths. There is, of course, a set of myths that are widely shared and that organize the national imaginary. These national myths are broad, vague, and open to various interpretations. The smaller interpretations are the malleable stuff of partisan imaginaries.

Three myths have been particularly important to the United States and were woven into the competing political imaginaries of the 1930s: the frontier myth, American Exceptionalism, and the American Dream. Those who inhabited a political imaginary compatible with the New Deal tended to ignore the frontier myth, perhaps finding its emphasis on individualism incompatible with their vision of the need for shared political community. When tapping into the myth of American Exceptionalism, they relied on the idea of the nation as chosen in a way that emphasized the importance of changing the nation's economic hierarchies. For them, the American Dream was primarily a moralistic rather than a material myth.[1] Those who inhabited a political imaginary opposed to the New Deal wielded the mythic element of their political vocabulary differently. Their imaginary relied on the American Dream as the material expression of individual hard work that depended on individual actions. Institutional structures should be designed and managed so as to impede those actions as little as possible. Their version of the frontier myth evoked the centrality of rugged individualism to national success. And their understanding of American Exceptionalism meant that for those who inhabit this imaginary, the impetus behind their version of the American Dream and the frontier myth is the superior nature of the American system of government; that government should, therefore, resist change and rely on time-honored practices and structures.

Political vocabularies order the differing political realities associated with political imaginaries precisely because they appear to transcend the details of a specific moment in political time and organize those details into a coherent understanding of their relationship to one another. Policy is legitimized by authoritative depictions of human experience that justify the existing social order. If those definitions and justifications are to have national political heft as fair representations of the preferred order, they must be grounded in terms that cohere across the nation—and political myths are one mechanism for this grounding. Not everyone must believe in these myths, and not everyone must connect the definitions and narratives as representative of the nation or see the order as fair. But foundational myths authorize for at least some citizens the nation's political hierarchies and the vocabularies through which we legitimate them. Myth, because it is both eternal and changeable, is especially useful as a means of legitimation.

The mythic element of political vocabularies pervades the American political culture, and thus circulates from both national elites to the local level and from the local to the national. Because this element organizes ideology and has clear ties to the nation's history, it is widely accessible and its circulation is continuous, as myth is used as a warrant for all our political actions and beliefs.

Writing with very different purposes in mind, V. William Balthrop summarizes the role of myth in ways that explicate what I see as their role in political vocabularies: "If there exists a strong, yet clear, relation between culture, myth, and ideology, then a similar relation appears to exist between them and public argument. It is, after all, through public expression that myths are handed on and that ideologies are used to explain away or to create inconsistencies between ideals and practices. Similarly, the cultural ideal exerts an important influence upon the form and content of those arguments used to attack and justify."[2] Balthrop here demonstrates the entangled nature of political vocabularies: they must resonate with the broader culture while doing specific kinds of political work, and one important way they do so is through myth.[3] Ideology can, in fact, become myth. This chapter looks at constituent parts of our most dominant myths as they are differently used by inhabitants of competing political vocabularies associated with the 1930s.

Myth in Political Culture

All cultures cohere on the basis of collective identity derived from a communal belief in a shared history.[4] Myth is thus integral to national identity because it sustains a belief in shared origins and purpose.[5] Myths orient us, rationally and affectively, toward the political world,[6] creating a sense of identity and purpose. As a starting point then, it is important to note that human societies are built upon and organized around a sense of shared history. The details of that history lead to and authorize the national sense of purpose. That purpose is affectively oriented in that it is the product of shared symbols and the beliefs attached to them. It is also rational in that we muster arguments, summon reasons, and take collective action based on those arguments and reasons.

Myths are patterns of perception, belief, and behavior,[7] orienting people to their shared world and providing guidelines for how to live appropriately in it. They "set forth values that inform public debate over important questions and thus impel action."[8] In James Jasinski's words, they "explore the world and suggest ways of coping with it."[9] Myths connect, in a coherent and communicable way, a people's values and the courses of action that they are supposed to take based upon those values. They are thus guides to the structuring of a community and its behavior; myths allow collectivities to justify their forms of social organization and action as moral and to police that organization and behavior. Myths thus exercise considerable disciplinary power.

Myths are conveyed through symbols and employ social stereotypes.[10] Those stereotypes, which also appear in this book as part of the ideological element of political vocabularies, serve as key elements of myth and sustain social hierarchies in which things that might properly be the subject of dispute are naturalized.[11] Myths naturalize the social order by relying on essentialized characters who represent significant elements of that order. Members of any given group are placed within the order with mythic references as they appear—or equally significantly, as they may fail to appear—in a nation's stories. But because they divide people into those who are chosen and those who are not, they are also potentially divisive and even possibly dangerous.[12]

Michael McGee, of course, noted that defining "the people" is an ideological move that legitimates the nation and its constitution.[13] Maurice Charland argued that these definitions are always presented as already accomplished, as if they are both "pregiven and natural."[14] "The people," then, are a narratively constructed fiction, a consequence of the choice to "live within a political myth."[15] To assent to a nation is to accept the nation's myths as constitutive of national identity and to one's sense of belonging to that community. Myths, in other words, set the terms for membership in a community, a key element separating competing political imaginaries and the political vocabularies that order them. If a given individual rejects utterly the idea of the protection of individual liberty as an important aspect of democratic governance, that individual is unlikely to find in the American Revolution a source of a strong affective connection to the nation or its government.[16] Americans are, according to the mythic revolutionary history, a people who are united by their commitment to individual liberty, so much so that they were and are willing to die in its defense. That the descendants—whether biological or ideological—of those revolutionary patriots would continue to be characterized by this commitment is both natural and inevitable. Forgoing that commitment is to also forgo a connection to national identity and national belonging. Myths, according to Leroy Dorsey, "constitute an essential community-building force. They bridge differences and promote commonality among human beings by framing their everyday reality in an almost mystical way."[17] That is, they are a "kind of cultural glue."[18] By assenting to the national myths, citizens also bind themselves to the culture and to the nation that governs it. They are affectively connected.

By establishing these terms, then, myths help integrate an individual into society in part by offering role models and rules for behavior.[19] Just as myths provide communities with guides for collective action they also provide individuals with a sense of commitment to the terms of that action, and therefore also guides to behavior as citizens. Definitions of citizenship, of course, vary over time and across context, even within one nation.[20] This is why I consider that there is one, overarching national political imaginary, but also at any given time smaller partisan iterations of that general imaginary. But because mythic elements are subject to change as well, the same elements can be repurposed and used as parts of a variety of political vocabularies, and in each one provide different indications of the boundaries and requirements of citizenship while invoking the same ideals. Elements of a national myth can be used to different purposes and help sustain competing political vocabularies. The plasticity of myth helps authorize those variations while also naturalizing them through the fiction of stability.

Because of the ways that myths connect members of the community to its ideals they also point toward those ideals. While myth may for some erase or elide the more deleterious elements of our collective history, communities are not necessarily blind to the ways in which they may collectively fail to live up to their own vision for themselves. Myths allow them to measure the distance between present action and a hoped-for future and plan ways to lessen that distance. This, of course, is why in the United States members of minority groups can be so quick to point out their erasure from national narratives and why they may work so hard to demonstrate their presence at key moments of the nation's generative history. The work of demanding inclusion and authorizing continuing exclusion is also, for members of different political imaginaries, the work of bringing the nation closer to its own vision of itself.

The language of myth is thus also important for it flags such important inclusions and exclusions and provides a language through which these things are negotiated. In general, myths are articulated as a kind of vernacular common sense. They tell the stories of the common person as well as heroes and villains, and do so from that person's point of view. National myths have both large and small elements. The myth of the American Revolution, for instance, is a large landscape that provides context for its smaller pieces. So the midnight ride of Paul Revere tells of a heroic action that makes a typical individual into someone extraordinary: it is a singular incident that relies on and reinforces the narrative that the revolution was itself a compendium of extraordinary actions by a collection of common individuals. In this example, details of gender, class, and the privileges they convey are erased by a focus on Revere's heroism in the face of the British threat to American liberty.[21] His famous ride was commemorated by the poet Henry Wadsworth Longfellow, is the centerpiece of the Old North Church as a national memorial, is featured as part of Boston's "Freedom Walkway," and is thus marked as integral to the history of the revolution. It is readily accessible to a wide range of audiences and tells the moral tale of individual heroism as homologous to the heroism of the revolution and to the centrality of individualist narratives of U.S. history.

Myths like those of the Revere ride and the U.S. Revolution are mobilized not as invention but as recall; not as creation, but as memory.[22] That is, it is important that citizens be able to see the myths as perhaps exaggerated but as ultimately grounded in past empirical reality. Otherwise, their capacity to engage with and accurately describe present political reality would be cast into question. If tour guides were to assert, in this example, that lanterns were never hung in the steeple of the church or that the ride itself never occurred, then both Revere himself and the elements of national character he symbolizes would be sundered from their connection to the lived experience of the nation and would be less powerful as tools for collective identity and national action. We must believe that the original story, however romanticized, is connected to the nation's actual history for it to serve as a foundation for the present. So tour guides are at liberty to explain to the tourists filling the pews in the Old North Church that there were actually a number of riders, that Longfellow was a poet, not a historian, and so on. Those explanations serve to reinforce the historical grounding of the midnight ride and thus also the historical veracity of the revolutionary myth in general. This historical connection is what allows myth to remain as a viable element of competing political vocabularies; they are both open to various interpretations and root the new by calling on the continuity of the nation's past.

The stories of Paul Bunyan and Babe the Blue Ox are entertaining childhood tales that help convey a sense of the enormity of the frontier at a particular time in the nation's development. But the frontier myth itself is a bigger, more capacious set of stories that both purport to explain national history and provide a continuing mechanism for national self-understanding. As these examples indicate, myths carry a clear ideological element.[23] In broad terms, they authorize the entire nation. In more specific iterations, they provide warrants for partisan imaginaries. The heroism of Revere's ride serves as a metonym for the revolution itself and for the national history that follows, and Paul Bunyan and Babe authorize the idea that size is an important indicator of virtue. These tales justify the act of rebellion against British rule and the insistence on individualism and conquest that has characterized dominant narratives of the nation's identity.

But even a mythic element as simple as Revere's ride has inherent complexities. Myths are useful because they can be used both to affirm an existing social or political order or to challenge one.[24] Paul Revere, as a portent of things to come, can be mobilized in arguments that defend a prevailing social organization as rooted in the founding and therefore worth preserving. He can just as easily be used as a warrant for claims that revolutionary change is required by the presence of a system inimical to individual liberty. Myths that appear to have only one use are unlikely to be sustained across a nation's history. Only those with continuing utility on various sides of a political argument will be present across competing sets of political vocabularies, a point that is made here in the reliance of one side of the 1930s political debate on the frontier myth and its absence among the letters advocating a different set of positions.

If a myth is to be available for use across contexts, it must contain and also resolve cultural tensions. Myths require tension; without obstacles the narrative collapses.[25] There must be obstacles for a hero to overcome, evil to conquer, an Other to vanquish. These characters can stand in for cultural tensions. So in one version of the frontier myth, for instance, the savage is represented as an American Indian, whose presence prevents the instantiation of a Christian nation spanning the continent. In another iteration of that same myth, the savage might be the white Euro-American who slaughters indigenous people to claim imperialistic control over the continent. Both iterations of the myth explain the nation and its history; both involve the same characters in the same relationship; both can claim correspondence with empirical history. And both illustrate relevant national hierarchies and the appropriate behavior of citizens within them. Defining the people connects the past to the present.[26]

As this example indicates, because myths are complete moral tales they help reconcile a culture's ideological inconsistencies.[27] "Myth is plastic, open to mutation and change."[28] So we interpret and reinterpret overarching myths to make sense of a particular moment. For myths to remain relevant they need to retain "familiar narrative structure" while being flexible enough to respond to societal change.[29] The more threatened a culture or subculture feels, the more tightly it will hold to its mythic identity, even when (perhaps especially when) that identity is no longer useful.[30] As myth always recurs in the present, it allows citizens to ignore inconvenient elements of the nation's past.[31] Because we can repurpose a mythic element—by say, figuring the Indian fighter as hero in one era and as villain in another—the more recent version enables a kind of cultural amnesia about prior iterations. The potential for change is not unlimited, however, for communities that find themselves under threat may well harden their allegiance to one interpretation of a myth and resist other options.[32] This element of myth makes it possible to understand it, as does Larry A. Williamson, as "part collective dream, part prophecy, and part rhetorical narcotic."[33] Chiara Bottici and Benoit Challard, on the other hand, find it more useful to think of myths as complicated articulations of a social imaginary rather than just as ideological masks.[34] While these scholars make different kinds of judgments about the workings of myth, they make the same analytic point: myths are deeply embedded in and reveal important aspects of a culture's ideology. They adapt and evolve as the ideology adapts and evolves. They thus find different expressions in the partisan iterations of the larger national political imaginary.

In sum, the nature and operations of the "rhetoric of myth" work as "a tropic narrative form" that "contains either religious or secular representations of iconic agents, acting on stylized scenes, to fulfill moral purposes consonant with the pieties of an authoritative order. Thus construed, myth is potentially transformative in function."[35] This element of myth is particularly important to its work as political vocabularies are being formed and re-formed. As the political context changes and as the nation's moral valences change, myths allow for that shift to occur within an apparently consistent framework that provides stability amid the chaos of change. In the American political context, two myths, both of which rely on and enable a third, are particularly useful in getting at the mythic elements of competing sets of political vocabularies: the frontier myth and the American Dream both animate our national history that depends on and reinforces a key ideological cultural element, American Exceptionalism.[36] Inhabitants of different political imaginaries used different elements and even different myths to sustain different understandings of the political world.

Myth and the 1930s Political Imaginaries

Political vocabularies have national traction to the extent that they can mobilize elements of our important national myths. In the 1930s, the competing political imaginaries included competing visions of the nation's mythic elements. The imaginary I associate with the Democrats contained a vision of the nation as a community, destined to become ever more equal. Its potential was enacted through continuous experimentation. The Republican imaginary, on the other hand, understood the nation as dependent upon individual initiative and achievement, protected by a reliance on time-honored institutional structures, and resistant to political experimentation. Both understood the polity as a community of individuals. One, however, foregrounded community, the other individualism. These mythic elements were prominent in the discourse of the era and can be clearly seen in the clergy letters, as the various ministers and rabbis interpreted and reinterpreted those elements as warrants for their specific policy preferences.

The clergy noted that they were encountering a difficult moment defined by political change and that this required a rethinking of—or a recommitment to—national values and practices. As Eugene Spiess wrote, "It seems to me, Mr. President, confidence will never again be restored as long as such conservative papers as the New York Times are at liberty to give full page propaganda to the cause of Soviet government, as was done last Sunday, in the Times Magazine. With a Soviet Ambassador at Washington, with Bolshevic ramifications all over our land, with a hand full of Dillingers down in Mexico City dictating to a helpless people, can you expect that men of means in our own country cast aside all prudence and invest their wealth as of old?"[37] For Spiess and for others like him, the world was in the grip of complex and confusing changes, and finding the correct way forward was both complicated and made more so by the nature of the "propaganda" being offered by the national news. The only conceivable response was to respect the needs of "men of means" and to act with "prudence." He was searching for reliable anchor points in a moment of upheaval. This is precisely what the elements of national myth provide.

LOOKING TO THE FRONTIER

The frontier myth is probably the nation's most important foundational myth.[38] According to Sacvan Bercovitch, it dates back to the first permanent European incursions into the Americas and was articulated through the idea of the Puritan errand into the wilderness.[39] The myth generally involves a scene of untamed wilderness into which white European immigrants are impelled. Those immigrants bring with them a civilizing element, taming the wilderness and its original inhabitants, rendering the continent suitable for development and progress in keeping with the will of God. As Richard Slotkin puts it, the defeat of savagery is exterior, requiring developing the scene of action (the wilderness), and interior, requiring that individuals overcome their own savage impulses, and thus bringing the nation closer to the ideal image.[40]

Like myths in general, the frontier myth establishes and regulates the nation's ideology.[41] It thus has implications for national identity.[42] Most importantly, the frontier myth marks the centrality of expansion to American national identity.[43] That is, the frontier myth focuses always on the boundaries between Americans and the world, between us and them, and the territory that connects the two groups as the scene of conflict between civilization and savagery and the American mission of bringing civilization into the wilderness. This myth has provided generations of Americans with a natural justification for all manner of governmental policies. It authorized various waves of Indian removal, the taking of indigenous land, the incarceration of tribal members into government boarding schools, and the genocidal wars that accompanied such actions.[44] And it did so not by recognizing the implicit and explicit violence of these policies, but by hiding that violence under the cloak of benign intentions or even as the enactment of God's will.

The myth is not seamless. It contains, in fact, an important tension between the valorization of (often violent) individual effort and the requirement that this effort be placed at the service of the community. Janet Hocker Rushing argues that this tension is critical to the myth's continued resonance.[45] These elements are especially difficult to reconcile.[46] In my view, this is part of why inhabitants of only one of the 1930s political imaginaries relied on it. That is, national expansion often required behavior that was inimical to the health of a community—the acquisition of land, the violent treatment of indigenous peoples and others on the frontier. We can collectively only tolerate that behavior to the extent that it serves the larger community. So in the simplest version of the tale, the lone frontier hero rides into a troubled town, executes the outlaws who have disrupted the order, and instantiates a new order. The hero then leaves, as his (it is almost always a male) capacity for violence makes him unsuitable as a member of an ordered community. As a strong, often (overly) masculine figure, the frontier hero embodies the values of citizenship. He also marks the boundaries of acceptable behavior and enacts his respect for those boundaries. The frontier myth thus justifies specific social hierarchies, especially in its ability to naturalize the United States as a settler nation. By justifying the acquisition of territory, the myth also erases and justifies social and political stratification, especially those involving women, American Indians, Latin@s, and African Americans.

Despite the changes in our nation since the closing of the frontier, the frontier myth has significant staying power.[47] A number of presidents have relied on it, including John Kennedy and Ronald Reagan.[48] Certainly, one president who relied heavily on the myth predated and influenced FDR—his cousin Theodore. TR used and adapted the frontier myth to tell different versions of the American story and, in so doing, authorized changes in how Americans understood themselves, their community, and their relationship to the national government. TR is a good example of the ways in which mythic elements can be defined and repurposed to allow for continuity on one level while authorizing change on another.[49]

Like all myths, this one can help integrate new members into a polity by serving as a primer for citizenship and by symbolically treating them as already included.[50] So some versions of the myth are populated entirely by white people (often only men) and often include racist elements, delineating the subordinate places of African Americans, Latin@s, and especially American Indians in the national hierarchies. Other versions may include minorities and others and in doing so both offer them inclusion in the nation as a whole and delimit the terms under which such inclusion will be managed. This variety, of course indicates that like all myths, this one is not stable but adaptable to specific arguments and circumstances.[51]

This narrative has been integral to the nation. Its various elements—the ideas that the United States has a special mission authorized by

God, that this mission involves ordering a chaotic landscape, and thus establishing natural hierarchies while at the same time being radically egalitarian—are integral to the myth in all its historical manifestations. These elements combine differently across political imaginaries, and different political vocabularies will probably foreground some elements over others. In the 1930s, those inhabiting the political imaginary connected to the New Deal did not rely on this myth, choosing instead to refute it in the name of community, while those more comfortable within an opposing imaginary tended to use it in ways that emphasized individualism as central to the nation's value system.

For many of the clergy who resisted FDR and the changes wrought by the New Deal, the frontier myth provided a reliable touchstone by which the contemporaneous world could be measured. A. R. Beck, for instance, professed that while he was concerned about national prosperity, other concerns dominated. He was, he insisted, more interested in national "INTEGRITY which is based on these fundamental virtues which we so much praise in the pioneer fathers, but which our generation has practiced all too little. The depression was not brought on by those virtues but by their opposites. True prosperity must ever be based on integrity, thrift, industry and those abiding foundations which alone can make a people strong and great. And they are found in the Christian home, the church, the school, and in the observance of those fundamental principles which alone can build up true manhood and womanhood."[52] Beck here explicitly referenced the frontier myth, attributing his preferred values to "the pioneer fathers," whom he labels as the progenitors of the nation. He equates the values articulated through that myth as identical to those of Christianity. He does not feel the need to list the foundational values and virtues, except for integrity, thrift, and industry, but instead seems to assume that they are so widely shared as to need no elaboration.

The mythic element of individualism, so closely connected to the frontier myth, found its clearest expression among these clergy in opposition to relief. J. O. Johnson, for example, wrote, "The present program of waste is political in every way, is making beggars out of an industrious people; is understood by most every one and can never succeed, but will in the end be a rock around our democratic neck."[53] For Johnson, individual initiative was the root of democracy, and the New Deal was antithetical to individuals in that it wasted their resources, inhibited their prosperity, and ultimately sank both their material well-being and their political system under the weight of failure. Clerics like Johnson saw individualism as integral to national well-being on every level.

The centrality of individualism was often implicitly connected to the frontier myth as the clerics modified "individualism" with the adjective "rugged." The modification of "individualism" into "rugged individualism" underscores the plastic nature of myth and also indicates the ways in which myth operates metonymically. Russell H. McConnell, for example, saw the stress on individualism as more prevalent among the president's opponents than among his supporters: "The republicans, and there are a good many of them here, are again asserting that rugged individualism is the thing. The democratic administration, in their estimation, is dangerously close to socialism."[54] For clerics like McConnell, "rugged individualism" was a marker of the past, and he argued for an interpretation of it that would provide a guide in present conditions. While Charles W. Neill stated that he approved of relief, he had reservations and based them in the importance of maintaining an independent and individualistic citizenry:

> But as relief has continued, I have been appalled at the effect on the morale of many of the workers. With a childish confidence that Uncle Sam can continue indefinitely to play Santa Claus, they have ceased to plan for their own future, use more of their funds for amusement than employed people can afford, patronize the liquor stores until the increase in drunken driving caused the state Automobile Association to circularize the ministers of the State last week with an appeal to aid in curbing the evil. Large sums for relief has undoubtedly helped the growing belief that the national Government can provide luxurious old age pensions and thus bring back prosperity. The effect on another class of people is more alarming to me than the effect on improvident laborers and credulous old people. Normally thrifty men are questioning the value of thrift.[55]

Here, Neill summoned a whole host of mythic characters, including workers, children, Uncle Sam, and Santa Claus, in the service of the centralized value, thrift. Citizens were configured as "workers," as those whose morale was suffering as a result of national policy that had turned them from adults into children, who regressed to their childish belief in Santa Claus. This childishness manifested in all manner of social ills. And the contagion was spreading beyond the working class, who perhaps could not be trusted to maintain their adult responsibilities, and infected even "normally thrifty men." The New Deal was thus a disease of sorts. By weakening individualism and self-reliance, values that presumably built the nation, it was also understood as weakening that nation.

The Santa Claus metaphor recurred quite often.[56] Richard Greeley Preston, for instance, argued, "This idea of 'Uncle Sam' as an indulgent 'Papa,' forever able to do the Santa Claus act, is mighty bad for moral fibre."[57] Santa Claus operated as a mythic figure often accompanying Uncle Sam and undermining his power. Rather than a stern father, this Uncle Sam represented an easy indulgence, a giver of gifts, an emblem of a system that risked turning citizens into children by undermining their self-reliance and independence. The frequent invocation of Santa Claus indicates overt concern about the paternalistic nature of government programs. Arthur S. Lewis argued, "America is suffering from a collapse of initiative and self-reliance, due largely to the paternal character the government in Washington has assumed. Through many of your alphabetical administrations, you are training Americans to look to Congress for everything. . . . We are growing soft, anaemic, and dependent."[58] This recalls Theodore Roosevelt's stress on the strenuous life, which he overtly associated with the frontier, as a requirement for a healthy democracy. Citizens in this understanding needed to be properly independent. They could only make trustworthy political judgments if they were free of economic obligation to the government.

This formulation valorizes a cultural fiction of citizen independence and masks all the ways in which any governmental action offers financial incentives to only some of its citizens. It attributes economic interests to only one class of citizen and presupposes that members of this class will act on those incentives alone, ignoring the greater issues at play in democratic government. The reliance on individualism, which is undoubtedly a pivotal cultural value, thus supports a vision of the nation that is on the surface free of class considerations but in which those considerations are actually quite central.

Individualism, whether plain or rugged, was an important mythic element in the politics of the Republican political imaginary in the 1930s. It authorized policy preferences on the Right and has interesting associations as a marker of both economic class and appropriate political behavior. Lacking a proper individualistic spirit made one dependent on the government. Individualism was thus clearly available as an inventional resource in the political imaginary occupied by those opposed to the New Deal. Other myths were employed by members of both competing political imaginaries, but to very different ends.

THE AMERICAN DREAM

The myth of the American Dream is of considerably more recent vintage than the frontier myth, but also exerted a powerful influence in American culture in the 1930s. It is separate from, but not unrelated to, the frontier myth. Like the frontier myth, it involves tensions between the individual and the community but also valorizes individual achievement in a much less ambiguous way. The American Dream is an importantly democratic myth and relies on the possibility that institutional structures are less important than individual initiative. It stresses the values of freedom, equality, democracy, religious independence, and the Puritan work ethic while offering a vision of success centered on wealth, consumption, and leisure.[59] The American Dream can be understood simply as the idea that one's progeny can earn for themselves, through hard work and dedication, a better life, at least in material terms, than that of their parents. This myth relies upon and reinforces the cultural fiction that the United States is an essentially classless society, one that is economically as well as politically democratic.[60] The use of these mythic elements in one or another of the competing political vocabularies at any given moment provides warrants for the associated political arrangements on precisely these grounds.

According to Walter Fisher, there are two versions of the myth: a materialistic version and a moralistic one.[61] Each version provides inventional resources for opposing political imaginaries. The materialistic version is "grounded in the Puritan work ethic and relates to the values of efforts, persistence, 'playing the game,' initiative, self-reliance, achievement, and success."[62] It privileges "competition, personal wealth, the free enterprise system, and the notion of freedom defined as freedom from controls, regulations, constraints that hinder the individual's striving for ascendency in the socio-economic hierarchy of society."[63] This version is radically individualistic and accounts for an individual's place in the national hierarchy solely on the grounds of merit. It ignores the ways in which ascriptive elements may structure opportunity. This myth is thus an especially useful one for rhetors who seek to authorize more explicitly hierarchical institutional arrangements and is here associated with the political imaginary opposed to the New Deal.

The moralistic version, according to Fisher, is more communitarian in orientation. It valorizes tolerance and charity; it looks to others rather than to the self.[64] It demands, rather than assumes, equality and stresses the ability to be rather than to do.[65] This version of the American Dream is, I stress, more communitarian than the materialistic version; it is not necessarily communitarian. Because of its emphasis on the freedom to be what one desires, it can also indicate a kind of political withdrawal, favoring the private over the public sphere, and so it is possible for those clergy inhabiting a political imaginary opposed to the New Deal to offer a communal vision that does not require national political action, while those in favor of the New Deal might well have a communal vision that does require such action. So for members of one political imaginary, the American Dream was best fulfilled by a government that fostered political community and individual equality, while for members of an opposing imaginary, such action destroyed community and was inimical to the principles of political equality. These elements led to very different conclusions regarding the way that Roosevelt and his policies were understood as upsetting national hierarchies.

Political Community

For many of the clergy who supported the New Deal, the American Dream was strongly connected to a communal vision of civilization as a collective enterprise. Only by seeing the individual as part of a community could the nation and the individual both advance. Ernest M. Whitesmith, for example, wrote, "I am happy to say, Mr. President, that you have not only given the nation a new hope in a time of deepening gloom, but you have also had a large part in developing a new and healthier nationalism,—a sense of the individual's duty to the nation, and the sense that the nation includes all of its people with the right of each individual to self-respect and to the sacredness of his own personality."[66] For Whitesmith, the nation's gloom was lifted by an enlightened commitment to "a new and healthier nationalism," one that looked away from the rugged individualism of the past. Daniel W. Fielder agreed, informing the president, "In a good many places I hear considerable criticism discounting the new Social Security Legislation, but on investigation I find it is only the propaganda of those whose private prosperity depend on the rugged individualism of the old order."[67] Fielder thus both challenged the use of individualism as a warrant for opposing Social Security by defining it as "propaganda," an explicitly inappropriate form of democratic communication, and then attributed class-conscious behavior to the upper rather than to the lower classes.

That kind of community favored by those inhabiting this political imaginary tended to be understood as one in which individuals were accorded personal dignity and economic security. They were thus able to see themselves as exercising autonomous agency and, because freed of dependency, able to make independent political judgments about the common welfare. Charles C. Wilkerson noted that while he "received a pathetic letter just a few days ago from a lady with several children who is under the yoke of poverty and begging for relief of some kind," in the main, "people of this country, especially negroes, who were hungry, and without clothes, and some even without shelter, have good clothes, plenty to eat, homes and money and are happy. Not all of them, but a majority of them."[68] This letter underlines the importance of community on several levels. First, Wilkerson articulated the general and the specific needs of his community, which were varied and complicated. Some remained in poverty while others were recovering. Those fortunate ones were understood as happy because their most basic material needs had been met; they had achieved a degree of independence. And for this minister, the idea that African Americans should have food and shelter was a sign that he thought they had equal status to other citizens.

For the clergy opposed to the New Deal and unwilling to inhabit a political imaginary in which federal activity served community, such activity was seen as destructive of the individual and thus also of the polity. For these clergy, the federal government fostered dependency, which destroyed individual initiative and community spirit. D. W. Hawkins, for example, warned the president that "unless the Social Security legislation can be kept clear of politics, it is going to prove a curse rather than a blessing. Already I have heard many of the older people talking in terms derogatory to the system as a citizen producing, and a citizen protection, agency. To be sure, all of us alike believe in taking care of the dependent. The crippled and the helpless, but to encourage this among the able-bodied is dangerous indeed."[69] Surely, some people, this cleric implied, could be equally citizens and also dependent; their dependence was either temporary or occurred through no fault of their own—they were somehow "crippled" and "helpless." But if the "able-bodied" were to succumb to the dangers of political and economic dependency, the consequences would be "dangerous indeed," ominous, if unspecified. The community would suffer if the proper boundaries of individualism were not maintained. Hawkins acknowledged a communal responsibility toward its most vulnerable members but regarded that responsibility warily, as its exercise threatened communal health.

There were other valences here as well, not least of which was fear of increased federal power, which could result in the loss of local autonomy, triggering in a political community the same pernicious sense of dependency that was seen as destructive to citizenship. E. J. Lemine, R. E. Sullivan, and James R. Flynn coauthored a letter that asked, "As matters stand in our dear United States people live in dread and fear of countless prying, snooping investigators, inspectors, census takers of County, State, and Federal Departments. Is the cost of this for-the-most-part-political jobs compatible with the good derived?"[70] The provision of political jobs incurred a community debt to the national government and undermined local citizenship. These clerics were not alone in expressing this fear. Government "snoopers" were of some concern. Claude R. Cook also took up the theme: "I should also suggest a moratorium on 'New Dealism': a minimum of activity on the part of the next Congress; and the culling of all snoopers, whose chief vocation seems to be annoying and harassing legitimate business interests, to more desirable pursuits."[71] With federal support, these clergy argued, came federal interference in local matters.

Governmental surveillance was not understood by them as benign but as unwarranted. It was not productive of good citizenship but was understood as "snooping," the kind of behavior that was destructive of strong communal bonds.

Members of different political imaginaries thus used foundational mythic values to authorize their different understandings of the nation. In one imaginary, the nation was grounded in the individual actions of independent citizens. In the other, it was a political community in which governmental action was understood as promoting, rather than impeding, self-reliance. The single nation, then, was structured around two competing views of equality and citizenship.

Equality and Citizenship

Equality is a key America value, and while the nation itself has always been hierarchically structured, it has also prided itself in its ability to enact the value of equality. But the gap between the nation's dedication to equality in the abstract and its ability to depend upon it in political practice have also motivated calls for political change. Given the overarching American political imaginary, good citizens are understood as independent. Only independent citizens can be equals. Political equality, especially in a system that, under the precepts of the American Dream, specifically encourages economic inequality, is difficult to achieve and creates a certain tension among the nation's mythic elements.

So for members of the Democratic political imaginary, political equality should be facilitated by governmental action promoting economic equality. Manning M. Patillo, for example, wrote, "I fervently believe that social security, if provided at all, should be provided for every citizen. No individual or class should be excluded."[72] Similarly, E. Herrington argued, "This community and all other communities can best be served by you when the barrier of inequality shall be broken down by you and each man be allowed to make an honest living regardless to creed or color and not beggars at the relief stations."[73] For these clerics, the exclusions written into the legislation authorizing Social Security hardened the exclusions already present in the nation.

These clergy approved of FDR's policies as specifically encouraging a greater degree of national political equality. S. H. Markowitz, for instance, told him, "Your administration is the first to recognize the obligation of the government to the citizens who suffer the hazards of life and who are unable to protect themselves against the incidence of illness, old age, accident, and unemployment."[74] This list marks a significant change in at least some people's thinking on matters of equality. The nation had long supported assistance to those it considered among "the deserving poor," and widows and orphans were often depicted as the archetypes of this category. But Markowitz specifically added the unemployed to this list, underlining a change in the ways notions of equality might be understood by adding economic dislocations to the vagaries deserving citizens might experience. For people like Markowitz, the mythic significance of equality facilitated an expansion of the category of the deserving poor.

Inhabitants of the Republican political imaginary, on the other hand, understood the promotion of economic protection as inimical to political equality because it undermined both citizenship and individual initiative. These clerics agreed with G. Robert Forrester that "any system of direct relief that does not require of men and women who are able a just return in honest and constructive work will break down the moral and industrial fiber of our citizenship. Any man who lives of the efforts of other men is a parasite and a menace whether he be on relief or a son of the rich."[75] John W. Starie summarized the complexities inherent in helping the needy while avoiding the dependency he considered inimical to democratic citizenship: "The danger of any system of relief is always obvious when the relief does not involve the recipients in any honest attempt to share their labors; and even when labor is required, if that labor does not demand an outlay of energy similar to that required by ordinary conditions of industrial employment, there is the danger of loss of morale, and the following, more or less permanently, of lines of least resistance."[76] Similarly, Gus Dattilo thought relief was producing bad citizens: "I believe, along with my brother members [of the St. Vincent De Paul Society] that all Federal relief of every kind should be abolished. The dole that is being put out in the United States, if not stopped in the very near future, will have a tendency to make parasites out of the American people."[77] Parasites are not good citizens; they suck the lifeblood of a system and are inimical to the health of the body politic.

These examples summarize the conflict over how equality was defined differently by inhabitants of opposing political imaginaries. There was widespread agreement on the centrality of equality as a national value and a belief that dependency marked citizens as less equal because they were less able to exercise independent judgment. These beliefs relied on stable components of American myths. But they also led to different conclusions that illustrated the capacity of the same myth to be mobilized to variable political ends. On the one hand the clergy could argue that debilitating dependency would be eliminated by government aid, and on the other hand they could argue that such aid increased dependency and its debilitating effects. This conflict was clearest when the clergy wrote about economic hierarchies.

Economic Hierarchies

The American Dream derives part of its mythic power from the implicit claim that in the United States, individuals are, if not free from the constraints of social class and ascriptive hierarchies, at least freer from them here than they are elsewhere. This sense of the United States as the land of opportunity helped fuel the nation's westward migration and encouraged millions of immigrants to venture here. This element masks national hierarchies by treating them as if they did not exist. It also provided a warrant for members of one 1930s political imaginary to level them when they are discovered to exist. Members of the opposing imaginary saw hierarchies as connected to political order and worried that upsetting them threatened the integrity of that order.

Participants in both political imaginaries understood overturning hierarchy as a key characteristic of the New Deal. George Long, for instance, told the president,

> You must be reminded that you have done one of the most daring things men have ever attempted—to befriend the poor expecting on the one hand, the gratitude of the poor who are helped, and on the other hand, to escape the enmity of the holding classes. Few men have ever succeeded in one or both of these hopes. Friendship for the poor is one of the most costly friendships any man ever covets. . . . You must expect

> increasing conservatism as the nation more and more recovers its sanity and its income. That means you will meet with more and more resistance to all socially-minded legislation.[78]

Long, in common with a large number of his fellow clergy, clearly understood the nation as stratified by class. He also expected citizens to act on the basis of class. William Tober, equally sure of class-based national stratification, actively encouraged the president to act on that basis, repeating, with increasing numbers of exclamation points, a simple stricture: "Soak the rich" and "feed the poor."[79]

Those who agreed with the president saw class hierarchies as destructive of national community and sought their removal. Phillip W. Sarles exemplifies this tendency, arguing that the "backward conditions" of his community were "caused by class conflict there and the racial difficulties. The low standard of living of the negro holds down the whole community."[80] For him, the tendency he observed among his parishioners of acting on class-based interests was actively working against the interests both of the specific classes and of the entire community. The intersections of class and race made the problems of hierarchy more intractable.

When the centrality of class was acknowledged—which was quite often—the clergy saw it as pathology. Charles J. Allen, for instance, wrote, "Your Administration has never lacked Ideas or Plans. What it has accomplished in view of the opposition of selfish interests is quite remarkable. These Interests are subtle and vicious and they are at work in small as well as large communities. We have something of this kind in our own midst. I talk to all groups from time to time, and am convinced that most Moneyed men and Lawyers as well as some Politicians are not in sympathy with your Social Legislation. They do not want the Old Order disturbed. They do not want to give up their power."[81] Those at the top of the nation's hierarchy are characterized here as "subtle and vicious" and as wielding vast power, even in smaller communities. FDR's social program, on the other hand, is clearly marked as a mechanism through which the "Old Order" can be upended and power more equally distributed, for this correspondent an implicitly desirable result.

Others saw in the nation's instability a chance to improve its policies without regard to the old order. C. Robert Ardry told the president, "I am in favor of what you have been doing. It is difficult to revive or replace an old economic system that is destroying itself because of its own inherent selfishness."[82] John S. Johnson urged FDR to "give men jobs at useful labor. Work for the distribution of buying power among the masses. Dare gently yet certainly to oppose those benevolent barons of industry. Evolve peaceably toward the socialization of the basic sources of production. Move left, Mr. President, move left!"[83] Norman Joseph Kilbourne wrote, "I am certain that the ethics of the man of Nazareth demand that you *go further toward the left*."[84] Arthur B. Patten agreed: "I have been in general accord with your policies—even wishing that you had made them more thorogoing. The capitalistic system must be more drastically changed."[85] W. A. Settlag contributed his opinion that "public ownership is the cry of many."[86] Warren E. Mosley agreed: "Your social vision is one that has been needed for a long time and I hope you will continue to enlarge upon it. I further wish that you might make it part of your purpose to obtain for this government and the people full and complete control of all public utilities such as railroads and lights, etc. if our banking system could also be made a function of government so much the better."[87] For all these clergy, and the many more like them, the dislocations of the New Deal were a product of the selfish and wrongheaded behavior of the previous ruling class and also presented an opportunity to correct the balance and move the nation forward. They hoped for a dramatic rather than incremental change in the national economic structures.

In the main, these clerics saw the president as adapting the nation's policies in ways that staved off disorder. W. H. Ezell, for instance, told the president, "You have borrowed from the rich to care for the poor, and thus you have saved us from a bloody revolution."[88] Similarly, John E. Rees stated, "If the New Deal did nothing else, it saved Iowa from chaos."[89] Orlo J. Price asserted his belief "that without the New Deal and its policies we would now be governed in this country by an American type of fascism, which would be more ruthless than European forms since we are greater extremists than the Germans or Italians in everything we do."[90] These clergy saw the president's actions as offering at least some degree of stability in what would otherwise be a chaotic, even violent, political world.

Members of the political imaginary opposed to the president saw

FDR as acting in ways that tended to increase the potential for chaos. In particular, they thought his policies were inimical to members of the business class, who did not deserve the treatment he was meting out. Sidney H. Babcock, for example, wrote, "Between youth and old age is the producing business class. The present policy is inimical to this class. It has levied upon business: a bureaucracy that is dictatorial . . . a liquor traffic . . . a tax burden."[91] For these clerics, the president was using government in oppressive ways that worked against members of the business class, which those like Babcock considered central to the American order.

So while clerics supporting FDR saw him as preserving order, those opposed to him understood him as threatening it. Gaston W. Duncan, for example, wrote, "Further, let me say, the masses are ignorant and restless. Never were conditions more favorable than now for the radical agitator. We must stabilize conditions and that quickly, or I tremble to visonise what will come to pass in revolutions."[92] For clerics like him, the situation was increasingly urgent, and the government needed to provide order. For some, the potential for disorder was heightened by Roosevelt's administrative actions. William B. Heagerty, for example, argued, "There is widespread satisfaction that some Social Security Legislation has been enacted; the good points are noted, but many express a fear that Socialism implied or expressed may kill much of the private initiative, this is noticed among those, the best people of the community, who have planned to build up much of their own security for old age and other chances of life."[93] For him, Roosevelt's policies leaned too far leftward and imperiled national stability. Middle-class citizens lived in fear of socialism to such an extent that their security was threatened.

There was tremendous concern among these clergy that FDR was going too far to the left and was threatening national stability by doing so. C. S. Newsom, for instance, advised FDR that he could help the country by "forsaking Russian ideals, and discontinuing the attempt to Russianize America; and by driving out the Russian Idealists from your 'Brain Trust.' Let your government give up the desire to destroy the Constitution of the United States and the United States, or alter it in such a way that will remove all its ability to hold despots in check."[94] And Walter P. Hill, who stated he was "not a 'Roosevelt' man," deplored the "*Europeanization* of our government," which he seemed to associate with the appointment of Catholic Jim Farley to the national administration.[95] These clerics made it very clear they considered Roosevelt's policies literally un-American. J. T. Michael agreed, writing, "Lets give no ground whatsoever to the Anti-American Propaganda which is abroad in the land today. We have no place in our philosophy of life for a Red, Russian Socialistic, and Atheistic doctrine."[96] Fred Anderson similarly saw the nation as imperiled by alien policies: "There is another great danger threatening our beloved Nation, and that is the red hand of communism there is strething over the land."[97] Members of this political imaginary saw in the upending of national economic hierarchies a dire threat to the very nature of American government.

These clerics, like H. Spencer Edmunds, urged the president to act more conservatively. Edmunds wrote, "If the government would quit passing unconstitutional measures, and experimental socialism measures, holding over us the increase of taxes,—for someone has to pay;—I believe that is the answer."[98] Robert T. Craig argued that "since human history has been recorded, every attempt that has been made to control the economic welfare of a nation, aside from the law of demand and supply has resulted in failure, and your attempt to do the impossible will fail. The ignorant have hoped that you would succeed, the educated have known that you were doomed to fail."[99] They sought a preservation of the prior order and saw that as the best hope of national stability.

Both opposing sets of political vocabularies thus relied on elements of the American Dream in authorizing their visions of the nation. That myth offers a sense of individual possibility amid an ordered and expanding nation. Each imaginary configured individualism, community, and order differently. But they both incorporated the notion that the United States was unique among nations.

AMERICAN EXCEPTIONALISM AND MISSION

According to Robert I. Ivie and Oscar Giner, the myth of American Exceptionalism is "the nation's sacred covenant, its sense of responsibility and duty, but also the legacy of presumed privilege and righteous indignation."[100] It is the idea that the United States is particularly ordained by

God to correct the evils of the Old World. By instantiating a New Jerusalem in the New World, it will become a shining city on a hill, a light that will illumine the world and will lead all people toward a better life, less corrupt, and more in line with divine mandates. This myth, which dates back to the mission Bercovitch and others associate with the Puritans and their vision, is a foundation of the American ideology and a critical component of the national political imaginary from which the smaller partisan versions are derived.

This myth underlies both the frontier myth and the American Dream, which depend upon and reinforce it. It underpins the frontier myth by providing a vision of the United States as uniquely civilized and therefore as uniquely capable of spreading civilization to other, less favored, places and through its emphasis on the importance of individual action in furtherance of civilization. It provides the purpose behind the errand into the wilderness even as that purpose is understood differently by different citizens. For those inhabiting a political imaginary opposed to the New Deal, it mobilizes elements of the frontier myth in its stress on individualism and self-reliance. It justified their sense of hierarchy and their faith in American political institutions as consisting of structures inherited from the past and needing to be preserved into the future. For those inhabiting an imaginary consistent with the New Deal, this myth justified their sense that the American enactment of its social order was a work in progress and authorized demands for more equality and the changes in political structures necessitated by progress toward a fuller realization of the national vision.

The frontier myth and the American Dream share important elements. They both depend on the idea that the United States is unique and special, reinforcing the idea that the nation is chosen. They both also depend on the idea that it is engaged in a great experiment and that this experiment is fundamentally democratic. Because of this fundamental commitment to democracy, both the frontier myth and the American Dream valorize the efforts of individual citizens. Both place individualism as central to the nation and understand individual action as important to the maintenance of social order. But different imaginaries configure both the community and the order upon which it depends differently. So inhabitants of both partisan political imaginaries could use the claim that the United States was a chosen nation and a great experiment in democracy to different ends: one that resisted political change and innovation, and one that endorsed them.

The Chosen Nation

There is perhaps no more deeply embedded mythic element than the understanding of "America," however imagined, as a select nation. The belief that the United States is special and has been chosen by God and endowed with a special mission has been integral to the nation's history, extending into its earliest colonial roots. This belief undergirds our national political imaginary. The different partisan variants of this imaginary, however, consider our national status as chosen to lead to very different ends. In general, the clergy thought that the nation would restore its economic and political health only after it returned to the precepts ordained by God. They had different views of what that meant.

Approving the president's social agenda, for instance, Paul Tanner reminded Roosevelt that his obligation was more to God than to the American people: "It is my settled conviction that no such social program can succeed without an unqualified Christian philosophy as its basis; faith, not opinion, built the Cathedrals. The insufficiency of the philosophy of materialism or mere humanitarianism to overcome the inherent greed and selfishness of our age must be apparent to thoughtful men. Enlightened interest as a motive for social security is not nearly enough. Frankly I cannot see how your excellent program will ever materialize without this deeply religious, Christian philosophy as its basis. . . . True religion, not sociology, is our ultimate hope."[101] For Tanner and others like him, FDR was moving in the right direction but without the proper mythic justification. To build a structure of lasting grace and power, the president and the nation needed to heed their highest calling, the calling of God. Myth, in the form of a divinely ordered nation, not social science, was the true basis for policy.

Thus, the clergy tended to argue that the nation's current wounds were self-inflicted. They were often understood as originating in its moral failures. S. C. Cornell, for example, wrote,

> In my sincerely humble opinion the subtle dangers that insidiously work to destroy the spiritual values of life are far more dangerous to our fellow beings than the more apparent subnormal conditions that affect primarily their physical life. That the physical has its inevitable effect on the spiritual is, of course, recognized. It is yet an irreparable disaster if the physical needs of folks are met at the expense of such intangible, indispensable, character values as personal initiative and self-respect. These values seems to me very gravely threatened at this time and I am quite confident that many of our people have already acquired a state of mind decidedly undesirable and distinctly dangerous to moral, spiritual, and physical progress of our nation. If I discern clearly, an alarming number of persons are looking toward government as tho it were a super–Santa Claus that will become aware of and provide for their needs. . . . Thrift and conservation seem to have little or no place in their plans or conduct.[102]

In offering this social analysis, Cornell argued that there were two related dangers, a material one and a spiritual one. He acknowledged that spiritual strength was easier in times of material prosperity, but argued that such prosperity also hinged upon adherence to the values of self-reliance and self-respect. Here, he mobilized the element of individualism, especially in his fear that the national government was acting against its material and spiritual self-interest in acting as a "super–Santa Claus." But the whole argument rests on the implicit understanding that the United States was, at heart, a spiritual nation, and that its well-being, however understood, depended upon adherence to Christian values. For clerics like Cornell, the nation was looking to the government rather than to God, and the national suffering would therefore continue.

Those who inhabited an imaginary opposed to the New Deal understood those policies as inimical to divine will. As H. F. Crim put it, "I believe that our people believe the Dole System has had its day, for the people seem to have the slogan, 'he that will not work, must not eat.'"[103] Here, Crim finds a biblical warrant for his policy preference, citing 2 Thessalonians 3:10. In Crim's view, then, his community's understanding of the proper way to administer social policy was in line with biblical warrants. That policy was implicitly authorized and approved by God. The administration's action in providing the dole were in direct contravention of the will of God and were thus both practically unworkable as inconsistent with human nature and morally wrong, inconsistent with biblical teaching.

These letters were, after all, written by clerics, so it is unsurprising that the idea that the nation had strayed from its divinely authorized goals was prevalent. What is interesting is the fact that they would so consistently argue, as did Hugh H. Ellis, that "I believe that the time has come for our prodigal national to cease bemoaning its loss of goods and to begin to bewail its loss of God."[104] By likening the nation to the prodigal son, Ellis both underlined the idea that it was possible to return to the Father and that there would be rewards for doing so. These clergy relied on the notion that because the United States was divinely favored it had special responsibilities to be obedient to the will of God. Agreeing broadly about that, the clergy had opposing views of whether that obedience led to endorsements of innovation or resistance to it.

Experimentation

Americans see themselves as nationally independent and innovative. We valorize "Yankee ingenuity" and self-reliance.[105] But these traits can be mobilized to opposing ends. Inhabitants of the New Deal imaginary saw innovation as pushing into the future while those opposing it often argued that the truly American innovation was the extant system of government, which allowed for incremental social and economic change. Altering those structures for them threatened the entire American experiment.

Howard A. Gibbs represented those conservative clergy when he wrote, "Government experimentation is often carried on too drastically."[106] Similarly, Gregory A. Sheradon instructed the president to "cease further experiments."[107] For these clerics, national experimentation was properly carried out by individual citizens, acting alone or as members of their local communities. It should not be conducted by the government, and it should not extend to governmental institutions.

Others, occupying a different imaginary and using an opposing political vocabulary, argued that the government was an appropriate place for experimentation. Paul L. Rider, for example, told FDR, "I admire greatly your advocacy and practice of intelligent social change in view of our widespread maladjustment. I hope that as the years of the depression lengthen, while you continue to experiment boldly and scientifically, you will strive to develop a more coherent and thorough-going philosophy envisioning the kind of social order our human welfare demands, as well as more stable institutions to carry what may have been only an 'emergency program.'"[108] Here, he displayed both a faith in science and a sense that as human society developed and changed, its governmental and societal orders should adapt and change as well.

These clergy equated the mythic elements of progress and experimentation. C. Arthur Sadofsky thus found FDR's course appropriate: "Let it be clearly understood that our nation is NOT GOING BACK TO CONSERVATISM—it must not be Communistic, but it must be LIBERAL and continue to experiment until we have perfected legislation that will fit the need of and serve the present age."[109] He favored experimentation as a means toward societal perfection, but also thought it should remain within clearly demarcated boundaries—good experimentation did not, by definition, encompass "Communistic" ideas. H. O. Pritchard argued that, "So deeply ingrained is the idea of 'every fellow for himself; the devil take the hindmost,' 'competition is the life of trade,' etc.—that it is going to take nearly a generation to implant the opposite concept, upon which the New Deal primarily rests, into the minds of the average American."[110] He implied that the New Deal represented a new way of thinking, a new kind of political culture, but that it was not yet fully inculcated.

A large number of the clergy, in fact, chastised Roosevelt for not experimenting enough. Isidor B. Hoffman, for instance, wrote, "I regret to inform you that I am on that increasingly large group who are dissatisfied with the Social Security legislation recently enacted. It is a step forward to be sure, but when a house is on fire it is not very adequate to take one step towards getting out of it if it takes ten steps to save oneself from being burned up."[111] A similar thought was expressed by E. H. H. Holmes, who thought recovery "cannot be done under capitalistic ownership and therefore a socialized industrial plant including distribution and the elimination of the profit-takers is necessary. More explicitly, a co-operative commonwealth organized and conducted in both its productive and distributive phases under democratic control must be realized."[112] George W. Pendes added his conclusion: "After much thought and study I have reached the conclusion that progressively increased production can only be balanced by consumption when the Government takes over all production and distribution."[113] It was seconded by clerics like Raymond O. Hall, who asserted, "With many others of the liberal clergy I would say to you that often we have been cheered by your words which seemed to promise undeviating allegiance to human welfare, but again and again it has seemed that the 'money-changers' were being served. We do realize the tremendous power of the interests, and the battle one must fight to resist them. Please reassure us that the welfare of the 'forgotten man' is your first interest, and the liberal clergy are with you!"[114] These clerics saw the moment as one in which ideological battle had been joined, and while the opposing forces were arrayed in great strength against the president and his progressive allies, with determination they could prevail and take advantage of the general instability to forge a more just economic and political order.

Conclusion

We think of myths as timeless, enduring, and stable. And in some senses, they are. But myths remain relevant only because they continue to speak to us, because they help us understand and participate in the world. They contain our national values. Political myths are especially important because they legitimate the political order and help guide communal action. The broad outlines of our national myths remain stable. The constituent elements, however, are more flexible, more open to interpretation, giving myth the capacity to adapt to changed times and remain relevant to evolving nations. American history has been marked by the continuing relevance of American Exceptionalism, which has been especially evident in various iterations of the frontier myth and the myth of the American Dream. These myths are used in different ways by members of opposing political imaginaries to help ground their competing political vocabularies.

The nation's most fundamental belief is that it is a chosen nation, somehow special, with a divinely ordained mission. Belief in American Exceptionalism has brought out both the best and the worst in the nation, impelling it to enact a communal life that is directed toward constant improvement in an effort to live up to its ideal of itself, and also justifying horrific acts of violence based on the belief that the nation has a divine mandate to bring its version of democracy to the rest of the world. American Exceptionalism operates both backward and forward, allowing the nation to see a divine presence in its past and using that presence as a warrant for various visions of its future. Every iteration of the nation, however, entails a tension between valorizing the individual and requiring individual service to the community. This tension has a variety of stasis points, and different eras will reflect different balances between community and individual achievement. The dominant political vocabulary in the Gilded Age, for example, valorized individualism and vested power in the private sector; the one that dominated during the New Deal was much more communitarian in orientation and vested power in the presidency.

The frontier myth was useful to Roosevelt, who often stressed the need for citizens of the 1930s to display the kind of hardihood he associated with the pioneers. It was less apparently useful to clerical inhabitants of his political imaginary, who found its emphasis on rugged individualism an uneasy element in a project designed to reduce national economic hierarchies and promote a sense of national unity. Conservatives, who occupied an imaginary opposed to that of the president, on the other hand, objected to the New Deal because they believed its programs, especially those dedicated to relief, were destructive of the individualism that had made the nation great.

The American Dream, a relatively recent arrival as a national myth, is closely connected to the nation's increasing commitment to democracy for it offers the faith that the nation's goods, whether understood as material or in other ways, are equally accessible to all. American Exceptionalism declares that the nation is special and that its actions both reflect that fact and must also live up to it. The American Dream renders that collective vision on an individual level, authorizing the idea that all individuals are equally able to attain the best the nation has to offer and that they are limited only by their own capacities. This mythic element was hard hit by the Depression, for the widespread dislocations laid bare the often hidden role of political and economic structures. As the clergy strove to find new political vocabularies, this element was used to justify both main sets of political positions, which were aimed at differently freeing the individual from oppressive structures and enabling individual potential.

These positions were enabled in turn by the national belief that the nation is engaged in a great, ongoing experiment in democracy and that it must constantly evolve and change to bring it closer to enacting God's purpose while preserving the best of the past. This flexibility means that the nation's foundational myths can also remain flexible, for it provides a ready warrant for arguments advocating change. This mythic element encourages change on the one hand, in that there is a belief that much is possible, and also discourages it in that moments of political change make it clear that democracy is fragile and often teetering on a razor's edge. There is at the same time a possibility that the nation can come closer to but also be more alienated from its destiny. The stakes for policy are always high, and the various interlocutors argue as if the nation's very soul is at stake.

This means that mythic decisions are ideological decisions. The belief that the nation is committed to a great democratic experiment and exists as an exemplar of democracy implies that our political vocabularies must always reflect those commitments. It is constantly in the process of reinventing itself. This makes the role of myth even more central to a political vocabulary, because that element provides a sense of continuity with the nation's past and projects it into the future in ways that provide reassurance to a mass public in a time of upheaval. Some interlocutors will, as Balthrop predicts, cling more tightly to old iterations of the national self. Others will employ mythic elements in the service of authorizing a new version of national identity.

The mythic element of political vocabularies provides an interesting case study for rhetorical circulation. For while those in power, especially presidents, rely on these myths in their broadest forms to authorize their national policies and visions of national identity, the vernacular articulations are probably those most sensitive to the ongoing processes of adapting those broad templates into contemporaneous forms. FDR, for example, was fond of the frontier myth and used it often. But it was circulated at the local level more frequently by his opponents than by his supporters.

Both the overall contours of our national myths and their constituent elements, then, are important aspects of opposing sets of political vocabularies, providing both a sense of continuity with the past and the capacity to authorize change without threatening national stability. As "cultural glue," myths enable the nation to understand itself as a collective.[115] It also allows the nation to act collectively, to engage in deliberation, and to create policy.

CHAPTER FIVE

Making a City on a Hill: Political Vocabularies and National Policy

At any given moment in time, citizens inhabit both an overarching national political imaginary and a smaller, more partisan one. That is, we agree on certain abstract values and the myths that support them, but disagree—sometimes substantially—on how those values ought to be understood and translated into national policy. Policy is integral to political imaginaries because it is the material enactment of our values and beliefs. Political imaginaries are rhetorically structured by political vocabularies, which delineate the role of authority, describe and rank members of the polity, ground these elements in specific iterations of national myths, and justify policy choices. This chapter concerns the last of these elements.

Clerical policy choices have been elements of every chapter of this book because the components of political vocabularies can be treated as analytically separate but are entangled and inseparable. So we have seen evidence that clerical views on repeal of Prohibition, for instance, were related to the ways in which they ranked citizens in the national hierarchy. Here, however, I place policy in the foreground because when one political imaginary dominates the national political scene, its preferences concerning both processes and outcomes are more likely to be enacted into law; the dominance of one political vocabulary over its competition thus has important consequences for the nation.

I talk about policy here in two senses. First, different inhabitants of different political imaginaries prefer different kinds of deliberative structures. Changes in regimes entail changes in administrative institutions, and so as those regimes change so do the institutions. The contestation between political imaginaries is also a contest between different decision-making procedures. These structures locate authority in different places and entail different protocols for managing political disputes. So the clergy make procedural arguments that are worth our attention.

The clergy who were aligned with the New Deal, for example, favored policy making at the federal level with strong presidential influence. They were also willing to expand the federal bureaucracy, what we now think of as the administrative state. They thus accepted a more nationalized state, operating under more generalized rules, which regularized political processes. With the important exception of Jim Crow, they were willing to enable wider citizen participation in the nation. There is a tension here: endorsing more regulation on the one hand would seem to reduce the role of the individual on the other. Democrats reconciled this tension through a belief, as we have seen, in the state as a mechanism of citizen empowerment. Republicans, on the other hand, did not endorse the same degree of federal or presidential governance, resisted the growth of the administrative state, and preferred the kinds of policy innovation they associated with strong state and local control over policy. More strongly individualist than the Democrats, inhabitants of the Republican imaginary understood the state as an obstacle to citizen empowerment and preferred deliberative mechanisms that emphasized individual rather than interest-based policy deliberation.

Second, members of different imaginaries have different policy preferences. Even if the nation is operating under one set of institutional rules, the policy preferences associated with the imaginary that prefers those rules are not guaranteed. The clergy, like their fellow citizens, were divided over issues like Repeal, relief, Social Security, and matters of foreign policy. Some of these issues, like Repeal and the anticlericalism of Mexico, were more salient for the clergy than for many members of the mass public. This indicates the way this element of political vocabularies circulates. Some elements are national in scope, and begin at the elite level, with the president and Congress. Debates over process, for instance, begin at the national level, as do policies that maintain national scope, like the National Industrial Relief Administration or the Agricultural Adjustment Administration (AAA). Other policies circulate through more local, or even niche, pathways. The White House was entirely unconcerned, for example, with the clerical opposition to Repeal. I discuss them briefly here, however, as indicators of the kinds of issue divergence we see among inhabitants of different political imaginaries.

The Structures and Processes of Political Deliberation

Scholars conceive of public deliberation and deliberative democracy on at least two levels: as a set of processes and as structures designed to facilitate those processes. Deliberative democracy is generally considered to consist of political structures that facilitate and enable some form of public opinion as influential in communal decision-making—democracy rests on the idea that public opinion should matter. So proponents of deliberative democracy look to both constitutional and extraconstitutional ways of encouraging public participation and the amalgamation of public opinion in ways that can be useful to policy makers. This aspect of deliberation has to do with developing the capacities for citizenship among members of the mass public such that they are able and willing to engage in decision making. Education is highly valued and so are the skills associated with respectful debate—including instilling tolerance, developing listening skills, and so on. These conceptions connect to political vocabularies, since those vocabularies authorize both the means of policy judgments and the results of those judgments. Our differing understandings of what it means to have democracy and how we can judge the proximity of our ideals and practices as well as the results of those practices are articulated through competing sets of political vocabularies.

At times of political rupture such as the 1930s, when hierarchies are disrupted and the meanings of political verities are unstable, deliberation becomes crucially important. Not only do new political decisions have to be made within changed contexts, but the rules of debate themselves are open to challenge. Roosevelt himself recognized this and argued at great length for an educated populace newly engaged in robust forms of political debate. He also argued for new institutional arrangements that, in his view, were better suited to his more democratic age.[1] He was more successful in some areas than in others, and the nation, increasingly seeing itself as more of a democracy than a republic, worked within republican political structures as it sought to instill more responsive policies. In the rest of this section then, I look at deliberative democracy as a set of political practices with specific reference to the 1930s before turning to a discussion of the clergy letters as they reveal opposing views of the way American democracy should be practiced and the kinds of policy that should therefore be enacted.

DELIBERATIVE DEMOCRACY IN THE 1930S

When scholars talk about deliberative democracy, they are often referring to a set of political structures that facilitate citizen participation. Thus, one of the central things at issue in any discussion of "public deliberation" is the role of the public. As Gerard A. Hauser notes, "A democracy is based on the premise that public opinion should matter in deciding the course of society."[2] The founders, of course, referred to the importance of public opinion as far back as the writing of the Declaration of Independence, and political actors since then have used it as a warrant for political action. But the meaning and measurement of public opinion have not remained stable. Indeed, it is an important element of the deliberative aspect of our political vocabularies, and thus its meaning cannot remain stable—new definitions and uses of it must develop as political vocabularies change.

As J. Michael Hogan points out in his discussion of public opinion polls, classical democracy did not rely on numerical majorities but on the weight of ideas as they were tested and deliberated in public forums. Aggregated public opinion is not, he notes, the same as collective wisdom.[3]

A focus on aggregated public opinion arose out of need to incorporate increasing numbers of citizens into the polity. There is a tension between the quality of deliberation and the number of participants involved in it.[4] So as notions of deliberative democracy have changed from classical times at least until the present moment, political actors and analysts have looked for ways to aggregate and understand public opinion. This has caused no small amount of tension in the U.S. context, for the battle for political legitimacy is closely tied to competing definitions of who gets to be included in the polity and under what terms their participation will be managed.

In a republic that role is restricted; one of the things that happened in the 1930s is an increased emphasis on the idea of the United States as a democracy. As a result, another one of the things that happened is the increase in ways to connect the public to the government, such as the rise of public opinion polls. This meant that pollsters rather than the public increasingly defined which issues were important and defined the terms through which they would be understood.[5] But this element of our national politics was in its early stages in the 1930s, and polls were but one way through which the president apprehended the mass public.[6]

The clergy letters are a useful gauge of public opinion not least because they responded to prompts from the president who wrote, "I am very anxious that the new Social Security Legislation, providing for old age pensions, shall be carried out in keeping with the high purposes with which the law was enacted. It is also vitally important that the Works Program shall be administered to provide employment at useful work, and that our unemployed as well as the nation as a whole may derive the greatest possible benefits." But he also asked what we would now call an open-ended question and requested that the clergy "write me about conditions in your community. Tell me where you feel our government can better serve our people." In this regard, Roosevelt encouraged the clergy to announce their own priorities.[7] The clergy letters represent a kind of aggregation of public opinion in that they served to augment information the president was receiving from a wide variety of other sources and so provided both perspective and depth.[8] This reflects the ways that FDR was pragmatically seeking legitimacy for his actions and simultaneously recrafting the mechanisms of political participation. It is no surprise that the president and his wife received something like five thousand letters a day over the course of his time in office. Inhabitants of the national political imaginary were encouraged to understand and act upon an increased role for public opinion in national affairs.

FDR tended to understand existing mechanisms as antiquated, facilitating elite rather than mass influence. Under Roosevelt, the nation increasingly understood public opinion as central to political legitimacy. It reflected not the narrow concerns of those increasingly called "interests," but somehow reflected "the common good," a fiction that animates democratically inclined politics.[9] Deliberative democracy, in other words, requires that individuals be obliged to look beyond their own interests and attend to some sense of commonality. This is a fiction not least because the only practical way to decide the common good is by amalgamating parochial understandings, and this amalgamation is always merely equal to the sum of its parts. And indeed, the problem with pluralism in general is that it must assume that everyone has equal access to political debate, are equally well organized, and that competition occurs on a level playing field.[10] These assumptions are untenable if politically useful and may actually impede progress toward democracy. This understanding marks one way in which we can measure the distance between our era and the 1930s.

If we understand deliberation to be about the act of political discussion, then that mandates certain kinds of political structures and behaviors.[11] Those mandates depend upon the capacities of the mass public to engage in those behaviors. The centrality of deliberation to ideas of democracy has roots that date back to the Enlightenment, and there have always been qualifications about the capacity of the public to engage in deliberative practices. In the context of the 1930s in the United States, it is important to note that Walter Lippmann had recently been making his thoughts on these limits plain. In his 1927 volume, *The Phantom Public*, Lippmann argued that the future democracy depended more on elites than on the informed participation of the mass public.[12] John Dewey, who was in general more supportive of the mass public than was Lippmann, also worried that modernity endangered, rather than facilitated, democratic potentials.[13] The problems caused by fragmentation, media, and the increasingly technical character of public issues, for both Lippmann and Dewey, were obstacles to effective participatory democracy. These views were largely reflected in the political imaginary that resisted FDR's view of the mass public and democracy and that was more skeptical of the mass public and its ability to guide public policy in useful ways.

In a large-scale representative democracy like the United States, it might be helpful, as Hauser implies, to think about public deliberation as coalition building.[14] At any given moment in time, inhabitants of both competing political imaginaries understood their coalition as representing the nation's overall public opinion. This is an especially productive way to think about it because it gets us to both the actual ways in which political actors understand their political tasks and because it enables us to focus on the ways in which deliberation not just requires consensus but also accommodates dissension and difference. Kendall Phillips offers an analysis of some of the ways deliberation understood as leading to consensus is problematic.[15] Thinking of deliberation as coalition building minimizes each of these ways. Coalition building accepts, as basic premises, both openness and exclusion, depends upon partiality, requires at least a degree of intersubjectivity, is both rational and affective, and exploits the fact of fragmentation. Not all interests are ever included in political coalitions, but artful politicians, especially at moments of national political redefinition, look for ways to capture and exploit constituencies while positioning their coalition as the one best representing the will of the entire nation. Coalition building does not get us to a public sphere that is unconcerned with consensus, nor does it get us to one that is refigured to highlight rather than occlude the kinds of differences that concern Phillips. But it does get us to an understanding of the public sphere as a place of institutionalized and even ritualized conflict. It accepts the rowdiness and messiness of what Hauser calls "rhetorical democracy," while also trying to order it. It is a way of thinking about what Calvin Troup thinks of as a more robust progressive, as opposed to a merely liberal, democracy.[16] And it helps us connect the local and the national. Finally, coalition building helps us centralize the material aspect of deliberation—policy.

The clergy letters reflect this notion of pluralistic coalition-building that underlay the understanding of deliberative democracy in the 1930s. They comprised a single-issue coalition against repeal of Prohibition, for example, and their thoughts on that reflect a limited kind of policy circulation. But occupants of different political imaginaries also participated in larger coalitions with a much broader policy circulation, in which the issue of Prohibition played only a very minor role. Out of the clergy letters we can find evidence for the different political imaginaries of the 1930s and the competing set of political vocabularies through which they were articulated. That articulation depended upon both a systemic understanding of how democracy would proceed and individual voices committed to engaging in the practices mandated by that system.

DELIBERATIVE RHETORIC

Deliberative rhetoric is, of course, one of the three genres of rhetoric first defined formally by Aristotle. It concerns that which may or may not take place, things that can be controlled by human action.[17] This matters because rhetoric only comes into play on matters of contingency.[18] But deliberative rhetoric can be distinguished from other kinds less by the element of contingency and more through the consideration of the question of whether a given course of action is desirable or not. Like forensic rhetoric it involves judgment; unlike forensic, deliberative rhetoric primarily concerns the future rather than the past, but can involve judgments about past actions as well.[19] Deliberative rhetoric then, is about both the shared commitments of a community and the rules by which those commitments will be debated, for all matters of judgment are concerned with both process and outcome.

It is also, as Jasinski notes, about "public business."[20] Deliberative rhetoric as a genre is, if nothing else, about the discussion of overall policy goals.[21] So it is not only the mobilization of private interest through public advocacy but is also the use of public reasons to advance public interests. Just as democracy, at least in theory, seeks the articulation of the common good, deliberative rhetoric, to the extent that it contributes to democracy, transcends narrow interest and serves the public interest. This, of course, is more easily required than accomplished.

One important danger here is a descent into what Simone Chambers calls "plebiscitary reason," or shallow, poorly grounded reasoning that appeals to the lowest common denominator precisely because of the need to make reasoning public.[22] That is, while the "public interest" can be understood as somehow greater than or even transcending private concerns, in striving to articulate it, political actors can easily be reduced to mass appeals that find numerical support because it debases rather than elevates our sense of both "the public" and "the public good." While groups in power have always tended to closely identify their interests with those of the entire mass public, and thus narrow the sense of the public good, plebiscitary reasoning widens but also debases that sense. The challenge of democracy, understood as a set of institutions and practices that promote the public good, is to locate "the public good" as broadly as possible without also demeaning our conception of the public and our communal life. Even more challenging is finding ways to do this that also involve as many members of the mass public as possible. Deliberative democracy, at least from the Progressive Era forward, requires the participation of citizens.

Citizenship, Robert Asen tells us, is motivated by certain acts; it is a participatory mode of engagement.[23] It is thus a discursive phenomenon that is both about what citizens do—how they participate—and the claims they make: the policies they prefer.[24] Public deliberation is best understood not as problem solving but as facilitating discussion using practical reason.[25] So in widening the arena of deliberation, we also need to account for different modes of citizen engagement as they occur in different kinds of political vernaculars.

Rhetoric is a kind of "creative reasoning," a "technology of deliberation" that draws attention to the materiality of power.[26] Citizenship as a set of rhetorical practices and the systems and processes through which these practices occur are clearly connected. Different kinds of political structures will facilitate different forms of participation engaged through different vernaculars. Even though it is unevenly accounted for, the element of practical reasoning is important; it marks "the direct participation of the audience and justifies and qualifies the conduct of advocates" as well as those of the audience.[27] So in the 1930s, for example, while the president encouraged more and more (white) citizens actively to participate, and to do so on their own terms (rather than through the enforcement of the kinds of Americanization practices that had been prevalent in previous decades), some citizens—especially African Americans—continued to be excluded. Their place in the national hierarchies altered at the margins, but the political vocabularies of power, which on the surface would have mandated their inclusion, came up against institutional structures that prevented such inclusion.

This example underlines the fact that deliberative practices, especially at the intersection of the institutional and the individual levels, are not about abstractions but concern concrete issues.[28] The key is to find ways to link public deliberations to public policy-making.[29] And as we will see in the clergy letters, some of their most strongly held beliefs had no impact on policy at all. Vernacular rhetorics are the expression of public opinion.[30] But on the individual as well as the institutional level, the opinions are public—they are not merely about private interest.[31] While the "common good" is a fiction that too often represents the interests of a narrow class, reaching for commonality remains an important element in how we understand representative democracy in the United States.[32]

Hauser notes that "it becomes a *public* opinion when a pattern of *sentiment*—thoughts, beliefs, and commitments to which a significant and engaged segment of the populace holds attachments that are consequential for choices individuals are willing to make and actions they are prepared to support in shaping their collective future—emerges from deliberative exchanges among those within a public sphere."[33] Deliberative rhetoric thus involves the evocation of argument. To qualify as deliberative rhetoric, reasons must be evoked.[34] It is a cooperative activity that is least implicitly dialogic.[35] And it leads to shared commitments—over process as well as policy. This element of shared commitment is integral to the ways in which deliberative rhetoric is an important element of political vocabularies. Those vocabularies provide a language through which these commitments are negotiated and contested. Without the stress on process, engagement, and outcome, there is no way in which the political vocabularies can cohere. They do so to the extent that they are widely shared and express a set of common concerns.

In sum, I understand political imaginaries as ordered rhetorically through the placement of authority and the depictions and hierarchies of citizens and grounded in myth. They are coalitions of essentially like-minded individuals who share a vision of the nation. That vision leads to a preference for different modes of deliberation and different kinds of deliberative rhetoric, in that they rely on different reasons for their preferences, and they result in different policy outcomes. These visions circulate generally from the top down, but also through more narrow local pathways that might cross partisan imagination. In the 1930s, Democrats wanted public policy to be aligned with public opinion understood in majoritarian terms. Their idea of good policy was that it was preferred by the largest number of citizens. So they approved structures and policies that facilitated public involvement and favored inclusion (for whites). Republicans, on the other hand, who occupied a more hierarchical imaginary, saw the best public policy as serving a public interest that was not determined by the number of people who approved of it but by its adherence to long-standing values and practices. They sought to preserve an existing order rather than to adapt the nation to an emerging one.

The Clergy Deliberate

Over eight thousand members of the clergy took the opportunity Roosevelt offered and expressed their opinions on a variety of policies, indicating, among other things, the increased legitimacy of the federal role in a wide range of matters that were previously under the purview of state, local, or private authorities. By conceding that FDR had a legitimate interest in many of these policies, many of the clergy also acceded to new institutional arrangements that had consequences for policy outcomes. By arguing against federal involvement, other members of the clergy were recognizing that this role was expanding and resisted the kinds of policy outcomes that entailed. In what follows, I first discuss the ways in which the clergy letters reveal contours of their views on proper deliberative practices. I then move to a discussion about specific policies. I conclude with a discussion of these as important elements differentiating competing sets of political vocabularies.

THE DELIBERATIVE PROCESS

Inhabitants of different political imaginaries understand the deliberative process differently. In keeping with the overall national imaginary, both partisan imaginaries find a role for public opinion in political deliberation.

Those in the Democratic imaginary, however, saw a greater role for mass participation; those in the Republican imaginary worried more about mass participation and saw the polity as better off under locally administered policy making. For those opposed to the New Deal, the best policy was local, which minimized corruption, meant that only the truly needy would get aid, and relied on local knowledge rather than governmental rules. Their opposition was as much about how policy was managed as it was about the content of that policy. John W. Jeffries, for instance, wrote, "I suggest that in order to bring about recovery, that the first thing to do is to Balance the Budget; Second, give out relief money so that it reaches the needy and does not go to Political henchmen as it does now; Third, revive local charity organizations who actually understand the need of the poor, and not bring in some stranger who only does it for the money involved; Fourth, you follow the teaching of the Constitution of the United States and not that of some Brain Truster."[36] For Jeffries, the prime concern was economic recovery, but he also understood the nation's economic problems as interwoven with a broad spectrum of entangled issues. He implied but did not make explicit his judgments of federal management of relief and the philosophy of government that undergirded the national administration. Examples like this indicate the ways in which deliberation operates through both vernaculars and a kind of shorthand—for people like Jeffries, use of the term "Brain Truster" condensed affective and rational responses to the national administration and its policies. His letter, which on cursory examination appears to be simply a list of rather poorly connected policy preferences, is better understood as articulating a response to policy as both a process (which rules governed the dispersal of relief) and content (a balanced budget), preferences widely shared by members of the Republican imaginary.

Similarly, L. J. Pederson wrote, "The country has been flooded with the cursed liquor; the murderous communistic government in Russia has been recognized; the food supply has been destroyed, though millions are in want; and now there seems to be a strong inclination to change the Constitution of our country for political reasons. How can genuine Americans but feel grieved and disgusted by such transactions? I am one of them, and I know my people concur with me in the matter."[37] Reasoning from the specific to the general, Pederson here argued against both individual actions and the philosophy that authorized them. He underlined his arguments with reference to what he considered to be a widespread affective disposition, in this case, grief and disgust. The federal government, in this view, was straying from the Constitution, and doing so in ways that led to poor policy outcomes. Don M. Chase was even more pointed, telling the president, "First, your 'relief' program has not solved unemployment. . . . Second, the agricultural program is unsound and morally indefensible. . . . Third, your government has shown itself to be a stronger proponent of militarism than any other in peace time history."[38] Here, Case connects ineffective and immoral policy-making, indicating that for him at least, effectiveness depended upon morality. His reference to militarism also indicates that he was reasoning from general principles.

Sometimes these general principles were clearly articulated. C. Arlin Heydon, for example, thought the president should "understand certain policies of our government in light of existing social conditions: a. Why spend so much on army and navy when that money is needed for food, clothing, education, and opportunities for work? b. Why destroy food stuff when our problem is not that of production, but that of distribution? c. Why seek to help support our government by legalizing and taxing life-destroying narcotics, including alcohol?"[39] For Heydon, policy making was a social task and, because it affected the nation's social life, should be undertaken with that in mind. He connected military spending to economic need and chastised the government for ignoring both material and spiritual necessities. For him, the broad context of policy provided the lens through which policy outcomes should be judged.

Those who advocated policies associated with the New Deal favored different kinds of deliberative processes, more dependent upon the needs of the public than on the preservation of existing political institutions and structures. Helen M. Heligman, for instance, who wrote on her father's behalf, asked FDR to "please pardon my being a bit personal. I want both you and Mrs. Roosevelt to know just what the Emergency Educational Program meant to this home. I was one of the thousands of unemployed teachers last year. In the Spring of 1935, I was placed in the EEP Program. This enabled me to provide the necessities of life for my mother."[40] Like those clergy who used local examples to make the larger case, Heligman mobilized private reasons to make a public argument. Because she was "one of the thousands," her voice spoke for those thousands; she could claim both direct experience and abstract knowledge, both of which culminated in a policy judgment: the EEP enabled her and, by implication, those in similar circumstances to "provide the necessities of life" to her aged parent.

Not all those seeking to invest the president in their private reasoning were disinterested or even necessarily sensible. The letter from Edward B. Lund, for example, was difficult to parse. After noting that "IDLE MEN SUPPORTED BY CHARITY SUSTAINED BY AGITATORS" were an issue, he wrote, "Distributing of the Abundance of Vitals creates rebellion and hatred so long as agitators and Disciples of Mammon do not repent and turn to God and do work meet for repentance." He may well have had either a public or private logic animating these rather obscure claims, but telling the president "Stumbling Blocks stepping stones into God's Promises" failed to clarify the course of action he preferred.[41] Examples like this foreground the problems of inclusion: some models of deliberative democracy strive to include as many citizens as possible, but the questions of what kinds of arguments ought to be privileged are always difficult.

W. H. Brightmire, for instance, told the president of his son, who had "a SURE CURE" for "our present economic trouble that is constitutional—legal in every respect and if adopted, would mark you as one of our greatest Presidents that ever ruled our country." Sadly, we do not know the specifics of this policy, for "my son will be very angry if he finds out that I wrote you it is his opinion that you are nothing more than a very astute politician trying your best not to help the people but to help the Democrat Party retain its hold on the American Public at any cost."[42] This letter indicates a certain naive sensibility: not only did Brightmire appear to have faith in his son and his economic ideas, but also evidenced little concern that his son's thoughts regarding the president might be offensive to Roosevelt. He seemed to consider that all ideas were welcome in the public arena no matter how unartfully conveyed.

He was not alone. Theodore C. Williams reported "I had a talk with a man whose work is taking him around the world. He knows something about a score of languages. He says that if you would stop the export of petroleum products to Italy the slaughter of Ethiopians would stop."[43]

Where Brightman depended upon his son's expertise, Williams relied on that of a man who had traveled widely. In their own way, each was trying to mobilize local experience while relying on a very democratic idea of participation: everyone's voice, it seemed, had a right to be heard.

Others, like J. J. Sharpness, used their local experiences to make recommendations for national policy: "Would it not be better to help the younger families to a piece of land and a little home with some equipment so they could provide for themselves? Just about all the dependents in the rural districts, as in our community, know how to farm."[44] Writing from a rural district himself, Sharpness was relying on his local knowledge to offer recommendations that in his estimation would provide for the entire nation. He was both making his local community representative of the nation and also reducing the nation's complexities to those of his own community. National deliberation as it proceeds from local experience is not without problems.

These examples illustrate different views of whose voices should be heard in national policy. Those opposed to the New Deal favored a local system of policy making; those who preferred a more national system were willing to provide local knowledge and individual expertise to the national government as a way of improving its ability to engage in national policy-making. These imaginaries also had differing views on the political structures that facilitated their preferred processes.

GOVERNMENTAL STRUCTURES

The changes in the relationship between the national and state and local governments were very much a part of the politics of the 1930s. The debates centered on the question of Roosevelt personally as a dictator, savior, or some combination of both, but also involved questions of institutional arrangements. By 1935, given the recent judgment in *Schecter Poultry Corp. v. the United States*, in which the Supreme Court invalidated the National Industrial Recovery Act, the centerpiece of New Deal legislation, the question of whether and to what extent Roosevelt's programs were constitutional were very much at issue. The debate over the constitutionality of the New Deal consumed the nation and was reflected in the clergy letters as well.

For the nation's clergy occupying the imaginary opposed to the president, the problem posed by the New Deal was one of subverting the capacity of local communities to care for their own, which led in turn to a kind of social breakdown within those communities. Samuel Jefferson Hood, for example, objected to relief programs because of what he considered the unwarranted and dangerous "centralization of power" they entailed.[45] Others made more extended arguments. Paul Little asserted, "Each State, city and town should do its utmost to take care of its own dependents rather than lean too much on the federal government."[46] Samuel M. Zwemer agreed: "Although I appreciate all that the present Administration has done in the abolition of child labor and other social measures, I deeply regret the plunge made in the work of relief by the appropriation of such large amounts for various local enterprises. In my opinion the pyramid of benevolence and aid for those in dire need has been put on its apex instead of its base. The first call for relief should be attended to by local agencies, then the State, and only in great emergencies by the National Government."[47] Finally, General Lee Phelps informed the president, "Frankly, I am fearful of the entire 'new deal,' of course I believe that some social security plan should be worked out for the security and protection of the aged and helpless, but I believe that each Municipality, and County and State should provide for their own."[48] These clerics saw some of the benefits of an increased federal presence, which manifested itself in the abolition of social ills like child labor, and the positive necessity of relief, but also worried about the consequences of the loss of local connections to policy, especially in terms of relief. They well understood that these changes had consequences for political attachments and institutional structures that would extend beyond the immediate moment.

Those occupying the imaginary aligned with FDR, on the other hand, sought a strengthened federal government and a stronger president. Charles R. Bell Jr., for example, writing about the situation of African Americans in Alabama, told the president that "it would be a hard task to describe the horror of this situation and to trace its dreadful effects upon our people. Living in the most degrading circumstances, hounded by loan sharks—and getting nothing for a crop is a fair description of the life so many of our people know. Our government should do something about it."[49] Here, he laid claim upon the government, insisting it both belonged to and owed its African American citizens. In examples like this one, it is clear that some of the clergy were implicitly arguing for more inclusive political processes facilitated by a more active federal government. These changed structures and processes would also lead to different kinds of policy outcomes than those advocated by members of the opposing political imaginary.

POLICY OUTCOMES

Policy discourse is unlikely to always fall neatly into one political imaginary or another because people may favor or oppose the same policy for widely different reasons. Certainly that was the case in the 1930s. The nation in general, for instance, favored repeal of Prohibition; the clergy, regardless of which political imaginary they aligned with, generally despised it. The AAA was widely loathed nationally and was criticized heavily in these letters. But there were also policies that indicated clerical preferences that align with the main opposing political imaginaries. Those who participated in the Democratic imaginary preferred a more inclusive polity governed by a more active federal government with a strong president. They favored policies like Social Security and relief and advocated presidential action in foreign policy. Those opposing that world view, on the other hand, were more cautiously supportive of Social Security or against it, worried about relief in general, and tended toward an anti-interventionist position on foreign policy. I want to focus on the reasoning behind the policy commitments as well as the commitments themselves as a way of illuminating the ways in which members of different political imaginaries figure policy in different ways.

Repeal of the Eighteenth Amendment

Of the federal government's actions, none aroused more ire among the clergy than Repeal. Opposition to Repeal marked the largest degree of clerical consensus in the letters. It was also one that the White House dismissed out of hand, noting in the report on the letters that, "It must be taken into consideration that the criticisms of the clergy concerning the liquor question are more a reflection of their own personal opinions than that of their congregations."[50] The president, having asked the clergy for their advice, was advised to be selective in listening to it. There is no question that this advice was sound; Repeal was far more popular than the Eighteenth Amendment had been, and legalizing alcohol meant that the government could accrue much-needed taxes from its sale. But even if the clergy spoke for a minority on the subject, they spoke very loudly indeed.

I want here to focus on the ways in which the clergy argued against Repeal rather than the fact that they argued against it. Members of the imaginary aligned with Roosevelt argued that repeal was inconsistent with his stated policy preferences. Those clergy opposed to the president, on the other hand, viewed it as completely consistent with his stated priorities. This difference indicates the ways in which the same policy can be evaluated by inhabitants of different imaginaries. In endeavoring to find a place for this policy within their general understanding of FDR and the New Deal, the clergy exemplify the ways in which we strive to order our political imaginaries neatly, if not always successfully.

Harold Francis Branch, in general an advocate of the president's program, wrote, "Your Administration is a strange anomaly. You lay one hand upon the Bible, swearing to defend the Constitution of the United States; with the other hand you encourage your great political organization to disregard the 18th Amendment. Long before it is repealed and while it is still in the process of orderly repealment. With this same hand you redonize the Government of Russia, than which the Constitution of the United States has no more bitter, relentless, subtle and ingenious foe on the face of the earth."[51] For Branch, the contradiction between caring for citizens through policies like Social Security and yet allowing the consumption of alcohol and recognizing an atheistic government in the Soviet Union was a matter of concern. He generally considered Roosevelt's policies as consistent with Christian doctrine and had difficulty accounting for his willingness to repeal Prohibition or his recognition of the Soviet government.

Others, like W. H. Whitlock, also found inconsistencies between the president's avowed concern for the nation's well-being and his support for repeal. After praising the administration for its policies on relief, Social

Security, and neutrality, he told the president, "A shame, however, will clowd the record because the very class who most greatly need the relief and security are the ones most cursed by the ravages of the liquor traffic which you have turned loose upon them."[52] Like Branch, Whitlock agreed that it was the government's responsibility to care for its weakest citizens and saw FDR as committed to that goal. He saw Repeal as explicitly failing to do just that, a fact that distressed him.

The clergy offered evidence in support of their claim that the federal government was failing its responsibility to the vulnerable. Many members of the clergy, like Hugh N. Ronald, blamed repeal for the fact that "we see more drunkenness on our streets."[53] Some thought it was a significant blot on the Roosevelt presidency. Lorenz I. Hansen, for instance, wrote, "With the exception of the return of liquor which has filled our streets, subways, and buildings with reeling 'drunks,' you have helped our nation to reform itself for a new and better day."[54] They saw and offered contrasts between the president's willingness to intervene in local affairs on some matters and not on others, seeming to imply that it should be all or nothing where federal intervention was concerned.

Those clergy opposed to the New Deal, on the other hand, understood repeal as part and parcel of the president's program. L. J. Powell told him, "Your wild schemes have quite eclipsed the glory of the flag; and will all the good that has been done, it will be at dreadful cost. . . . Personally I hold you responsible more than any man for the present order of intemperance, the nation-wide scheme of distilleries and brewers to make the present generation of drinkers."[55] Frank H. Haydenfork similarly fumed, "To me, your leadership which legalized the sale of intoxicating liquors and brought in its train moral and spiritual degradation, is a crime and a sin of which you need to repent before God."[56] FDR's actions were not understood here as proceeding from an institutional vantage but from a personal one, for which he would be held personally accountable. Theodore Bauer's rage was perhaps the most clearly expressed: "You pledged the nation repeal and we have repeal. We also have a hell of a mess. I suppose you are proud of your achievement when you read or hear of someone, perhaps a child, being killed by a drunken driver."[57] Bauer saw repeal as the direct result of the president's program for which the president was uniquely responsible.

Perry F. Webb noted the interconnections of policies, seeing in repeal the signs of other problems: "You have flooded this country with liquor, violating promises, as well as bringing a fearful tide of misery and suffering, which has increased the sadness of homes and hearts, and at the same time frustrating the very 'Social' work in which you say you are so interested."[58] Others agreed with A. M. Harrington, who wrote, "No country can drink or legislate her way back to prosperity. Material security cannot abide where morals decay and the souls of men are impoverished."[59] These clerics argued that the federal government should do less than it was doing, but also argued that they wanted it to do different things: it should stay out of relief, but should enforce prohibitions on gambling, on alcohol, on pornography. They were similarly united on the question of the administration's agricultural policy.

Farm Policy and the AAA

Repeal was undoubtedly the policy on which the clergy expressed their strongest and most united feelings, but the sentiment against the AAA was almost as strong. The AAA, an omnibus agricultural relief bill, represented the president's effort to repair the nation's farm economy, which, he considered, had been damaged by an overabundance of supply driven by the widespread inability to pay for protein and produce. When the Depression destroyed the ability of people to pay for groceries, farms continued to produce, but prices feel so drastically that farming became financially impossible. Coupled with widespread drought and the dust storms that decimated farming in the Midwest, the American farmers' plight was dire. The New Deal included a plethora of farm policies, ranging from plans to plant trees to mitigate the winds in the Midwest to the AAA's mandated killing of livestock and the plowing under of crops in an attempt to restore balance to supply and demand of farm goods. This latter policy enraged many, for the destruction of food at a time when people were starving was seen as perverse and illogical. That rage is clear in these letters, although it was fueled by differing kinds of reasons.

The clergy who opposed FDR found the AAA sinful; for them, the policy indicated the ways in which God and the president parted company. J. W. Storer told FDR, "The pig-killing crime is indefensible, and the doctrine of planned scarcity such a fantastic perversion of nature that people just dismiss it with a shrug, except when they go to the store to buy food."[60] For him, the president's agricultural policy was so preposterous as to be unworthy of serious discussion; it was "dismiss[ed] with a shrug" by all thinking people. Martin B. Quill was equally vehement: "You have asked me for my opinion and I shall give you my opinion with kindness consistent with sincerity. I believe that you are honest, but I am not going to vote the democratic ticket again until I can be assured that your policies will not prevail. Your orgy of spending is unjustifiable. Your killing of pigs and sows and cows has no moral defense. Neither has the plowing up of cotton any defense."[61] By naming the policies an "orgy," Quill was also labeling it, as had Storer, as a perversion, immoral, a sin, and without justification.

Others, like Reginald Shepley, who were in general aligned with the president, had some difficulty reconciling their approval of the New Deal with their disapproval of "the slaughter of pigs and cattle."[62] "Slaughter" was often used when the clergy voiced their opposition to the AAA, as in this example from Holden H. Clements:

> I am in hearty accord and I am willing to aid in every measure which creates greater social welfare, especially for those who are dependent and helpless. But the conscientious, thinking people of my parish join me in saying, I am against some of the policies which have been adopted and employed for recovery, namely, the slaughter of hogs and cattle and the plowing under of crops, when thousands go hungry and are in need of clothing, and most of all, the use of revenue derived from alcoholic beverages, which, to my mind, is using literally the "life blood" of our nation.[63]

Clements, like Storer, placed the president on one side of the debate and "conscientious, thinking people" on the other, dissociating the president from even the possibility of wise policy. He also dissociated the administration from life in general, calling his policies inimical to feeding the hungry, clothing the needy, and in opposition to the nation's "life blood." These examples indicate the ways in which inhabitants of a political imaginary can disagree with some policies while in the main supporting others associated with their partisan preference; members of a coalition cannot be taken for granted.

At least some of the clergy felt competent to advise the president on social as well as economic policy and did so by referencing local experience, economic theory, and moral beliefs, although many declined to offer their thoughts on matters they considered outside of their areas of expertise. When it came to the New Deal's signature policy, however, the majority of Roosevelt's correspondents were happy to share their thoughts. And, as we might expect, in this policy area, there was a wide gulf between those who endorsed Social Security and those who opposed it. There was a smaller gulf between those who endorsed Social Security and those who favored different kinds of social insurance, such as Share the Wealth or the Townsend Plan.

Social Insurance

The support for some form of social insurance was nearly unanimous among the clergy who approved of the president's overall program although some fretted that its benefits were not equally available to all workers, including the clergy themselves, and that these exclusions reflected problems with the nation's political hierarchies. The author(s) of the White House report on the letters wrote Social Security was "hailed as the greatest measure of the New Deal and the most Christian legislation of the century. Small minority worried about it's cost, about it's being the states' right and duty, and about it's becoming a tremendous political weapon compelling regimentation."[64] The report's summary is accurate, if ungrammatical. The clergy were, in general, wildly enthusiastic about Social Security, although those inhabiting the Republican imaginary worried about the effects on the nation's morality, budget, and independence.

James W. Hailwood approved of the legislation, although he did not see such support as widespread in his Michigan community. He wrote, "I stand alone in this community among one hundred ten Protestant pastors, not to mention Catholic and Jewish ministers, as an exponent of the principles of social security. . . . I believe that the Social Security Program, which you initiated and conducted to successful issue, is definitely the finest answer to the problems made by any nation at time in the history of the world."[65] Such hyperbole was not uncommon. Kenneth Danskin assessed it this way: "The Social Security Legislation, though inadequate in amounts, is one of the most forward looking steps of our national history."[66] These clergymen tended to place the president and his specific policies in the context of world history and frequently told him that his place in that history was secure.

Equally common, however, was approval tempered with concern. Robert Ray, for example, wrote, "I am favorable to the Social Security legislation and am sorry that so much of it was ruined by its failure to pass because of the foolishness of one man. Because there is so much gambling, dishonesty and disloyalty to trust in our country, I believe that the people generally are afraid that money spent in this program will miss its mark by way of some politician's pocket."[67] Similarly worried about corruption, William Hart complained about "too much favoritism" and announced his preference for the Townsend Plan.[68] For these clergymen, the policy was one thing; its administration was quite another. They were happy to support the one but had major concerns about the other and urged the president to safeguard the policy by appropriate administration of it. This tendency of course, reveals the continuing influence of Progressive Era thought in the nation; the idea that government existed to serve the people and that administration of government policy should be rule- rather than interest-based was one of that era's most important influences. But it also reveals the way in which partisan political imaginaries and political coalitions are constructed. These clergy had to choose between a policy that they admired and an administrative structure that they did not.

Others among the clergy supporting the president were less able to support Social Security and found themselves favoring the Townsend Plan. Enthusiasm for the plan, along with support for Huey Long's Share the Wealth proposals, is often credited with helping to pass Social Security.[69] But even after its passage, enthusiasm for the Plan remained high among the clergy. G. W. Austin, for instance, wrote, "I earnestly ask you to read the Townsend Recovery Plan . . . it is not a radical plan and cannot, in any way, be compared to Father Coughlin, Huey Long, or any of their type."[70] It is interesting that Austin felt the need to defend Townsend as mainstream rather than radical; one of the ways FDR defended his administration was by situating it in the middle between extremes, making even his most revolutionary policies appear mainstream, which is often an advantageous frame in our national politics.

Others among the clergy offered political assessments of support for the plan. Walter L. Thompson observed, "Of course San Diego as well as most of southern California is a hot bed of enthusiasm for the Townsend Pension Plan. Most thinking men know that this is financially and practically impossible of realization. But California is filled with aged and retired people who are suffering greatly from depressed conditions and loss of investments and having nothing to lose they are grasping at any straw which will relieve the insecurity of their condition."[71] Unlike the clergy who dissociated FDR from "thinking men," Thompson associated his ideas with thoughtfulness. At the same time, he excused those who were rendered incapable of wise consideration by financial need. Here, Thompson privileged rational deliberation as important to policy making and also noted the factors that mitigated citizens' capacities to engage in such deliberation.

But many claimed to be both rational and also Townsend supporters. Jesse Marhoff offered a financial analysis of the Townsend Plan before concluding that it "is beneficent and good business, workable and just."[72] O. M. Showalter found in the Townsend Plan the key to the nation's spiritual and economic recovery: "Mr. President, there is a way out. The Townsend recovery Plan, though it is ridiculed by the monied interests, holds the solution to our spiritual and material wellbeing. It will loosen the rusted bearings of the wheels of industry, without which we can never recover. It will be an immediate help to our government, to its every citizen, young and old alike."[73] For Marhoff, the plan was defensible both as good for business and as serving justice, two things that were often treated as incommensurate given the political divisions of the era. The debates over Social Security, the Townsend Plan, and other social insurance programs indicate the degree to which pre-1930 ideas about the role of government vis-à-vis the nation's needy were in flux and how various interlocutors attempted to reconcile the tenets of "good business," "responsible government," and national values demanding individual self-sufficiency to make sense of their political worlds.

Clerical interlocutors opposed to the New Deal imaginary also opposed Social Security. A. Quello, for example, wrote: "*The simple fact is that the modification of the homestead act so as to apply to the present conditions would cure troubles as we see it has been done before and remake America as it is made in the first place needs to be re-realized. It is the* OLD DEAL *that we need.*"[74] Like others among his brethren, Quello here wanted to see people given land rather than relief; he sought a return to an idealized past as the best way out of present difficulties. He made his preference for the previous order explicit. Others were harsher in their criticism of Social Security. Carl J. Nolstad argued, "The Social Security Bill is like handing the baby a piece of candy to make it stop crying."[75] In this one sentence, he defined the national government as paternalistic and the nation's needy as fractious children. Like Quello, Nolstad argued for a return to old ways of doing things, even though his reasoning appears to be quite different. H. L. Thomas offered these reasons for his belief that Social Security would fail: "The Federal Government has to deal with all 48 States, all with different laws. . . . The recipient must take an oath that he or she is a pauper in order to get this pittance. . . . Besides it puts no additional circulating funds into the channels of trade—the thing most needed to give back prosperity."[76] He grounded his arguments in political rather than social analysis. And this, of course, is precisely how deliberative democracy as a coalitional endeavor proceeds: people with very different kinds of reasons for preferring one policy need not agree on reasoning to work together toward a shared goal. As much as debates over social policy revealed the emerging issue cleavages of the contesting New Deal political vocabularies, the issue of relief brought those issues into even sharper focus.

Relief

Again, the White House report summarized the letters:

> From the standpoint of the moderate, there is no question in the minds of the clergy that the recipients of the Dole are losing their ambition, honesty, and initiative; are looking to the Government to take care of them; are becoming class-conscious, which is turning the struggling

> tax-payer class into a resentful group, for they see their hard-earned money going toward the maintenance of non-workers. They agree that it was necessary, at the beginning; but since that time has passed the necessity of preserving our national inherent traits demands a cessation of the Dole for all except widows and orphans, etc.[77]

As we have seen consistently in these letters, one of the big issues animating the New Deal political order circulated around whether the government should offer relief and, if so, under what terms and conditions. The White House summary, which naturally presents the debate in the administration's preferred terms, depends upon the national fiction that the United States was free of class prejudice, even class awareness. The danger of the dole was that it threatened to inculcate class into the nation's political life. That Roosevelt was largely able to avoid sanctioning Social Security and relief in class terms was one of his great political successes. It also meant that class remained an unacknowledged feature of national political policy, although it was an important force helping to structure the competing political imaginaries of the time.

The clergy who opposed the president were leery of creating a political class that depended upon relief.[78] Clifford E. Hay, for instance, called it "a political football" that resulted in "grief to the unemployed and the indebtedness of the country."[79] W. C. Cranston claimed that "There is increasing criticism of the various relief measures, occasioned largely by the obvious political manipulation of funds. Professional politicians are growing fat, while many of the needy go uncared for."[80] R. B. Lee agreed: "it is true that the Relief is some help to some, but I am sure it costs 80 c of each dollar to get it down to the needy, and then such a few get the 20 c."[81] Kiddoro P. Simons objected to "the lies, intemperance, corruption and graft sponsored by your group," which he thought "already exceeds the administration of any other I can find in the history of our nation."[82] For these clergy, relief was damaging to the poor in that it inculcated dependency. It was also bad for the nation in that it created two classes of parasites—those on relief and those who administered it. As George A. Percival put it, "This has been commonplace for Republicans, and Democrats have not been free from it, but somehow many of us had believed that, under you, politicians would not trade on human misery."[83]

This comment reveals the level of mistrust many conservatives harbored for the federal government and the political class; they feared political actors would damage the nation's moral structure in return for power.

Some, like Ernest E. Ventres, told FDR, "We resent the unprecedented enormous and extravagant expenses of administration, and the unrighteous taxes that must result."[84] Kenneth W. Moore agreed, considered funding New Deal programs tantamount to "taxation without representation," and complained about the "heavy tax burdens."[85] In making his argument against relief, he referenced important political mythologies dating back to the revolution. Others relied on prospective rather than retrospective appeals. W. S. Thornton wrote, "While the government's Work programs have given employment to many—many who would be on public charity otherwise—yet I continually hear the cry, 'Who is going to pay for all this?' And again, 'is it right to burden future generations with the cost of our extensive expenditures?' I wonder myself."[86] Many of these clergy, like Alexander Hood, called for a balanced budget.[87] Frederick W. Hatch argued that "thrift is as valuable for governments as for individuals."[88] And Harry N. Young insisted that while New Deal programs "have put our country on the road to recovery. But now that business is recovering, the government should curtail expenses and start working in that promised 'Economy in Administration.' Our federal debt is staggering and should not be increased unnecessarily."[89] These clergy often reasoned from the individual to the government, analogizing household and national budgets and rendering the huge sums being spent nationally into terms that could be more readily understood.

Those inhabiting the New Deal political imaginary, on the other hand, were more likely to defend publicly administered programs by defining them as a social good—as protecting the vulnerable, for example—as well as arguing for the government's role in providing that social good, as a neutral arbiter. So those opposed to that view criticized government and its programs on both counts: those being protected were not vulnerable but lazy, and the government was not administering programs neutrally. Once programs like Social Security or relief were firmly established, those opposing the government's administrative role were fighting a rearguard action.

The clergy supporting the president worried that relief, not yet fully established, was temporary and uncertain. J. R. Griffith, for instance, made it plain that his main concern was the impermanent nature of relief: "Now, as for conditions in our community, I would say that I consider them very bad, though much better than they once were in some respects at least. Many more people are at work than once were working, but thousands of them are being paid out of Government funds, of course, and are working at almost starvation wages. I am wondering what will become of them when this appropriation is exhausted."[90] As for most people at the time, for Griffith, relief was, by definition, temporary. He could not conceive of it as ongoing, and its temporary nature meant that the nation's vulnerable citizens had only a limited kind of security.

The clergy thus both illustrated the range of issues that comprised the deliberative consequences of New Deal political argumentation and demonstrated the range of ways in which those arguments can be considered deliberative. They exemplified limited, qualified, and full support for federal policies; they argued against those policies; and they did both these things by mustering vernacular discourses, abstract theory, and common sense. They had a wide variety of opinions and expressed them with considerable passion as well as with rational argumentation. When it came to foreign policy, the range was considerably more restricted and the number of participants considerably fewer.

Foreign Policy

Given the depth of the Depression and the administration's concentration on domestic policy, it is unsurprising that the political debate was largely restricted to domestic policy and the nation's relationship with itself. When it came to the nation's place in the world, a much smaller number of clergy offered opinions, and in general, those opinions were restricted to a demand that the United States remain free of "foreign entanglements." There was also strong feeling among the Catholic clerics that the president should intervene militarily in Mexico, given its anticlerical policies (he did not) and that the recognition of the Soviet government was a mistake. But in general, the clergy, like the nation, remained focused on matters of domestic concern. In the national political imaginary of the time, foreign policy remained a minor element; that is reflected in the minor role it played in the partisan iterations of that imaginary. As in the case of repeal of Prohibition, the clergy were largely united in their views on foreign policy; to the extent that this reflected national public opinion, it reveals the scale of the task Roosevelt faced as he sought to bring the nation into the international arena in response to events that were starting to simmer in Europe.

Unsurprisingly, the clergy in general were advocates of political neutrality. In this, of course, they reflected the national preoccupation with anti-interventionism that characterized the decade.[91] Walter F. Troeger, for instance, wrote, "Earnest efforts to remain at peace with the world and to maintain neutrality during European conflicts are essential to the happiness and wellbeing of our people."[92] J. E. Flew wanted "to commend you on your stand against becoming involved in Foreign wars. Let us be 'Good Neighbors' but not get mixed up in their quarrels."[93] William Lasley made his opinion clear with all available typographical resources: "KEEP US OUT OF WAR!!!"[94] Robert S. Sidebotham asserted, "We thank God for the neutrality legislation. We are all with you fully in your effort to keep us at peace with our neighbors."[95] These arguments indicate the role of American Exceptionalism in the national political imaginary, for they rely on the claim that conflict was somehow restricted to the Old World and was not part of New World ideology or practice. Given that the United States had been at war—with the British, the Spanish, the Mexicans, and hundreds of indigenous nations—for most of its existence, this claim was grounded more in ideology than empirical reality, but it reveals the power of that ideology as well. Like many Americans, the clergy were not entirely blinded by this ideology. They were quite willing to resort to force of arms when U.S. interests were at stake. But they were attentive to events in Europe and reluctant to believe that our national interests were involved there. As Harold F. Shimeall put it, "personally, I believe America should never fight on foreign soil nor in foreign waters—regardless of the circumstances."[96]

Some, like Shimeall, advocated neutrality on general principles. Others did so because of its perceived connection to other policies. Rolla Earl Brown asked, "may I urge that you use your utmost power to lift from our people to terrible expense of armament and the prevention of any future war."[97] These clergy argued that the money spent on munitions could be better spent on other things. Similarly, Winfred H. Johnson found himself "opposed to the increasing millions that are being spent for war, and I feel the navy game in the Pacific waters was an incitement for militaristic sentiment in Japan. Why not use some of the money for social security?"[98] Llewelyn A. Owen agreed: "According to your budget we will spend for old age pensions, crippled children and unemployment insurance a mere pittance in comparison with the expenditures for past wars and present military and naval expansion . . . of what permanent value is your program of social legislation if you are building on the defeated philosophy that war is inevitable?"[99] They considered the federal budget a zero-sum game and wanted the money dedicated to the military spent elsewhere or not at all. F. L. Raney wrote, "So far as the Church folks are concerned, your consistent stand in matters of peace and war are very pleasing. Most of us perhaps are confused as to why it is necessary to spend so much money for the military activities of our government while the unemployment situation remains as it is."[100] Raney here provides evidence of thoughtful balancing of interests—his reasoning and his priorities are both evident.

Partly, the clerical ordering of national priorities was a matter of the hierarchies implicit in their partisan iterations of the national imaginary. And partly, it reflected the widely shared suspicion of the armaments industry that many blamed for American involvement in the Great War.[101] Charles S. Owen, for example, wrote,

> I sincerely hope that this neutrality legislation may be strengthened; made a permanent policy of the nation so that we may be spared the stupid mistake of participating again in another foreign war. . . . On the other hand I join emphatically with those who feel that you should show more leadership in bringing the munition racket under control; and with those who protest against such extravagant waste as the unparallel peace time expenditures on the army and navy; and with those who resent such sets of international bad manners as the recent naval maneuvers in the Pacific. In these spheres I would like to see courage and leadership from you rather than bowing to the lop-sided Admirals.[102]

Some, like Lester R. Minion, went so far as to call for "universal disarmament."[103] Others simply sought to make munitions unprofitable. Ernest Baker argued that "Legislation should be enacted immediately, which would take the profit out of war. The American legion has such a program. Wealth should be conscripted as well as men."[104] There was considerable aggravation at the amount of money the clergy felt was going to the military.

American Exceptionalism was on display in other ways as well. Francis E. Stifer, for example, expressed both the prevailing ideology and its associated casual racism: "We are not an imperialistic nation as has been demonstrated by our actions with regard to Cuba and the Philippines. Furthermore, we are a self-supporting nation. These two facts added to our favorable geographical location and our popular distaste for militarism give us a splendid opportunity to lead the world in the way of peace. I believe that unless we do this no one will and I am convinced that another general outbreak of war in all western civilization means the beginning of its final decay and the opening of the door for the colored people of the world."[105] First, of course, his views on the United States as a non-imperialist nation are open to challenge, although this view was clearly widely shared at the time as Americans distanced their practices from European versions of colonialism. Second, Stifer here articulates one version of American Exceptionalism, calling for global American leadership premised on inherent moral superiority. And finally, this passage reveals the ends to which that leadership was to be aimed: at the protection of white Western civilization from the unspecified threats posed by "the colored people of the world." Stifer recognized that U.S. global leadership would be premised on the hierarchies that operated at home.

Not everyone favored neutrality, however. Franklin D. Southworth, for example, offered his opinion at some length:

> For the vast majority of our people, however, the problem of social security is eclipsed by the war-cloud in Europe. Without exception so far as I know the people of this region are in hearty sympathy with the League of Nations in declaring Italy to be the Aggressor and in the desire to cooperate with the League to the full extent of their power in the application of sanctions. We are prevented by the unhappily worded Neutrality Act from a direct embargo on Italian shipping. The President, however, has full power under the Neutrality Act to place an embargo both for Italy and Abbysinia on the full category of goods

> which the League would prevent shipping to Italy. Such a course would not only obviate any diplomatic friction with the possibility it might involve of our being drawn into war, but would relieve many patriotic Americans of the consciousness of blood guiltiness in standing coldly aloof while one of our fellow signers of the Kellogg Pact is wantonly attacking another member.[106]

Southworth exhibited here a kind of deliberative rhetoric that is most closely aligned with the idealized Enlightenment version. He connects foreign and domestic policy, refers to the important debate about the American role in the League of Nations, demonstrates knowledge of both the theory and practices of that League, demonstrates also his familiarity with the details of the most recent Neutrality Act and the constraints it imposed on the president as well as the president's remaining ability to act, and then postulates the consequences of his preferred course of action. And all of this was couched in a reasoned and reasoning tone. This passage is a very model of classically defined deliberative rhetoric.

On matters of war and peace, then, the clergy had strong views and mustered warrants that ranged from the impassioned demand that the president keep the nation out of the impending European conflict to reasoned discussions of domestic legislation and international law. These arguments were, most often, couched in an ideological understanding of the United States and its role in the world.

The clergy were equally happy to discuss that role regarding more specific foreign policies. Father Bonaventure spoke for the Catholic clergy in general when he wrote, "The situation in Mexico should receive some official attention. It cannot be denied that the United States put the anti-God crowd in power there and is now keeping them there contrary to the wishes of fully ninety-five per cent of the Mexican people. The helpless Mexican people are being treated far worse than the Jews in Germany."[107] Paul E. Meyer agreed writing, "As a Catholic priest, I am violently opposed to the lack of action of the administration in regard to the Mexican situation as regards religion. . . . I am also violently in opposition to the recognition of the Soviet government in Russia. Commercially, it seems to be a failure, morally speaking it was disastrous, and it appears to be a diplomatic blunder."[108] The Catholics felt especially strongly about the necessity for Mexican intervention and, like Bonaventure, associated anti-Catholicism with being "anti-God." FDR chose to encourage the Mexican government to change its anticlerical policies by working behind the scenes, a stance that the clergy resented.

That resentment, confined as it was to the Catholic clergy, revealed a narrow debate that might have affected FDR's immediate coalitional concerns but had little impact on the competing sets of political vocabularies. The recognition of the Soviet government, on the other hand, was translated far more broadly across the nation, indicating at least one place where the national political imaginary held broad policy agreement. Many Americans, and most of the clergy, considered Russian Communists, and Communists in general, unsavory, untrustworthy, and unreliable. Few clerics supported the president's decision to open formal relations with the USSR. Charles T. McKay, for instance, asserted, "Russia has proved herself unworthy of recognition. Her emissaries are openly advocating the violent overthrow of government."[109] Basil Maniosky was "very sorry that the UnSts recognized the Russian Government" avowing that "we Ukranians will never believe that bolsheviks can keep their promises, or stop their propaganda."[110] It was clear that the Soviets needed, in the minds of these clerics, to be treated very carefully indeed. When it came to foreign policy, adherents of the national political imaginary generally looked backward for moral guidance and forward for global leadership.

Conclusion

Over time, the United States has mustered different definitions of democracy, authorized by different conceptions of the role of the mass public and public opinion to justify different kinds of institutional and administrative arrangements. The dominance of one partisan iteration in every set of competing political vocabularies authorizes a different set of institutional arrangements and political processes. Those arrangements reflect and encourage sets of issue cleavages, which circulate through a variety of pathways. Debates about processes generally begin at the top and filter down; policy debates, on the other hand, circulate both from the bottom and the top and may be confined to smaller networks. This is critically important, because important material consequences follow from the dominance of one partisan imaginary over another. Different imaginaries understand deliberative processes in different ways and prefer different kinds of policy outcomes as a result of those processes. The clergy of the 1930s understood that the president was offering a more expansive view of what democracy might come to mean, and they expressed their thoughts on governmental organization. In doing so, they were contributing to the ongoing public debate about the parameters of the proper relationship between the president and the public. They were helping to organize the public sphere and to determine how deliberation would be conducted and judged.

They also did this by making arguments themselves, using forms and content that they considered appropriate modes of conversation between the governed and the president. They felt free to express their feelings, and the affective valences of these letters are quite remarkable. The clergy wrote with passion and expressed rage, gratitude, fear, and hope. They did so by using what we would consider classic deliberative rhetoric, based in good reasons, providing warrants for claims, and offering assessments of the past and predictions for the future. They also relied upon ideological assertions and idealized views of national history, grounded their arguments in (sometimes esoteric and sometimes incoherent) religious beliefs, and in general mustered all kinds of vernacular knowledge to inform their expressions of policy preferences.

In other words, they reflect the ways in which the nation can be understood as a set of deliberative interests that could be called upon in different kinds of ways to support different kinds of policy alternatives. The national administration was told it could rely on Catholics, for instance, to support intervention in Mexico, but not to support alliance with the USSR. It could depend on farmers to oppose the AAA, but might count on them to advocate extensions to Social Security. This information did not just circulate through letters like these, of course, but these letters provide a condensed frame for the national debate that was occurring in newspapers, and in bars, and on street corners around the nation. The letters reflect, in no uncertain terms, the centrality of deliberation to the competing sets of political vocabularies.

Conclusion

Historically, American politics is characterized by a relatively stable system of partisan conflict involving two major parties. Most of the time, most of those involved in politics find themselves comfortable with one or another of the partisan imaginaries that offer specific iterations of the more widely shared national imaginary. From time to time, that structured and stable system falls apart, and a new system develops. I examined one such moment of change to better understand the rhetorical patterns that underlie our national partisan political conflict. At these moments of change, when the mass public reorganizes itself, other changes follow. No configuration is permanent. Authority can be relocated from the government to the private sector, or from the private sector to the government. It can be moved from the states and localities to the national government or vice versa. We come to understand the composition of the polity differently and rank its members in different ways. We do so based on changing and evolving understandings of national history and the national mythology that binds us to that history. And we argue over different policies. These elements circulate from elites to the public, from the public to elites, from the national to the local, from the local to the national, and among vernacular networks in complicated ways. There is nothing inevitable about the structures or concerns of our national life; they are the products of our collective choices.

The conditions reflected in political vocabularies change, either as a result of sudden events or through slow erosion. When those conditions change, the symbolic organizations associated with them no long help us to describe and understand the world. They are no longer useful as guides for collective action. When that happens, the nation simultaneously reorganizes its material and rhetorical life in ways that appear to largely cohere. Remnants of the previous order remain and are refigured. Some themes are apparently eternal: the United States is perennially preoccupied with liberty and equality, for instance, although those terms take on different meanings over time.[1] Other terms seem to be more restricted to particular moments. It is hard to imagine an argument advocating slavery gaining any traction today, for example.

As a result of the 1929 stock market crash and the Depression it signaled, the forms of political organization, ideological commitments, and social hierarchies that dominated American political life were shattered, resulting in a cacophony of arguments aimed at a nationwide redefinition of the national self and the sets of institutional arrangements and symbolic justifications that entailed. As a result of this cultural negotiation, the New Deal coalition emerged politically, the bureaucratic state developed institutionally, and a new set of competing political vocabularies developed rhetorically. These vocabularies were reflections of a shared national imaginary but also offered very different ways of instantiating that imaginary in the contemporaneous world. The one I associated here with the New Deal located political authority in the federal government and the president so long as they respected the institutions of Jim Crow, saw a more economically equal nation while continuing other kinds of hierarchies, relied on a moralistic version of the American Dream and a version of American Exceptionalism that mandated change and experimentation as warrants for their view of the nation's history, and preferred policies that provided a measure of economic security for an increasing number of citizens.

Republicans, on the other hand, inhabited an imaginary in which political authority was properly located in the private sector and state and local governments. They placed more reliance on congressional than executive power. They had a more restrictive view of the nation and ordered it more hierarchically, in keeping with their stress on individualism. That stress was justified through the precepts of the frontier myth, a more material understanding of the American Dream, and a view of American Exceptionalism that required defending the American experiment understood as the founding. They preferred policies that minimized governmental action and facilitated the freedom of the individual. It is my hope that by understanding this one moment of political contestation we can also understand the routine ways in which political conflict is structured in general.

Political Vocabularies and Political Argument

Political vocabularies are reasonably coherent collections of the terms we wield in making political arguments. Those terms locate political authority, depend on depictions that allow the nation's citizens to envision one another and the community they share, justify the social order, connect the present nation to its past and future through myth, and result in both rules for public deliberation and structure debates over the policy outcomes of deliberation. These elements circulate through the polity and contain both broad and more vernacular permutations. Nonetheless, they are reasonably consistent. Members of the polity argue over the nature of political authority. But we do so at one cultural moment by arguing about the actions of Congress and the presidency and at others by arguing about the actions of the federal government versus that of the states. Authority is at issue in every set of political vocabularies, but it will be at issue in different ways at different times and it will entail different kinds of arguments—over the presence of a national bank or the extent of the national debt, for instance. Political authority determines the nature of the relationship between a government and its citizens and can be construed in a variety of ways, from the patrician to the plebiscitary.[2] These debates are consequential, for they have affective consequences as well as material ones and determine the kinds of legitimate expectations citizens have regarding their government, and whether they see it in personal terms, as close or more distant, as relevant or not to their daily lives. The way we configure authority as part of a political vocabulary determines a great deal about the day-to-day political life of a citizen.

Depictions of those citizens are also consequential. The circulation of these depictions allows the government to get a sense of the citizenry and allows citizens to envision one another. This has two kinds of consequences. First, it gives members of the polity a chance to participate in a community. By depicting the nature of that community, citizens are able to access parts of it that they do not directly experience. Of course, this also means that they think they know more about those parts of the community than they do, but such depictions can also convey themes of common humanity across the nationally diverse culture. In addition, these depictions can also structure the national community in invidious ways. By making the lives of some members of the community more visible than others, they can also make those citizens seem more important than the others. Heightened visibly can equate to heightened humanity, and can certainly equate to heightened chances of becoming the beneficiaries of policy. The national government is much more likely to address problems it can see than those that are rendered even comparatively invisible. So both the nature and the amount of depiction can have important consequences.

The depictions of the national political vocabulary are thus closely related to its hierarchies. Different understandings of these hierarchies mobilize political ideologies to challenge or support the existing social order. Competing sets of political vocabularies include different understandings of democracy and the nation's political arrangements as closely approximating it (or failing to do so). Different visions of the nation and it ends and means are naturalized by versions of the nation derived from the same documents—in this case, the Bible (or Torah) and the Constitution. Rhetors operating from opposing political vocabularies thus also operate from very different but equally natural understandings of how our shared political community ought to be constructed. So during the 1930s, poverty was widely understood to be widespread, but some considered it to be the product of aberrant behavior among the monied class and others to be a natural part of the ebbs and flows of capitalism. These definitions entailed prescriptions for the appropriate action to be taken in response to the situation so understood.

Those understandings have authority not only because they are grounded in foundational documents, but because they call upon and reference national myths. We treat these myths as if they are stable and unchanging, and this is an important part of their appeal—especially in times of political change. But our myths are malleable. Inhabitants of different political imaginaries make different uses of national myths. So while we may always depend upon individualism as part of the national imaginary, the way individualism is defined and mobilized and the political valences associated with it will have different meanings to inhabitants of partisan imaginaries. The mythic element of political vocabularies means that new political coalitions can be constructed on the bones of the old. Political stability can be pulled out of the uncertainty of political change.

Such stability is important because it is the first task of government. In a changing political environment new groups can be incorporated and the terms of the incorporation of all citizens are subject to change as well. So the deliberative element of a political vocabulary encompasses two kinds of deliberation: the rules and structures of how deliberation will proceed, and discussion over the policy outcomes of that deliberation. As political cultures change, and as the nation becomes more diverse, deliberation will be defined in different ways and may proceed according to different kinds of rules. It is imperative that the rules match the expectations of citizens because that is the only way that the system can be seen as legitimate. If the system itself is understood as legitimate, then policy outcomes will also be understood that way. The deliberative component may well be the first to show the fracturing of an existing political regime, because it is the element that most obviously connects to the legitimacy of the system. If policy outcomes and the ways they are achieved begin to lose their legitimacy, then the connections between political structures and citizens are endangered.

The dominance of one partisan imaginary over another in the New Deal era animated politics for decades. It authorized a connection between local and national power that was unprecedented in our national history. Equally unprecedented was the personal nature of that power. Under the terms of the New Deal, presidents have been expected to be involved in the personal lives of the nation's citizens, to understand that their actions have consequences that matter to individual lives. Depictions of those lives as warrants for action continue to animate our politics as well. From Rosie the Riveter to Joe the Plumber and Black Lives Matter, the ways in which citizens envision one another have important influences over the ways we can envision national policies. They do so by authorizing arguments over citizenship that justify national hierarchies, declaring some citizens—and their suffering—as more consequential, more worthy of national attention, than others. And this in turn, of course, helps determine both the ways in which we deliberate over policy and the kinds of policy outcomes we secure as a result of deliberation. Since the New Deal, we have, for example, tragically been unable to find a way to talk about race; it was largely absent from our national political imaginary then, and that absence is with us still as we do not share an imaginary that easily admits race as a deliberative topic. Race may well be a structuring absence in our national politics, one that may form the basis of an emergent political regime and a new set of competing political vocabularies.

The New Deal Political Vocabulary in the Twenty-First Century

The 1930s were characterized by passionate and extensive political debate. Those debates centered, I have argued, on the nature of political authority and on depictions of citizenship and the hierarchies they authorized by redefinitions of national myths and animated by policy debates. Out of that cultural negotiation came a reasonably coherent party system that stabilized political argument during the New Deal. As conditions changed, those competing political vocabularies have lost at least some of their power to describe shared political reality and provide a guide to political action. Some of its terms have been reworked to provide continuing relevance, and some have merely fallen away. But the slow erosion of the system is evident. Some have argued, for instance, that the Reagan era represented a new party system; others are less sure.[3] I want to argue here that we may well be in the midst of another realignment, in which all of the components I have identified as central to political developments are losing their ability to describe political life in ways that divide the nation more or less neatly into adherents of existing political parties. The stability that once characterized our national politics, especially at the presidential level, is less apparent than it once was.

It seems equally possible that we are in the midst of a continued dealignment, an end to the routines of politics as we understand them. Donald Trump may represent a disintegration of the ways in which these elements used to cohere, for in his political rhetoric there is little cohesion. Instead of offering cohesive arguments that tie these elements together, he offers a compendium of gestures that do not coalesce into a coherent imaginary and that does not call its adherents into the future but pulls them into a fragmented and imagined past. It remains to be seen if such cohesion will develop over time, if we can restructure our politics into a new set of institutions that can earn legitimacy among the mass public. The Democrats seem to offer a more coherent vision, although it remains to be seen what will come of that vision under a Trump administration.

POLITICAL AUTHORITY

Given the ways that authority itself was called into question during the 1930s, the clergy underlined, legitimated, and contested the president's institutional and personal authority. So one of the first things that became clear as part of the 1930s political debates was that there would be arguments concerning the nature and extent of the role of the president and the federal government. While initially the expansion of those roles was hotly contested, as the New Deal moved from what Stephen Skowronek calls the politics of reconstruction toward the politics of articulation, there was much less dispute over the nature and use of political authority, although there were always Republican voices making the case against prevailing practices.[4] But as the New Deal faded, and its institutional arrangements seemed less useful as explanations for political reality and less workable as guides to shared political action, those minority voices gained strength. The institutional arrangements, however, are deeply entrenched; they continue even as they have less support among the public and lose also their connection to symbolic forms.

For a long time, there were no important arguments against the fact of presidential power; concerns over the imperial presidency, for instance, gave way remarkably quickly to fears concerning the imperiled presidency. Authority was securely located in the federal government, and arguments about presidential power have been largely confined to debates over the uses of that power and over its legitimate extent in specific circumstances; the fact of such power has been largely beyond significant dispute. That may be changing. Republicans worked very hard to delegitimize Barack Obama as president; Democrats seem willing to work equally hard to avoid normalizing Donald Trump. These actions must have consequences for how we understand the role of the U.S. president in the political system.

At the same time, the personal elements of national leadership also seem less trustworthy than they did in the 1930s. There were many people who seemed to feel the same faith in presidents like Ronald Reagan or, more currently, Barack Obama as they did in FDR. Certainly, journalists made frequent comparisons between Obama at least and Roosevelt.[5] Obama, for a multitude of reasons, is no Roosevelt. More to the point, and with the important exception of Obama's personal comportment, the personal behavior of any number of presidents and political actors since FDR, increasingly open to public scrutiny, have provided significant evidence that personal character may not be the best guide to the efficacy of public action. As symbols of the nation, our leaders are not often exemplifying our better angels. There is no better example of this than the famously coarse, even vulgar, Donald Trump as the victor of the 2016 presidential election, despite his loss of the popular vote.

It is also true that given the institutional context of the presidency, individual presidents have been less able to exert the kind of personal leadership with which FDR is often credited and that he sometimes managed to achieve. The growth of the executive branch, the partisanship evident in Congress, the fractious nature of the political culture and its increasing diversity, and the changes in the national media have all contributed to a more professional, increasingly calcified, and much more difficult to lead federal government. Presidents are treated as if they can control all manner of national events and are held individually responsible for them. But that control and responsibility, encouraged by the New Deal, are more illusory than real. This provides evidence for how the element of authority in that vocabulary lingers, although its power and its utility are diminished.

There are significant levels of distrust among members of both parties toward the partisan establishment. As of this writing, that distrust is evident in the success of insurgent candidacies like Bernie Sanders's (D-VT) and Donald Trump's. Authority circulates from the top down. Trump's apparently random policy positions and lack of attention to the details of policy making appear unlikely to establish a revitalized and newly legitimate set of governing structures. His own willingness to profit from his institutional position and the wide circulation of the word "kleptocracy" to describe his new administration underscore both a new kind of authority—one explicitly tied to a union of political and financial power—and a lack of legitimacy conferred on it by a significant portion of the electorate. The contrast between Sanders and his determined assault on the inequities of the current financial system and Trump's assertion of business acumen as the warrant for his political power is stark and may herald a fault line between emerging partisan imaginaries.

DEPICTIONS OF CITIZENSHIP

For the federal government to assume responsibility for local matters in the 1930s, those matters had to be made present to that government and the government had to be made present in local communities. The depictive elements of the clergy letters are important evidence for the ways in which that dual relationship was being established in the 1930s. By bearing witness to the dislocations of the Depression, the clergy allowed the White House into their communities and offered evidence for the necessity of federal policies. They relied upon foundational texts as warrants for their interpretation of events, and while the narrative of inevitable progress was disrupted by the Depression, the interpretations of those texts, evident in the clergy letters, formed a bridge between present difficulty and the restoration of hope.

These interpretations were offered as guides to collective action and formed the basis for the set of arguments characterizing the New Deal coalition. On the one hand were those who with the president understood the Constitution as a living document that needed to be reinterpreted to allow for continuity as well as flexibility given changing conditions. On the other were those who argued that the Constitution provided an immutable set of practices and relationships that should be adhered to if the nation is to thrive. In practice, throughout the New Deal, the Constitution was treated as more flexible than immutable, but recent debates indicate that this continues to be a point of vigorous contention.

Depiction circulates from the local to the national. The clerical definitions of the citizenry, offered through metaphor, narrative, and analogy, seem both dated and relevant to us now. The vivid descriptions of suffering are less relevant if still painful reading, as the social programs put in place in response to that suffering have indeed ameliorated it in large segments of the nation. But that amelioration, as the clergy observed and predicted, has not been even. Some groups have benefited much more than others. The New Deal promised a more equal system, and perhaps achieved it. But equality remains elusive.

The questions of who should benefit and of how we should understand the poor have both remained with us and shifted. There remain important debates over the question of the deserving and the undeserving poor, debates that continue to be animated by depictions of members of both classes.[6] As the intensity of the recent economic crisis has ebbed, and as fears about the costs of social programs rise and fall with the nation's economy, debates over the nature and even the utility of programs like Social Security and welfare in general remain with us.

We will continue to debate questions about religious inclusion, about immigration and citizenship, and about whose lives matter, and to what degree, as the Black Lives Matter movement meets significant opposition in the form of All Lives Matter. This difference alone indicates the ways in which inhabitants of different political imaginaries have difficulty communicating across those imaginaries. It may be that the ways we currently configure our politics may not be facilitating that communication. For some of our citizens, the continued marginalization of African American citizens is life-threatening; for others among us, their place in the national imaginary is in danger of displacement. There is a great deal at stake in this debate, and it reflects the ways in which the depictions of our fellow citizens can be deeply consequential, as both sides are fighting for what they envision as a proper understanding of their place in the nation and the ways in which that place is in danger. These issues appear to have driven the behavior of at least some of the voters in 2016, as misogyny, racism, and economic anxiety fueled support from Trump's candidacy, which was premised on activating these toxic elements of the American community and which depended in part on the systemic disenfranchisement of a number of citizens, as their voter suppression efforts indicate. The Democratic imaginary remains more inclusive, but it is not clear to what extent it can craft a vision that is inclusive as well as electorally viable. It is equally unclear whether our current institutions, like the Electoral College, can retain legitimacy if they are perceived as contributing to inequitable results, instantiating inequality among citizens.

HIERARCHIES

As the example of the Electoral College indicates, depictions are relevant because the ways in which we describe citizenship have not entirely altered. Like depiction, the hierarchical element circulates from the public up but finds expression in the language of elites as well. Regardless of which partisan imaginary they inhabited, in general, the clergy feared and fought against cultural changes they saw as eroding what we now refer to as "traditional values." They expressed significant anxiety over what they understood as increasing licentiousness among their parishioners. They worried about drinking, gambling, and all manner of social behaviors that they saw as contributing to the loss of the nation's moral fiber. They feared that social insurance policies discouraged the kind of resilience and self-dependence, the rugged individualism upon which national success depended. For some of the clergy, these social behaviors were deleterious to the nation's virtue and thus to its material and moral success.

Certainly, many of them would be horrified at the current state of the United States. The nation has endorsed marriage as equally open to all citizens, and so some hierarchies appear to have been shaken. Those clergy who feared that Repeal would lead to a national moral decline and contribute to an excess of substance abuse, rampant gambling, sexual freedom, and a loss of respectability would find ample evidence for their claims. These battles continue, in general, under the rubric of the "culture wars," in which competing versions of what it means to be a moral nation contend with one another in the public arena and center most heavily in educational issues. The 2016 presidential campaign could not have presented a stronger contrast between candidates along this dimension.

Other elements of clerical concern also animate our present political arguments. Questions of national hierarchy and concerns over racial, ethnic, and gender inequities are very much at issue. Here, as in the case of the culture wars, the definitions offered by the clergy seem to us outmoded while the concerns are equally relevant. Prior to the Trump candidacy it would have been hard to imagine someone making overt arguments based on skin color or hair texture, for instance, being taken seriously in national debates. But that candidacy revealed many of the ways in which racial and racist arguments, like those based on ethnicity, sexuality, or gender, continue to have a strong hold. The nation is more equal, but it is not equal; it is not even uniformly committed to equality. The New Deal set up a set of expectations and provided a language that delegitimized exclusionary policies and political practices. But both policies and practices were part of the political structure then, and they remain part of it now. Trump's victory empowered groups like the Ku Klux Klan; individual citizens painted swastikas on synagogues, threatened Muslim citizens, and apparently rejoiced in the return of white nationalism. Those groups and those actions were and are being fought and resisted. National hierarchies and the placement of various groups in that hierarchy are likely to be an important and explicit dividing line between inhabitants of partisan imaginaries.

MYTH

In part, ascriptive hierarchies remain because they are deeply rooted in our national mythology. The competing New Deal political vocabularies, which reinvented and reinscribed many mythic elements, were grounded in and also reestablished the centrality of those national myths, which, in their broadest form, circulate from the national to the local; in their more specific iterations, they move upward from the local to the national. In relying on the frontier myth, a materialistic version of the American Dream, and a strong sense of American Exceptionalism as providing a warrant for adhering to previous political practices, opponents of the New Deal resisted many of the changes wrought by the president and his allies. They inhabited a political imaginary colored by a nostalgic vision of the nation and what it stood for. We can see similar nostalgic visions motivating Trump's claim that he can "Make America Great Again," a claim that he connects to the reversal of many political changes, especially those associated with racial, gender, and LGBTQ rights.[7]

The firm hold of these myths encourages some among us to believe and to act as if failure is always individual, never systemic. It also encourages some among us to understand success and failure in materialistic terms. Both of these have consequences for our shared political life. Internationally, the most important consequence at the present moment is the tendency among at least some of our national policy-makers not only to assert that the U.S. version of democracy is the best version but also sometimes to consider it the only version. This assertion leads us to use all manner of means to insure that our version of democracy dominates the world.[8]

Adherents of the New Deal, on the other hand, also have descendants who depend on the American mythology, and who use it to argue against these claims. They rely on communitarian rather than individualist elements of those myths, and like their forbearers in the 1930s, they do not wield the frontier myth very often but rely on a moralistic version of the American Dream and seem to articulate a version of American Exceptionalism that demands inclusion at home. There is less of a consensus apparent among Democrats on foreign policy at this point;[9] and foreign policy may well constitute a new line of fissure continuing to divide both the Left and the Right, or driving people into a different kind of political alignment.

POLICY

All of these elements are given material form in the policies that we collectively enact and to which we collectively adhere. The New Deal authorized a burgeoning administrative state, in which members of the polity were understood and constituted as interests, whose demands could be balanced off one another, accommodated, and postponed. This politics depends upon people being able to see themselves as constituted this way, tailoring their political demands to this understanding, and being willing to accept the balancing, accommodation, and postponement. The system depends upon the perception of fairness among and between interests. It is by no means clear that any of these understandings will continue to animate our political judgments.

We continue to debate cultural policy, although not those at issue in the 1930s. But the question of American cultural morality is very much at issue, not only in the culture wars, but in debates over abortion, in the so-called Republican War on Women, and in arguments over immigration that depend on specific understandings of classes of immigrants as inherently possessing specific characteristics. We continue to debate welfare, and as Mitt Romney's famous reference to the "47 percent" indicates, at least some among us have doubts about whether there should be measures of worthiness involved in determining who should receive such aid, and there are continuing fears about the moral consequences of dependence upon it. In different ways, and often to opposing ends, Bernie Sanders's and Donald Trump's campaigns centralized all of these concerns. Most interestingly for this analysis, those campaigns shared one element in common: both candidates made arguments about the need to find ways to provide increased security for members of the working class (which they seemed to understand as the white working class).[10] It is entirely possible that if there is a realignment, the party that can include the working class (and not just the white working class) will have an advantage in the search for partisan political dominance.

We also continue to debate the role of the nation in the world. The New Deal political vocabularies continue to animate much of that debate as well, although the parameters of that debate are beyond the scope of the data I have here, as foreign policy had such a minor place in these letters. But the clergy did seem to consider the United States as a powerful example and an important source of political wisdom for the world and would have not been reluctant to extend their views of a moral polity to other cultures.

The policy element of political vocabularies circulates in complex ways, involving bottom-up, top-down, and vernacular networks. By participating in quasi-public deliberation, the clergy both authorized national policy-making and also engaged in it. But they did so on the basis of practical reason and by advocacy that included an important figural and affective component. Like the president, they tended to organize the nation by groups and targeted policy at groups. In doing so, they also contributed to a conception of politics as coalition building, in which the local and the personal could be understood as ways of mobilizing on a national level and toward collective ends. It seems to me that the connections between the local and the national are frayed in our time and that this element of the competing political imaginaries is most in need of reinvigoration.

Throughout this book, I have argued that these competing sets of political vocabularies differently authorize specific mechanisms of political authority; they rest on depictions that describe the political world and hierarchies that order it. They resonate widely because they employ and redefine timeless elements of national belief. And they rely on these elements in guiding national action in the form of the rules of public deliberation and the outcomes of that deliberation. The New Deal vocabulary authorized federal and presidential power in the service of making a single nation of prosperous citizens, ordered along more fluid lines than had previously been the case. The myth of the American Dream was made more widely accessible by the addition of a strong federal government, acting to provide a context for individual action. Elements of individual and community were thus reordered by policies like Social Security and relief. That political vocabulary was eventually extended from the nation to the world; it continues to have power both domestically and internationally. It was opposed by those who wanted to locate authority in the private sector and in state and local governments. They saw a nation of hard-working citizens whose progress was at least potentially impeded by government action and by the government's tendency to support the undeserving. These citizens inhabited a political imaginary that had relatively strict hierarchies but understood those hierarchies as determined primarily by merit. They relied on the individualism inherent in the frontier myth and the materialistic version of the American Dream, and they preferred policies that restricted the role of government and allowed for more exercise of individual choice.

Many of these elements are clearly discernible in our current politics, which sometimes appear to mimic the chaos and virulence of the 1930s as well. Then as now, there are significant parts of the polity who no longer trust the political system, and who want to see political authority relocated; there are those who feel their political marginalization as a serious threat to their well-being; there are those who are uncomfortable with the current shape of the national hierarchies; there are those who feel that the nation's promise, as articulated by our national myths, is no longer possible. These things are all reflected in the tenor and intensity of our national debates over policy and how that policy should best be enacted.

The 2016 national election had elements of stability, personified by Hillary Rodham Clinton, who won the popular vote. It also appeared remarkably unhinged from historical precedent, as evidenced by the victory of Donald Trump, who won the Electoral College, and thus the presidency. The cacophony of voices competing for attention throughout the election—including Barry Sanders and Jill Stein on the Left, and Gary Johnson on the Right—ranged from people who identified as Socialists to Libertarians. This wide diversity indicates the ways in which mass opinion is less organized and more volatile than we expect during normal, routine, moments in our politics. The Democratic political imaginary, which in 2016 proved successful among a plurality of voters, is apparently not capturing the loyalty of significant numbers of voters. It is unclear at this point whether Trump's apparent incoherence will lead the way to the development of a new political reality, in which the elements of political argument fail to cohere but become, as they are in his public speech, unattached to a coherent political imaginary that authorizes a system of government that can provide for and protect its citizens. The success of his free-floating gestures, strikes me as evidence for the bankruptcy of the previous Republican imaginary rather than the basis for the development of a new, revitalized one. At the moment, however, neither party is offering a vision of politics that can attract and maintain the loyalty of more than roughly half of the nation; there is no dominant imaginary, only fragments, partial visions that seem to resonate in various vernaculars while being ignored or resisted in others. The compelling need is for a vision of the nation that can earn the allegiance of the nation. Without it we risk fragmentation and a loss of national purpose.

In forming his vision of the nation, Roosevelt could afford to overlook and ignore some citizens; he did not, for example, offer more than some small evidence of symbolic inclusion for African Americans. That is no longer possible. He was also able to rely on a nation that was presumed to be largely Christian and largely Protestant. No president or presidential candidate can authorize a national imaginary centered on any specific faith, or even faith in general. In the absence of a unifying transcendent ideal, presidents have tried to replace God with national values such as equality and freedom. But those values only unify us in the abstract; their enactment is precisely what divides adherents to different political imaginaries.

We are at a crossroads; the Democrats are no longer the party of FDR, and the Republicans are not the party of Ronald Reagan. It is not entirely clear what the parties are now or what they will become, but their new imaginaries will, I suspect, come to resemble previous imaginaries with new twists. The Democrats will continue to locate authority in the federal government; they will increasingly welcome new constituents whom they will try to order equally; they will rely on the American Dream and its promise of economic security; and they will offer policies that advance that goal. They will stress civil rights and economic equality. Republicans, to the extent that they can offer a coherent vision of themselves, will endeavor to relocate authority to the market and to the states and localities. They will offer a more restrictive understanding of the nation and will order its members ascriptively. They will depend on a nostalgic vision of the past, one that depends heavily on American Exceptionalism. Their policies will favor those at the higher reaches of the economy and will offer little to those who are more dependent upon institutional assistance.

This description sounds like a return to the New Deal set of political vocabularies, but there is an important difference. FDR created new sets of administrative structures; those structures have lost a great deal of their legitimacy. Trying to enact a Rooseveltian vision with FDR's apparatus seems unworkable. It seems likely that a Trump administration will be dedicated to dismantling what is left of the New Deal administrative apparatus. It remains to be seen what might be built in their place.

Notes

Introduction

1. There is an enormous literature on realignment. The basic outlines of the theory can be found in the work of those most commonly credited with developing that theory. See Walter Dean Burnham, *Critical Elections and the Mainsprings of American Politics* (New York: Norton, 1970); James L. Sundquist, *Dynamics of the Party System: Alignment and Realignment of Political Parties in the United States* (Washington, DC: Brookings, 2011); Stephen Skowronek, *The Politics Presidents Make: Leadership from John Adams to Bill Clinton* (Cambridge, MA: Harvard University Press, 1993); Raymond Williams, *Marxism and Literature* (New York: Oxford University Press, 1977), 128–135.
2. Vanessa Beasley, *You, the People: American National Identity in Presidential Rhetoric* (College Station: Texas A&M University Press, 2003); Mary E. Stuckey, *Defining Americans: The Presidency and National Identity* (Lawrence: University Press of Kansas, 2004).
3. See, for example, Benedict Anderson, *Imagined Communities: Reflections on the Origin and Spread of Nationalism*, rev. ed. (New York: Verso, 2006); Charles Taylor,

"Modern Social Imaginaries," *Public Culture* 14 (2002): 91–124.

4. On the stable and interrelated nature of partisan disagreement as expressive of political culture, see John Gastil, Don Braman, Dan Kahan, and Paul Slovic, "The Cultural Orientation of Mass Political Opinion," *PS* 44, no. 4 (October 2011): 711–714.
5. Realignments are generally thought to have occurred around 1824, 1860, 1896, 1936, and 1980.
6. Thomas S. Kuhn, *The Structure of Scientific Revolutions*, 4th ed. (Chicago: University of Chicago Press, 2012).
7. Not all of those I refer to as "clergy" would have used that noun to describe themselves. I mean the term ecumenically and use it because the collection at the Roosevelt Library is called the "Clergy Letters."
8. Different geographic regions also have important elements of variation, but they are variations on a theme rather than strong oppositions to the national narrative.
9. Stuckey, *Defining Americans*.
10. See, for example, Jerome M. Chubb, William H. Flanigan, and Nancy H. Zingate, *Partisan Realignment: Voters, Parties, and Government in American History* (Beverly Hills, CA: Sage, 1980). Even David Mayhew, who challenges realignment theory, finds evidence for a New Deal realignment. David R. Mayhew, *Electoral Realignments: A Critique of an American Genre* (New Haven, CT: Yale University Press, 2002), 47–49.
11. John Gerring, *Party Ideologies in America, 1828–1996* (New York: Cambridge University Press, 1998), 57–115.
12. Political Party Platforms, "Republican Party Platform of 1928," June 12, 1928, *The American Presidency Project*, http://www.presidency.ucsb.edu/ws/?pid=29637.
13. Herbert Hoover, "1928 Campaign Speech," New York City, NY, October 22, 1928, Speech Vault, http://www.speeches-usa.com/Transcripts/herbert_hoover-campaign.html.
14. Political Party Platforms, "Democratic Party Platform of 1928," June 26, 1928, *The American Presidency Project*, http://www.presidency.ucsb.edu/ws/?pid=29594.
15. Gerring, *Party Ideologies in America*, 221.
16. Political Party Platforms, "Democratic Party Platform of 1928."
17. Chubb, Flanigan, and Zingate, *Partisan Realignment*, 98.
18. Al Smith, "Address of Acceptance at the State Capitol, Albany, New York," August 22, 1928, *The American Presidency Project*, http://www.presidency.ucsb.edu/ws/?pid=75571.

19. Ibid.
20. Everett Carll Ladd Jr. with Charles D. Hadley, *Transformations of the American Party System: Political Coalitions from the New Deal to the 1970s*, 2nd ed. (New York: W. W. Norton, 1978), 25.
21. Ibid., 32–36.
22. Ibid., 42–60.
23. Mary E. Stuckey, *The Good Neighbor: Franklin D. Roosevelt and the Rhetoric of American Power* (East Lansing: Michigan State University Press, 2013).
24. Albert Fried, *FDR and His Enemies* (New York: St. Martin's Press, 1999), 2; Charles Hurd, *When the New Deal Was Young and Gay* (New York: Hawthorn Books, 1965), 10; Arthur M. Schlesinger Jr., *The Age of Roosevelt: The Coming of the New Deal* (Boston: Houghton Mifflin, 1959), 3.
25. Sundquist, *Dynamics of the Party System*.
26. "Report on Clergy Letters," Samuel I. Rosenman papers, The Public Papers and Addresses, Memos to Be Used for Annotation: China and Japan, Transportation of Munitions to Cotton, Box 34, File: Clergy Letters, Franklin D. Roosevelt Presidential Library, Hyde Park, NY, 1.
27. Merlin Gustafson, "Franklin D. Roosevelt and His Protestant Constituency," *Journal of Church and State* 35 (1993): 285–297. See also Merlin Gustafson, "The President's Mail," *Presidential Studies Quarterly* 8 (1978): 36–44; Gary Scott Smith, *Faith and the Presidency: From George Washington to George W. Bush* (New York: Oxford University Press, 2006), 202.
28. Gerard A. Hauser, *Vernacular Voices: The Rhetoric of Publics and Public Spheres* (Columbia: University of South Carolina Press, 1999), 264.
29. Gustafson notes that "newspapers unfriendly to the administration quickly seized upon the opportunity to publicize derogatory replies and to ridicule the New Deal." Gustafson, "Franklin D. Roosevelt and His Protestant Constituency," 285.
30. Smith, *Faith and the Presidency*, 199.
31. Christian Erik Kock and Lisa Storm Villadsen, "Introduction: Citizenship as a Rhetorical Practice," *Rhetoric and Democratic Deliberation* 3 (2012): 1–10; Christian Erik Kock and Lisa Storm Villadsen, eds., *Rhetorical Citizenship and Public Deliberation* (University Park: Penn State University Press, 2012).
32. For a sampling of the range of this scholarship, see among numerous others, James Arnt Aune, "Reinhold Niebuhr and the Rhetoric of Christian Realism," in *Post-Realism: The Rhetorical Turn in International Relations*, ed. Francis A. Beer and Robert Hariman, (East Lansing: Michigan State University Press, 1996),

75–93; James Arnt Aune, "The Argument from Evil in the Rhetoric of Reaction," *Rhetoric & Public Affairs* 6 (2003): 518–522; James Darsey, *The Prophetic Tradition and Radical Rhetoric in America* (Albany: SUNY Press, 1997); David A. Frank, "The Prophetic Voice and the Face of the Other in Barack Obama's 'A More Perfect Union' Address, March 18, 2008," *Rhetoric & Public Affairs* 12 (2009): 167–194; Richard W. Leeman, "Speaking as Jeremiah: Henry McNeal Turner's 'I Claim the Rights of a Man,'" *Howard Journal of Communications* 17 (2006): 223–243; Michael Leff and Ebony A. Utley, "Instrumental and Constitutive Rhetoric in Martin Luther King, Jr.'s 'Letter from Birmingham Jail,'" *Rhetoric & Public Affairs* 7 (2004): 37–51; Martin J. Medhurst, "Religious Rhetoric and the Ethos of Democracy: A Case Study of the 2000 Presidential Campaign," in *The Ethos of Rhetoric*, ed. Michael J. Hyde (Columbia: University of South Carolina Press, 2004), 114–135; John M. Murphy, "Barack Obama, the Exodus Tradition, and the Joshua Generation," *Quarterly Journal of Speech* 97 (2011): 387–410; Joseph E. Rhodes, "Reinhold Niebuhr's Ethics of Rhetoric" (PhD diss., Eastern Michigan University, 2012); Mark Vail, "The 'Integrative' Rhetoric of Martin Luther King Jr.'s 'I Have a Dream' Speech," *Rhetoric & Public Affairs* 9 (2006): 51–78.

33. Aune, "Argument from Evil in the Rhetoric of Reaction."
34. Martin J. Medhurst, "From Duche to Provost: The Birth of the Inaugural Prayer," *Journal of Church and State* 24 (1982): 573–588.
35. On religion and the American colonies, see, among numerous others, Catherine L. Albanese, *A Republic of Mind and Spirit: A Cultural History of American Metaphysical Religion* (New Haven, CT: Yale University Press, 2006); Sidney E. Ahlstrom and David D. Hall, *A Religious History of the American People* (New Haven, CT: Yale University Press, 2004); Robert Neeley Bellah, *The Broken Covenant: American Civil Religion in Time of Trial* (Chicago: University of Chicago Press, 1992); Patricia U. Bonom, *Under the Cope of Heaven: Religion, Society, and Politics in Colonial America* (New York: Oxford University Press, 2003); Alan Heimert, *Religion and the American Mind: From the Great Awakening to the Revolution* (Eugene, OR: Wipf and Stock Publishers, 2006).
36. Patrick J. Deneen, *Democratic Faith* (Princeton, NJ: Princeton University Press, 2005), xvii.
37. Eldon Eisensach, *Sacred Discourse and American Nationality* (Lanham, MD: Rowman and Littlefield, 2013).
38. Fiona Venn, *The New Deal* (Edinburgh: Edinburgh University Press, 1998), 1–2. For discussions about the depth and prolonged nature of the Depression and the

difficulties of recovery, see, among many others, Jonathan Alter, *The Defining Moment: FDR's Hundred Days and the Triumph of Hope* (New York: Simon and Schuster, 2006); Michael D. Bordo, Claudia Goldin, and Eugene N. White, eds., *The Defining Moment: The Great Depression and the American Economy in the Twentieth Century* (Chicago: University of Chicago Press, 2007); David M. Kennedy, *Freedom from Fear: The American People in Depression and War, 1929–1945* (Oxford: Oxford University Press, 1999); Amity Shlaes, *The Forgotten Man: A New History of the Great Depression* (New York: Random House, 2009).

39. For discussions of the extent of national economic dislocations, see Adam Seth Cohen, *Nothing to Fear: FDR's Inner Circle and the Hundred Days That Created Modern America* (New York: Penguin, 2009), 32; Kennedy, *Freedom from Fear*, 214; Jean Edward Smith, *FDR* (New York: Random House, 2008), 282–287; Venn, *New Deal*, 7.
40. Stephen W. Baskerville and Ralph Willett, introduction to *Nothing Else to Fear: New Perspectives on America in the Thirties*, ed. Stephen W. Baskerville and Ralph Willett (Manchester: Manchester University Press, 1985), 5.
41. George Wolfskill and John Allen Hudson, *All but the People: Franklin D. Roosevelt and His Critics, 1933–39* (London: Macmillan, 1969).
42. Graham J. White, *FDR and the Press* (Chicago: University of Chicago Press, 1979), 35.
43. For discussions of the accusations of FDR as a dictator, see among many others, Robert S. McElvaine, *The Great Depression: America, 1929–1941* (New York: Three Rivers Press, 1993), 251; Shlaes, *Forgotten Man*, 251.
44. Jeffrey Shesol notes that FDR's popularity was "steadily declining." See Jeffrey Shesol, *Supreme Power: Franklin Roosevelt vs. the Supreme Court* (New York: W. W. Norton, 2010), 158. See also McElvaine, *Great Depression*, 286; Kennedy, *Freedom from Fear*, 189. Mary E. Stuckey, *Voting Deliberatively: FDR and the 1936 Presidential Election* (University Park: Penn State University Press, 2015), 8–12.
45. Russell L. Hanson, *The Democratic Imagination in America: Conversations with Our Past* (Princeton, NJ: Princeton University Press, 1985), 257.
46. Wolfskill and Hudson, *All but the People*, 62–66, 94–119.
47. Ibid., 53.
48. On Cardinal Mundelein, see Edward R. Kantowicz, "Cardinal Mundelein of Chicago and the Shaping of Twentieth-Century American Catholicism," *Journal of American History* 68 (1981): 52–68. On Ryan and his influence and rhetoric, see Martin J. Medhurst, "Argument and Role: Monsignor John A. Ryan on Social

Justice," *Western Journal of Speech Communication* 52 (1988): 75–90.

49. He wrote that FDR "knew the forcefulness of plain Bible English on the American people." Robert H. Jackson, *That Man: An Insider's Portrait of Franklin D. Roosevelt* (New York: Oxford University Press, 2003), 160. Rhetoricians agree with this assessment, noting the centrality of such imagery in Roosevelt's speech. See Suzanne M. Daughton, "Metaphorical Transcendence: Images of the Holy War in Franklin D. Roosevelt's First Inaugural," *Quarterly Journal of Speech* 79 (1993): 427–446; Ronald Isetti, "The Moneychangers of the Temple: FDR, American Civil Religion, and the New Deal," *Presidential Studies Quarterly* 26 (1996): 678–693. But see also Davis W. Houck and Mihaela Nocasian, "FDR's First Inaugural Address: Text, Context, and Reception," *Rhetoric & Public Affairs* 5 (2002): 649–678.
50. See Richard Hofstadter, *The Age of Reform: From Bryan to FDR* (New York: Vintage, 1955). Frances Perkins, in fact, noted that "his Christian faith was absolutely simple." Frances Perkins, *The Roosevelt I Knew* (New York: Viking, 1946), 141. Patrick Maney argued that FDR's ideal polity would be a "Christian Commonwealth." Patrick J. Maney, *The Roosevelt Presence: A Biography of Franklin D. Roosevelt* (New York: Twayne, 1992), 56. On the president's religion more generally, see Thomas A. Greer, *What Roosevelt Thought: The Social and Political Ideas of Franklin D. Roosevelt* (East Lansing: Michigan State University Press, 1958), 4–5.
51. He thought, Amy Waters Yarsinske wrote, "in terms of human beings rather than abstract, unattainable objectives." Amy Waters Yarsinske, *Rendezvous with Destiny: The FDR Legacy* (Virginia Beach, VA: Dunning, 2009), 325. For details on his personal religious beliefs, and the ways in which those beliefs may have influenced his politics, see Merlin Gustafson and Jerry Rosenberg, "The Faith of Franklin D. Roosevelt," *Presidential Studies Quarterly* 19 (1989): 559–566; Andrew Polk, "'Unnecessary and Artificial Divisions': Franklin Roosevelt's Quest for Religious and National Unity Leading up to the Second World War," *Church History* 82 (2013): 667–677; Smith, *Faith and the Presidency*, 192–219.
52. Maney, *Roosevelt Presence*, 56; see also Lewis L. Gould, *The Modern American Presidency* (Lawrence: University Press of Kansas, 2009), 80;
53. Houck and Nocasian. "FDR's First Inaugural Address," 664–666. On his redemptive rhetoric see Gould, *Modern American Presidency*, 6.
54. Dan McKann, *Prophetic Encounters: Religion and the American Radical Tradition* (Boston: Beacon Press, 2011).

55. Leo P. Ribuffo, *The Old Christian Right: The Protestant Far Right from the Great Depression to the Cold War* (Philadelphia: Temple University Press, 1983), 3.
56. Max Wallace, *The American Axis: Henry Ford, Charles Lindbergh, and the Rise of the Third Reich* (New York: Macmillan, 2004).
57. See Alan Brinkley, *Voices of Protest: Huey Long, Father Coughlin, and the Great Depression* (New York: Vintage, 1981).
58. Paul Stob finds this, for instance, in Roosevelt contemporary Louis Brandeis; it was an important element in the Progressive tradition, which influenced them both and which resonated in many important elements in U.S. politics. In Brandeis's case, religious appeals were infused with Zionism, distinguishing him from mainstream reformers. See Paul Stob, "Louis Brandeis and the Rhetoric of Transactional Morality," *Rhetoric & Public Affairs* 14 (2011): 261–290.
59. For a discussion of the ways in which the first of these uses was gradually replaced by the second, see James Turner Johnson, introduction to *The Bible in American Law, Politics, and Political Rhetoric*, ed. James Turner Johnson (Philadelphia: Fortress Press, 1985), 4.
60. Franklin D. Roosevelt, "Radio Address Announcing the Proclamation of an Unlimited National Emergency," May 27, 1941, v. 10, 192, in *The Public Papers and Addresses of Franklin D. Roosevelt*, ed. Samuel I. Rosenman (New York: Random House, 1950).
61. H. Richard Niebuhr, *The Kingdom of God in America* (New York: Harper, 1937), 9. See also Perry Miller's discussion of the American errand in *Errand into the Wilderness* (Cambridge, MA: Harvard University Press, 1956).
62. Stuckey, *Voting Deliberatively*.
63. Hauser, *Vernacular Voices*, 30.
64. Ibid., 84–85.
65. John Dewey, *A Common Faith* (New Haven, CT: Yale University Press, 1934), 84.
66. For more on John Dewey, see Nathan Crick, *Democracy and Rhetoric: John Dewey on the Arts of Becoming* (Columbia: University of South Carolina Press, 2012).
67. On the ways in which reliance on the Judeo-Christian tradition creates political problems and opportunities, see Eisensach, *Sacred Discourse and American Nationality*.
68. There is also plenty of evidence that presidents following FDR relied on religious warrants for their preferred policies. See especially Smith, *Faith and the Presidency*.
69. On the ways in which the Bible influences U.S. culture, see, among many others,

Vincent L. Wimbush, ed., *The Bible and the American Myth: A Symposium on the Bible and Constructions of Meaning* (Macon, GA: Mercer University Press, 1999).

70. Matthew Josephson argues, for instance, that at least for some people, "in reality the Great Depression was not depressing. The lean years of the New Deal became a period of lively ferment. The old centers of power were being rudely knocked about, new opportunities opened for those able and ready to respond to them." Matthew Josephson, *Infidel in the Temple: A Memoir of the Nineteen-Thirties* (New York: Knopf, 1967), xi.

71. I am indebted to Matthew Klingbeil for the important reminder that national identity is always contested.

72. Samuel McCormick, *Letters to Power: Public Advocacy without Public Intellectuals* (University Park: Penn State University Press, 2011). A number of other authors also discuss letters as a rhetorical genre. See, for example, Janet Gurkin Altman, *Epistolarity: Approaches to a Form* (Columbus: Ohio State University Press, 1982); Rebecca Earle, ed., *Epistolary Selves: Letters and Letter-Writers, 1600–1945* (Burlington, VT: Ashgate, 1999); Brandon Michael Inabinet, "When Pastors Go Public: Richard Furman's Public Letter on Slavery," *Southern Communication Journal* 76 (2011): 169–190; James Jasinski, *Sourcebook on Rhetoric: Key Concepts in Contemporary Rhetorical Studies* (Thousand Oaks, CA: Sage, 2001), 470–471; Malinda Snow, "Martin Luther King's 'Letter from Birmingham Jail' as Pauline Epistle," *Quarterly Journal of Speech* 71(1985): 318.

73. McCormick, *Letters to Power*, 4–5. Without doubt, the most well-known and well-studied public letter in modern times is Martin Luther King Jr.'s "Letter from Birmingham Jail." On that letter, see Haig A. Bosmajian, "The Rhetoric of Martin Luther King's Letter from Birmingham Jail," *Midwestern Quarterly* 8 (1967): 127–143; Richard P. Fulkerson, "The Public Letter as a Rhetorical Form: Structure, Logic, and Style in King's 'Letter from Birmingham Jail,'" *Quarterly Journal of Speech* 65 (1979): 121–136; Snow, "Martin Luther King's 'Letter from Birmingham Jail' as Pauline Epistle." Finally, see the 2004 special issue of *Rhetoric & Public Affairs* (vol. 7, no. 1), dedicated to the "Letter."

74. In this, they bring McCormick's analysis of Christine de Pizan's letters as the rhetoric of exemplarity to mind. See McCormick, *Letters to Power*, 66. Stephen H. Browne also usefully analyzes the ways in which public letters can be understood as having an "ambivalent status." See Stephen H. Browne, "Edmund Burke's Letter to a Noble Lord: A Textual Study in Political Philosophy and Rhetorical Action," *Communication Monographs* 55 (1988): 219. See also Stephen H.

Browne, "The Pastoral Voice in John Dickinson's First Letter from a Farmer in Pennsylvania," *Quarterly Journal of Speech* 76 (1990): 46–57.

75. C. Joachim Classen, "St. Paul's Epistles and Ancient Greek and Roman Rhetoric," *Rhetorica* 10 (1992): 319–344. On the importance of placing letters within their cultural context, see John C. Hammerback and Richard J. Jensen, "History and Culture as Rhetorical Constraints: Cesar Chavez's Letters from Delano," in *Doing Rhetorical History: Concepts and Cases*, ed. Kathleen J. Turner (Tuscaloosa: University of Alabama Press, 1998), 207–220.
76. Fulkerson, "The Public Letter as a Rhetorical Form"; Snow, "Martin Luther King's 'Letter from Birmingham Jail' as Pauline Epistle," 331.
77. Fulkerson, "The Public Letter as a Rhetorical Form," 131.
78. While the clergy were of course relatively privileged, my sense of the political nature of their letters owes much to Paul Michael Taillon, "'All Men Are Entitled to Justice by the Government': Black Workers, Citizenship, Letter Writing and the World War I State," *Journal of Social History* 4 (2014): 88–111.
79. See, for example, Snow, "Martin Luther King's 'Letter from Birmingham Jail' as Pauline Epistle," 319, 331. On the didactic function of letters in general, see Martin Camargo, "Epistolary Rhetoric," in *Encyclopedia of Rhetoric*, ed. Thomas O. Sloane (New York: Oxford University Press, 2001), 259.
80. On jeremiads, see Sacvan Bercovitch, *The American Jeremiad* (Madison: University of Wisconsin Press, 1978); Ronald C. Carpenter, "The Historical Jeremiad as Rhetorical Genre," in *Form and Genre: Shaping Rhetorical Action*, ed. Karlyn Kohrs Campbell and Kathleen Hall Jamieson (Falls Church, VA: Speech Communication Association, 1981), 103–117; John M. Murphy, "'A Time of Shame and Sorrow': Robert F. Kennedy and the American Jeremiad," *Quarterly Journal of Speech* 76 (1990): 410–414; Kurt W. Ritter, "American Political Rhetoric and the Jeremiad Tradition: Presidential Nomination Addresses, 1960–1975," *Communication Studies* 31 (1980): 153–171; Robert C. Rowland and John M. Jones, "A Covenant-Affirming Jeremiad: The Post-Presidential Ideological Appeals of Ronald Wilson Reagan," *Communication Studies* 56 (2005): 157–174. My reading of jeremiads owes much to Richard Leeman's argument that the form can be understood less rigidly. See Leeman, "Speaking as Jeremiah."
81. Clergyman Bede Herrmann, for example, wrote that, "The root of this evil, in my humble opinion, lies in the curse of God. . . . God has been banished from the schools and children have been cruelly robbed of their native right to know God." Holy Trinity, Alabama, October 10, 1935.

82. On the capacity of letters to illumine social hierarchies and the ways in which authors may use them to negotiate those hierarchies, see Stacey K. Sowards, "Rhetorical Functions of Letter Writing: Dialogic Collaboration, Affirmation, and Catharsis in Dolores Huerta's Letters," *Communication Quarterly* 60 (2012): 295–315. See also A. C. Carlson, "Character Invention in the Letters of Maimie Pinzer," *Communication Quarterly* 43 (1995): 408–419; Fernando Delgado, "Rigoberta Menchú and Testimonial Discourse: Collectivist Rhetoric and Rhetorical Criticism," *World Communication* 28 (1999): 17–29; Lisa M. Gring-Pemble, "Writing Themselves into Consciousness: Creating a Rhetorical Bridge between the Public and Private Spheres," *Quarterly Journal of Speech* 84 (1998): 41–61; Catherine H. Palczewski, "Bodies, Borders, and Letters: Gloria Anzaldúa's 'Speaking in Tongues: A Letter to Third World Women,'" *Southern Communication Journal* 62 (1996): 1–16.
83. On the social functions of letters, see, among many others, Earle, *Epistolary Selves*; Malcolm Richardson, "The *Ars Dictaminis*, the Formulary, and Medieval Epistolary Practice," in *Letter-Writing Manuals and Instruction from Antiquity to the Present: Historical and Bibliographic Studies*, ed. Carol Poster and Linda C. Mitchell (Columbia: University of South Carolina Press, 2007), 52–66. It is this aspect of letter writing that makes them so useful to novelists. On epistolary novels, see Altman, *Epistolarity*; Robert Adams Day, *Told in Letters: Epistolary Fiction before Richardson* (Ann Arbor: University of Michigan Press, 1966).
84. A. Earl Morris, for instance, offered his advice as friend to friend, asking the president, "Will you permit me to call you friend? It has never been my good fortune to meet you, yet I do feel that you are a friend—not only to me, but to every well-meaning person in the land." Grandview, Indiana, October 19, 1935. Paul B. VanHorn resisted the urge to call him "Frank," but mentioned it nonetheless. Worcester, Massachusetts, September 28, 1935. On the importance of the president's "intimate" relationship with the public, see James MacGregor Burns, *Roosevelt: The Lion and the Fox, 1882–1940* (New York: Harcourt, Brace, Jovanovich, 1956), 203; Maney, *Roosevelt Presence*, 70.
85. Certainly, this was how the ancients such as Isocrates viewed them. See R. Sullivan, "Classical Epistolary Theory and the Letters of Isocrates," in Poster and Mitchell, *Letter-Writing Manuals and Instruction from Antiquity to the Present*, 7–20.
86. On this kind of practical reason, see Don Waisanen, "Toward Robust Public Engagement: The Value of Deliberative Discourse for *Civil* Communication,"

Rhetoric & Public Affairs 17 (2014): 287–322.

87. See, for instance, Carolyn Steedman, "A Woman Writing a Letter," in Earle, *Epistolary Selves*, 111–133.
88. On the narrowing of interests, see Ira Katznelson, *Fear Itself: The New Deal and the Origins of Our Time* (New York: Liveright Publishing, 2013), 478–479.
89. On the ways in which the "common good" gets confused with more narrowly defined interests, see Scott Welsh, *The Rhetorical Surface of Democracy: How Deliberative Ideals Undermine Democratic Politics* (Lanham, MD: Lexington Books, 2013).
90. For a more detailed version of this argument, see Stuckey, *Voting Deliberatively*.
91. Susan Herbst, *Numbered Voices: How Public Opinion Polling Has Shaped American Politics* (Chicago: University of Chicago Press, 1993).
92. On this point, see also J. Michael Hogan, "George Gallup and the Rhetoric of Scientific Democracy," *Communication Monographs* 64 (1987): 161–179; J. Michael Hogan et al., "Report of the National Task Force on the Presidency and Public Opinion," in *The Prospect of Presidential Rhetoric*, ed. Martin J. Medhurst and James Arnt Aune (College Station: Texas A&M University Press, 2008), 293–316.
93. On invoked public opinion, see Jeffrey P. Mehltretter Drury, *Speaking with the People's Voice: How Presidents Invoke Public Opinion* (College Station: Texas A&M University Press, 2014).
94. He did, for instance, use one of these letters in his famous "Quarantine Address," October 5, 1937.
95. On the distinction between civic engagement and spectatorship, see Robert Asen, "A Discourse Theory of Citizenship," *Quarterly Journal of Speech* 90 (2004): 189–211.
96. On the centrality of vision to the politics of the 1930s, see Cara Finnegan, "FSA Photography and the New Deal Visual Culture," in *American Rhetoric in the New Deal Era, 1932–1945*, ed. Thomas W. Benson (East Lansing: Michigan State University Press, 2006), 115–155; Cara Finnegan, *Picturing Poverty: Print Culture and FSA Photography* (Washington, DC: Smithsonian, 2003); Mary E. Stuckey, "FDR, the Rhetoric of Vision, and the Creation of a National Synoptic State," *Quarterly Journal of Speech* 98 (2012): 297–319.
97. It is notable in this regard that his letter to the clergy found a place in his public papers.
98. John Durham Peters, "Witnessing," *Media, Culture & Society* 23 (2001): 709.
99. Paul A. Lomax, Blythe, California, October 8, 1935.

100. Ralph Supplee, Dunkerton, Iowa, October 18, 1935. See also J. M. Stambaugh, Charleston, West Virginia, October 7, 1935.
101. Stuckey, *Good Neighbor*.
102. Richard Mervin Weaver, Richard L. Johannesen, and Renard Strickland, *Language Is Sermonic* (Baton Rouge: Louisiana State University Press, 1970).
103. Here, I rely on the arguments made in Tarla Rai Peterson, "The Rhetorical Construction of Institutional Authority in a Senate Subcommittee Hearing on Wilderness Legislation," *Western Journal of Speech Communication* 52 (1988): 259–276.
104. Calvin L. Troup, "Civic Engagement from Religious Grounds," *Journal of Communication and Religion* 32 (2009): 240–267.

Chapter 1. By Benefit of Clergy: Authoritative Political Vocabularies

1. See Gary Miller and Norman Schofield, "Activists and Partisan Realignment in the United States," *American Political Science Review* 98 (2003): 245–260.
2. See Walter I. Trattner, *From Poor Law to Welfare State: A History of Social Welfare in America* (New York: Simon and Schuster, 2007).
3. Thomas E. Cronin and Michael A. Genovese, *The Paradoxes of the American Presidency* (New York: Oxford University Press, 1998).
4. On the history of anticommunism and Red Scares, see Joel Kovel, *Red Hunting in the Promised Land: Anticommunism and the Making of America* (New York: Basic Books, 1994).
5. For a history of isolationism during the period, see among many others, Thomas N. Guinsburg, *The Pursuit of Isolationism in the United States Senate from Versailles to Pearl Harbor* (New York: Garland, 1982).
6. On the benefits of the federal system prior to 1932, see Daniel P. Carpenter, *The Forging of Bureaucratic Autonomy: Reputations, Networks, and Policy Innovation in Executive Agencies, 1862–1928* (Princeton, NJ: Princeton University Press, 2001).
7. See David R. James, "The Transformation of the Southern Racial State: Class and Race Determinants of Local-State Structures," *American Sociological Review* 53 (1988): 191–208.
8. Alan Brinkley, *The Unfinished Nation: A Concise History of the American People* (New York: McGraw Hill, 1993), 658–660; Sean David Cashman, *America Ascendant: From Theodore Roosevelt to FDR in the Century of American Power* (New York: NYU Press, 1998), 257.

9. Adam Seth Cohen, *Nothing to Fear: FDR's Inner Circle and the Hundred Days That Created Modern America* (New York: Penguin, 2009), 15.
10. Ira Katznelson, *Fear Itself: The New Deal and the Origins of Our Time* (New York: Liveright Publishing, 2013), 31.
11. John T. Flynn, *Country Squire in the White House* (New York: Doubleday, 1940), 81; Robert S. McElvaine, *The Great Depression: America, 1929–1941* (New York: Three Rivers Press, 1993), 161; George McJimsey, *The Presidency of Franklin Delano Roosevelt* (Lawrence: University Press of Kansas, 2000), 72–80.
12. Gary Dean Best, *The Critical Press and the New Deal: The Press versus Presidential Power, 1933–1938* (Westport, CT: Praeger, 1993), 97; Jean Edward Smith, *FDR* (New York: Random House, 2008), 350.
13. Stephen W. Baskerville and Ralph Willett, introduction to *Nothing Else to Fear: New Perspectives on America in the Thirties*, ed. Stephen W. Baskerville and Ralph Willett (Manchester: Manchester University Press, 1985), 9; Terry Golway, *Together We Cannot Fail: FDR and the American Presidency in Time of Crisis* (Napierville, IL: Sourcebooks, 2009), 40; Richard Hofstadter, *The Age of Reform: From Bryan to FDR* (New York: Vintage, 1955), 327; William E. Leuchtenburg, *Franklin D. Roosevelt and the New Deal, 1932–1940* (New York: Harper, 2009), 73; Arthur M. Schlesinger Jr., *The Age of Roosevelt: The Coming of the New Deal* (Boston: Houghton Mifflin, 1959), 13; George Wolfskill and John Allen Hudson, *All but the People: Franklin D. Roosevelt and His Critics, 1933–39* (London: Macmillan, 1969), 101.
14. Stephen Skowronek, *The Politics Presidents Make: Leadership from John Adams to Bill Clinton* (Cambridge, MA: Harvard University Press, 1993), 17–33.
15. This is the rhetorical problem of political reconstruction. On reconstructive presidents, see Skowronek, *Politics Presidents Make*. He discusses FDR specifically at 288–324.
16. Lynn Clarke, "Contesting Definitional Authority in the Collective," *Quarterly Journal of Speech* 91 (2005): 1–36; Edward Schiappa, *Defining Reality: Definitions and the Politics of Meaning* (Carbondale: Southern Illinois University Press, 2003), 29.
17. See Walter Dean Burnham, *Critical Elections and the Mainsprings of American Politics* (New York: Norton, 1970); Ronald L. Fineman, *Twilight of Progressivism: The Western Republican Senators and the New Deal* (Baltimore: Johns Hopkins University Press, 1981); Sidney M. Milkis, *Political Parties and Constitutional Government: Remaking American Democracy* (Baltimore: Johns Hopkins

University Press, 1999), 76–104; James L. Sundquist, *Dynamics of the Party System: Alignment and Realignment of Political Parties in the United States* (Washington, DC: Brookings, 2011); Nancy Weiss, *Farewell to the Party of Lincoln: Black Politics in the Age of FDR* (Princeton, NJ: Princeton University Press, 1983).

18. Peri Arnold, *Making the Managerial Presidency: Comprehensive Reorganization Planning, 1905–1996* (Lawrence: University Press of Kansas, 1998).
19. Mary E. Stuckey, "FDR, the Rhetoric of Vision, and the Creation of a National Synoptic State," *Quarterly Journal of Speech* 98 (2012): 297–319.
20. Mary E. Stuckey, *The Good Neighbor: Franklin D. Roosevelt and the Rhetoric of American Power* (East Lansing: Michigan State University Press, 2013).
21. In this, they enacted their part in the long history of those looking to the president to promote Christianity. See Gary Scott Smith, *Faith and the Presidency: From George Washington to George W. Bush* (New York: Oxford University Press, 2006); Gary Scott Smith, *Religion in the Oval Office: The Religious Lives of American Presidents* (New York: Oxford University Press, 2015).
22. As Malinda Snow notes, letters can also serve as sermons, and in judging as well as exhorting the president, the clergy were certainly exercising a sermonic role. See Malinda Snow, "Martin Luther King's 'Letter from Birmingham Jail' as Pauline Epistle," *Quarterly Journal of Speech* 71 (1985): 319.
23. On the capacity of letters to enact hierarchies and to provide opportunities for collaboration, affirmation, and catharsis, see Stacey K. Sowards, "Rhetorical Functions of Letter Writing: Dialogic Collaboration, Affirmation, and Catharsis in Dolores Huerta's Letters," *Communication Quarterly* 60 (2012): 295–315. See also Lisa M. Gring-Pemble, "Writing Themselves into Consciousness: Creating a Rhetorical Bridge between the Public and Private Spheres," *Quarterly Journal of Speech* 84 (1998): 41–61; Catherine H. Palczewski, "Bodies, Borders, and Letters: Gloria Anzaldúa's 'Speaking in Tongues: A Letter to Third World Women,'" *Southern Communication Journal* 62 (1996): 1–16.
24. They were thus entering into a national debate on policy issues. On the capacity of letters to allow authors to join such debates, see Richard P. Fulkerson, "The Public Letter as a Rhetorical Form: Structure, Logic, and Style in King's 'Letter from Birmingham Jail,'" *Quarterly Journal of Speech* 65 (1979): 121–136.
25. Martin J. Medhurst, "Argument and Role: Monsignor John A. Ryan on Social Justice," *Western Journal of Speech Communication* 52 (1988): 75–90.
26. On the ways in which arguments from authority can help rhetors establish authority, see Michael Leff and Ebony A. Utley, "Instrumental and Constitutive

Rhetoric in Martin Luther King, Jr.'s, 'Letter from Birmingham Jail,'" *Rhetoric & Public Affairs* 7 (2004): 37–51.

27. Brandon Michael Inabinet, "When Pastors Go Public: Richard Furman's Public Letter on Slavery," *Southern Communication Journal* 76 (2011): 169–190.
28. Robert Hariman, "Status, Marginality, and Rhetorical Theory," *Quarterly Journal of Speech* 72 (1986): 38–54.
29. This clerical claim to authority did not originate in the 1930s. See, for example, Inabinet, "When Pastors Go Public."
30. On the connection between authority and values, see Charles Alan Taylor, "Of Audience, Expertise, and Authority: The Evolving Creationism Debate," *Quarterly Journal of Speech* 78 (1992): 277–295.
31. Rex Mitchell, for instance, was critical of the president because rather than following previous practice and "calling upon the ministers to lead the people in prayer for divine wisdom," instead, "heretofore you have counseled the Atheistic, Communistic Brain Trusters." Paso Robles, California, September 28, 1935.
32. On such approaches, see John M. Murphy, "Inventing Authority: Bill Clinton, Martin Luther King, Jr., and the Orchestration of Rhetorical Traditions," *Quarterly Journal of Speech* 83 (1997): 75.
33. For a discussion of how place works in these contexts, see Richard Marback, "The Rhetorical Space of Robbin Island," *Rhetoric Society Quarterly* 34 (2004): 7–27.
34. Tarla Rai Peterson, "The Rhetorical Construction of Institutional Authority in a Senate Subcommittee Hearing on Wilderness Legislation," *Western Journal of Speech Communication* 52 (1988): 259–276.
35. Thomas B. Farrell, *Norms of Rhetorical Culture* (New Haven, CT: Yale University Press, 1993), 290.
36. Arabella Lyon, "Rhetorical Authority in Athenian Democracy and the Chinese Legalism of Han Fei," *Philosophy and Rhetoric* 41 (2008): 51–71.
37. See, for example, Brycchan Carey, *From Peace to Freedom: Quaker Rhetoric and the Birth of American Antislavery, 1657–1761* (New Haven, CT: Yale University Press, 2012); Victor B. Howard, *Religion and the Radical Republican Movement, 1860–1870* (Lexington: University Press of Kentucky, 1990).
38. Martin P. Simon, Eugene, Oregon, October 8, 1935.
39. Paul P. Meiser, Monroe, Iowa, September 26, 1935.
40. Samuel McCormick, *Letters to Power: Public Advocacy without Public Intellectuals* (University Park: Penn State University Press, 2011), 40.
41. O. B. Sarber, Indianapolis, Indiana, October 22, 1935.

42. George E. Keithley, Newman, Illinois, October 3, 1935.
43. W. W. Gunner, Rock Lake, North Dakota, January 15, 1936.
44. John Thompson, Chicago, Illinois, September 26, 1935.
45. O. L. Prentice, Cutler, Indiana, October 24, 1935.
46. Paul R. Johnson, Stratford, Iowa, November 5, 1935.
47. A. Davis, Chicago, Illinois, October 16, 1935.
48. M. Blanke, Leavenworth, Kansas, October 24, 1935.
49. Joseph M. Coulombe, Montequl, Louisiana, October 8, 1935; see also Constant M. Klein, Carlsbad, New Mexico, October 4, 1935. G. A. Baker, Haulka, Mississippi, October 12, 1935; see also C. K. Malmin, Florence, South Dakota, October 24, 1935. J. W. Bashore, Vinita, Oklahoma, September 25, 1935.
50. R. C. Nanney, Burnsville, Mississippi, September 27, 1935.
51. Robert Crawford, Omaha, Nebraska, September 26, 1935.
52. Clifford L. Moody, Thorntown, Indiana, September 26, 1935.
53. A. Freeman Traverse, Saint Joseph, Michigan, October 25, 1935.
54. W. H. Baring, Augusta, Georgia, October 29, 1935. See also Edmund G. Lindsay, Goshen Indiana, September 27, 1935; Meredith A. Groves, Portland, Oregon, October 1, 1935.
55. Benjamin Schwartz, Des Moines, Iowa, September 25, 1935.
56. Samuel Andron, Poughkeepsie, New York, October 12, 1935.
57. Henry W. Thompson, Decatur, Indiana, September 26, 1935.
58. George Truman Carl, Winchester, New Hampshire, October 14, 1935.
59. Alfred G. Fisk, San Francisco, California, October 7, 1935.
60. For examples of claims that he failed to keep his promises, see Humphrey O. Hughes, Jasper, Florida, September 26, 1935.
61. Albert Gasten, Gerster, Missouri, October 4, 1935.
62. Samuel A. Troxell, Baltimore, Maryland, October 4, 1935. This view seems especially strong in Massachusetts. See also D. S. Smith, Brookline, Massachusetts, October 19, 1935; Ralph M. Barker, East Gloucester, Massachusetts, September 28, 1935; Edson Gould Waterhouse, Swampscott, Massachusetts, October 2, 1935.
63. William J. Gordon, Scottsdale, Arizona, October 15, 1935.
64. Evert Leon Jones, Pipestone, Minnesota, October 5, 1935. See also David B. Ross, Newark, New Jersey, October 10, 1935.
65. James Lawson, Hammond, Indiana, September 27, 1935.
66. Clement Saiman, Los Angeles, California, October 21, 1935.

67. R. L. Bolton, Chapel Hill, North Carolina, no date.
68. N. B. Bynum, Camden, Arkansas, October 1, 1935.
69. Gustav A. Papperman, Chicago, Illinois, October 8, 1935. See also Patrick Rogan, Chicago, Illinois, October 4, 1935; G. M. Pencock, South Bristol, Maine, September 10, 1935; Jesse D. Frank, Columbus, Mississippi, October 8, 1935.
70. M. O. Clemmons, Clay Center, Kansas, September 29, 1935.
71. See, for example, Nirum P. Olmstead, Brainerd, Michigan, October 15, 1935. It is also worth noting, of course, that some members of the clergy also found the New Deal "unscriptural and Un-American." See L. L. Tucker, Stockton, Missouri, October 7, 1935.
72. Fred M. Essig, Fallbrook, California, October 1, 1935.
73. See also T. J. Drexler, Mill Valley, California, November 11, 1935.
74. Ben M. Bogard, Little Rock, Arkansas, October 2, 1935. For similar arguments, see M. E. Shanks, Brayton, Iowa, October 22, 1935; R. C. Harding, Erie, Kansas, September 23, 1935.
75. G. C. Meyer, Wathena, Kansas, October 1, 1935.
76. Truman was later criticized on similar grounds. See Smith, *Religion in the Oval Office*.
77. Jesse Tidball, Madison, Indiana, October 22, 1935. For similar arguments, see John Ward Rose, Tipton, Indiana, October 23, 1935; Noah Garwick, Mankato, Minnesota, September 30, 1935; M. L. Riley, Windsor, Missouri, October 16, 1935.
78. R. J. Lorance, Auburn, Nebraska, October 16, 1935. See also Edward A. Durham, Claremont, New Hampshire, October 10, 1935.
79. Noel Parker, Sacramento, California, October 4, 1935. See also similar recommendations by R. W. Everroad, Payson, Illinois, October 10, 1935.
80. George W. Blount, Warsaw, North Carolina, November 6, 1935.
81. M. Theodore Hamm, University of Colorado, December 31, 1935. For others who noted the educative value of the radio addresses and urged him to give more of them, see L. A. Crown, Litchfield, Illinois, September 25, 1935; Raymond B. Blakney, Williamstown, Massachusetts, October 6, 1935; S. C. Michelfelder, Toledo, Ohio, September 26, 1935.
82. Jeffrey Tulis, *The Rhetorical Presidency* (Princeton, NJ: Princeton University Press, 1987). Although Tulis also dates the inception of the rhetorical presidency after the New Deal.
83. Charles Alexander Richmond, Washington, DC, October 8, 1935; see also Harry Rimmer, Duluth, Minnesota, October 7, 1935; John D. Hammel, Valley, Nebraska,

October 14, 1935. Myles Hemenway, Portland, Maine, October 23, 1935.

84. M. T. Keizer, Chenon, Illinois, October 3, 1935.
85. Henry Sills Bradley, Atlanta, Georgia, October 14, 1935. See also William J. McCoy, Fairport, New York, no date; Henry Barnston, Houston, Texas, October 7, 1935.
86. E. J. Jarrell, Chicago, Illinois, November 7, 1935. See also E. Lansing Bennett, Merchantville, New Jersey, September 27, 1935; Arthur O. Wright, Cozad, Nebraska, December 2, 1935.
87. U. B. Johnson, Petersburg, New York, October 4, 1935.
88. Charles B. Lewis, Olathe, Colorado, November 25, 1925. A number of clergy expressed the thought that the letter may have been "a piece of political strategy." See also Alva E. Gilbert, Cascade, Idaho, October 22, 1935; W. D. Chamberlin, Louisville, Kentucky, October 7, 1935.
89. Albert Hale Plumb, Hartford, Connecticut, September 28, 1935.
90. W. C. Poole, Dover, Delaware, September 30, 1935.
91. Daniel S. Gage, Fulton, Missouri, September 26, 1935.
92. Franklin L. Graff, San Mateo, California, November 1, 1935. See also Perry F. Webb, Pine Bluff, Arkansas, October 20, 1935.
93. Thomas S. Hickman, Mt. Pleasant, Arkansas, October 7, 1935.
94. R. O. Sutton, North Little Rock, Arkansas, October 8, 1935.
95. See also George H. Schuster, Inglewood, California, November 11, 1935.
96. See, for instance, D. W. Harrell, Tampa, Florida, October 7, 1935.
97. M. E. Seltz, Atlantic, Iowa, October 11, 1935.
98. John W. Meecham, Lompoc, California, October 4, 1935.

Chapter 2. Witnessing Politics: The Depictive Element of Political Vocabularies

1. James C. Scott, *Seeing Like a State: How Certain Schemes to Improve the Human Condition Have Failed* (New Haven, CT: Yale University Press, 1998).
2. On Hoover, see David Bruner, *Herbert Hoover: A Public Life* (New York: Alfred A. Knopf, 1979); Joan Hoff Wilson, *Herbert Hoover: Forgotten Progressive* (Boston: Houghton Mifflin, 1975).
3. Jean Edward Smith, *FDR* (New York: Random House, 2008), 287.
4. Robert S. McElvaine, *The Great Depression: America, 1929–1941* (New York: Three Rivers Press, 1993), 168.
5. On the history of Social Security, see Daniel Béland, *Social Security: History and*

Politics from the New Deal to the Privatization Debate (Lawrence: University Press of Kansas, 2005); Kirstin Downey, *The Woman behind the New Deal: The Life and Legacy of Frances Perkins—Social Security, Unemployment Insurance, and the Minimum Wage* (New York: Anchor, 2009).

6. This thought may go a long way toward explaining the centrality of visual language during the era. See Cara Finnegan, "FSA Photography and the New Deal Visual Culture," in *American Rhetoric in the New Deal Era, 1932–1945*, ed. Thomas W. Benson (East Lansing: Michigan State University Press, 2006), 115–155; Cara Finnegan, *Picturing Poverty: Print Culture and FSA Photography* (Washington, DC: Smithsonian, 2003); Mary E. Stuckey, "FDR, the Rhetoric of Vision, and the Creation of a National Synoptic State," *Quarterly Journal of Speech* 98 (2012): 297–319.
7. Bradford Vivian, "Witnessing Time: Rhetorical Form, Public Culture, and Popular Historical Education," *Rhetoric Society Quarterly* 44 (2014): 204–219.
8. For a contemporaneous view of Christian witnessing, see, for example, Reinhold Niebuhr, "The Christian Witness in the Social and National Order," in, *The Essential Reinhold Niebuhr: Selected Essays and Addresses*, ed. Robert Macafee Brown (New Haven, CT: Yale University Press, 1986), 93–101.
9. John Durham Peters, "Witnessing," *Media, Culture & Society* 23 (2001): 707–723.
10. Vivian, "Witnessing Time," 204.
11. Ibid., 206.
12. On presence, see Chaim Perelman and Lucie Olbrechts-Tyteca, who argue that events only come to have meaning through their rhetorical depiction. Chaim Perelman and Lucie Olbrechts-Tyteca., *The New Rhetoric*., trans. John Wilkinson and Purcell Weaver (Notre Dame, IN: University of Notre Dame Press, 1969), 115–120. See also John M. Murphy, "No End Save Victory: FDR and the End of Isolationism, 1936–1941," in *Making the Case: Advocacy and Judgment in Public Argument*, ed. Kathryn M. Olson et al. (East Lansing: Michigan State University Press, 2012), 127–160; Richard E. Vatz, "The Myth of the Rhetorical Situation," *Philosophy and Rhetoric* 6 (1973): 157.
13. Barbie Zelizer, "Finding Aids to the Past: Bearing Personal Witness to Traumatic Public Events," *Media, Culture & Society* 24 (2002): 687–714. See also Arabella Lyon and Lester C. Olson, "Special Issue on Human Rights Rhetoric: Traditions of Testifying and Witnessing," *Rhetoric Society Quarterly* 41 (2011): 203–212.
14. Carrie A. Rentschler, "Witnessing: U.S. Citizenship and the Vicarious Experience of Suffering," *Media, Culture & Society* 26 (2004): 296–304.

15. Samuel McCormick, *Letters to Power: Public Advocacy without Public Intellectuals* (University Park: Penn State University Press, 2011), 8.
16. The White House specifically notes this connection in the report on the clergy letters, arguing in one place that the 8,294 responses "represent the opinion of about 100,000 people," and in another that "it must be taken into consideration that the criticisms of the clergy concerning the liquor question are more a reflection of their own personal opinions than that of their congregations." See "Report on the Clergy Letters," Samuel I. Rosenman papers, The Public Papers and Addresses, Memos to Be Used for Annotation: China and Japan, Transportation of Munitions to Cotton, Box 34, File: Clergy Letters, Franklin D. Roosevelt Presidential Library, Hyde Park, NY, 1, 13.
17. Melford Loske Brown, Mount Vernon, New York, September 24, 1935; Philip C. Diamond, Georgetown, Illinois, October 17, 1935.
18. Rentschler, "Witnessing."
19. On those distinctions, see Herbert J. Gans, "Positive Functions of the Undeserving Poor: Uses of the Underclass in America," *Politics & Society* 22 (1994): 269–283.
20. Lyon and Olson, "Special Issue on Human Rights Rhetoric," 204.
21. Michael M. Osborn, "The Trajectory of My Work with Metaphor," *Southern Communication Journal* 74 (2009): 83.
22. Ibid., 84.
23. James R. Andrews, "The Imperial Style: Rhetorical Depiction and Queen Victoria's Diamond Jubilee," *Western Journal of Communication* 64 (2000): 53–77.
24. Janis L. Edwards and Carol K. Winkler, "Representative Form and the Visual Ideograph: The Iwo Jima Image in Editorial Cartoons," *Quarterly Journal of Speech* 83 (1997): 289–310.
25. See Robert Asen, "Women, Work, Welfare: A Rhetorical History of Images of Poor Women in Welfare Policy Debates," *Rhetoric & Public Affairs* 6 (2003): 286–287.
26. Osborn, "The Trajectory of My Work with Metaphor," 84.
27. Lisa M. Gring-Pemble, "'Are We Going to Now Govern by Anecdote?': Rhetorical Constructions of Welfare Recipients in Congressional Hearings, Debates, and Legislation, 1992–1996," *Quarterly Journal of Speech* 87 (2001): 341–365.
28. Andrews, "The Imperial Style," 55.
29. Michael M. Osborn, "Rhetorical Depiction," in *Form, Genre, and the Study of Political Discourse*, ed. H. W. Simons and A. A. Aghazarian (Columbia: University of South Carolina Press, 1986), 79–107.

30. Jeanne Fahnestock, *Rhetorical Style: The Uses of Language in Persuasion* (New York: Oxford University Press, 2011), 335. She notes that the kind of description I am talking about would fall under the category of *demonstratio* rather than *depictio* in the classic canon.
31. Ibid., 336.
32. Allen R. Stowell, Chillicothe, Illinois, October 14, 1935.
33. B. M. Collins, Ventura, California, October 9, 1935.
34. C. B. Scott, Waterford, Mississippi, November 5, 1935.
35. John R. Leatherbury, Sparrows Point, Maryland, November 12, 1935.
36. George Graham, Washington, DC, October 10, 1935.
37. See, for example, Charles W. Caldwell, St. Cloud, Florida, September 30, 1935.
38. William F. Cochran, Gooding, Idaho, October 15, 1935; Kirk M. Dewe, Oak Lawn, Illinois, November 12, 1935. For other letters relying on detail as an argumentative strategy, see, for example, O. A. Smith, Nogales, Arizona, September 30, 1935.
39. John W. Nicholson, Markie, Indiana, October 7, 1935.
40. Quenton Hauer, Lukachukai, Arizona, October 9, 1935.
41. O. F. Jordan, Park Ridge, Illinois, September 25, 1935. See also W. H. Griffin, Cumberland, Iowa, October 18, 1935; Harvey S. Stoner, Massillon, Ohio, October 15, 1935.
42. J. Edwin Hemphill, Petersburg, Virginia, October 22, 1935. See also G. M. Hereford, Steptoe, Washington, October 16, 1935.
43. Joe W. English, Gentry, Arkansas, October 10, 1935.
44. Dwight W. Learned, Claremont, Colorado, September 28, 1935.
45. Michael Leff and Andrew Sachs, "Words the Most Like Things: Iconicity and the Rhetorical Text," *Western Journal of Speech Communication* 54 (1990): 252–273.
46. James Jasinski, *Sourcebook on Rhetoric: Key Concepts in Contemporary Rhetorical Studies* (Thousand Oaks, CA: Sage, 2001), 551.
47. On metaphors as truncated analogies, see Fahnestock, *Rhetorical Style*, 110; on argument by comparison, see Perelman and Olbrechts-Tyteca, *New Rhetoric*, 137; Jasinski, *Sourcebook on Rhetoric*, 38–39.
48. Osborn, "The Trajectory of My Work with Metaphor," 80.
49. George Lakoff and Mark Johnson, *Metaphors We Live By*, 2nd ed. (Chicago: University of Chicago Press, 2003); Jasinski, *Sourcebook on Rhetoric*, 258.
50. Kenneth Burke, *A Grammar of Motives* (Berkeley: University Press of California, 1969), 503.
51. Fahnestock, *Rhetorical Style*, 106.

52. Osborn, "The Trajectory of My Work with Metaphor," 84.
53. Ibid.
54. Robert Hariman, "Status, Marginality, and Rhetorical Theory," *Quarterly Journal of Speech* 72 (1986): 38–54.
55. George Lakoff, *Moral Politics: How Liberals and Conservatives Think* (Chicago: University of Chicago Press, 2002); George Lakoff, *Don't Think of an Elephant: Know Your Values and Frame the Debate* (White River Junction, VT: Chelsea Green Publishers, 2004).
56. Lakoff and Johnson, *Metaphors We Live By*, 9. Leah Ceccarelli has done especially good work on this aspect of metaphor; see Leah Ceccarelli, *On the Frontier of Science: An American Rhetoric of Exploration and Exploitation* (East Lansing: Michigan State University Press, 2013). See also David Zarefsky's important work on Lyndon Johnson and the War on Poverty, *President Johnson's War on Poverty: Rhetoric and History* (Tuscaloosa: University of Alabama Press, 2005).
57. Robert L. Ivie, "Metaphor and the Rhetorical Invention of Cold War 'Idealists,'" *Communication Monographs* 54 (1987): 165–182.
58. Jasinski, *Sourcebook on Rhetoric*, 24.
59. Osborn, "The Trajectory of My Work with Metaphor," 81.
60. Lloyd C. Kelly, Pineville, Kentucky, September 26, 1935.
61. Suzanne M. Daughton, "Metaphorical Transcendence: Images of the Holy War in Franklin D. Roosevelt's First Inaugural," *Quarterly Journal of Speech* 79 (1993): 427–446.
62. Don M. Chase, San Francisco, California, October 10, 1935.
63. William M. Maxton, DuQuoin, Illinois, September 27, 1935.
64. Thomas Quayle, Lakebluff, Illinois, November 19, 1935.
65. Such metaphors were common during the period. See Davis W. Houck and Amos Kiewe, *FDR's Body Politics: The Rhetoric of Disability* (College Station: Texas A&M University Press, 2003).
66. S. B. Coggins, Higginsville, Missouri, September 15, 1935.
67. James B. Dancey, Keokuk, Iowa, October 31, 1935.
68. George Lang, University of Alabama, November 3, 1935.
69. Barnaby Haran, "Machine, Montage, and Myth: *Experimental Cinema* and Politics of American Modernism during the Great Depression," *Textual Practice* 25 (2011): 563–584.
70. Lawrence Radcliffe, Daytona Beach, Florida, October 1, 1935.

71. Francis L. Baechle, Port Allen, Louisiana, October 21, 1935.
72. B. M. Shacklette, Bloomfield, Missouri, October 4, 1935. Others made similar recommendations. See W. H. Rogers, New York, New York, October 14, 1935.
73. Jas. A. DeMoss, Ayres, Kansas, September 19, 1936.
74. On narrative, see, most prominently, Walter R. Fisher, *Human Communication as Narration: Toward a Philosophy of Reason, Value, and Action* (Columbia: University of South Carolina Press, 1989); Walter R. Fisher, "Narration as a Human Communication Paradigm: The Case of Public Moral Argument," *Communications Monographs* 51 (1984): 1–22; John Louis Lucaites and Celeste Michelle Condit, "Re-constructing Narrative Theory: A Functional Perspective," *Journal of Communication* 35, no. 4 (1985): 90–108.
75. Fisher, of course, argues that narrative is compatible with rational modes of thinking; William Lewis makes a convincing argument that this assumption isn't supported in his analysis of Reagan's narrative. See William F. Lewis, "Telling America's Story: Narrative Form and the Reagan Presidency," *Quarterly Journal of Speech* 73 (1987): 280–302.
76. See Herbert W. Simons, "From Post-9/11 Melodrama to Quagmire in Iraq: A Rhetorical History," *Rhetoric & Public Affairs* 10 (2007): 183–193.
77. H. H. Harris, Macon, Georgia, October 10, 1935.
78. H. L. Owen, St. Charles, Minnesota, October 3, 1935. A similar letter was written by Albert E. Budd, Heuvelton, New York, October 21, 1935.
79. Walter N. Bump, St. Louis, Missouri, September 25, 1935.
80. C. L. Edwards, Harrisburg, Iowa, November 5, 1935. See also A. J. Cupp, Williamsburg, Kentucky, October 4, 1935.
81. Ralph M. Barker, East Gloucester, Massachusetts, September 28, 1935.
82. Frederick B. Niss, Andover, Massachusetts, September 26, 1935.
83. Joseph F. Panetta, Germantown, Pennsylvania, September 27, 1935.
84. Norman E. Richardson, Chicago, Illinois, September 25, 1935.
85. Joe Hulett, Jacksonville, Georgia, October 17, 1935.
86. Stanley O. Whitesill, Warren Indiana, February 10, 1935.
87. Karl G. Newell, Washington, DC, October 2, 1935.
88. Joseph Utschen, Hibbing, Minnesota, October 22, 1935.
89. T. B. Frost, Edwards, Mississippi, October 11, 1935.
90. Edward Berger, Hollywood, Colorado, November 5, 1935.
91. L. E. McEldowney, Tampa, Florida, October 15, 1935.
92. Robert C. Rhodes, Emory University, Georgia, October 23, 1935.

93. E. L. Edens, Ashland, Kentucky, October 1, 1935.

Chapter 3. Revelations: Naturalizing Hierarchies in Political Vocabularies

1. Kenneth Burke, *A Rhetoric of Motives* (Berkeley: University of California Press, 1969), 141.
2. Adam Seth Cohen, *Nothing to Fear: FDR's Inner Circle and the Hundred Days That Created Modern America* (New York: Penguin, 2009), 286; Albert Fried, *FDR and His Enemies* (New York: St. Martin's Press, 1999), 3; Arthur M. Schlesinger Jr., *The Age of Roosevelt: The Coming of the New Deal* (Boston: Houghton Mifflin, 1959), 567.
3. George Wolfskill, "New Deal Critics: Did They Miss the Point?," in *Essays on the New Deal*, ed. Wilmon H. Droze, George Wolfskill, and William E. Leuchtenburg (Austin: University of Texas Press, 1969), 51.
4. On FDR's relative conservatism, see James MacGregor Burns, *Roosevelt: The Lion and the Fox, 1882–1940* (New York: Harcourt, Brace, Jovanovich, 1956), 185, 243.
5. Robert S. McElvaine, *The Great Depression: America, 1929–1941* (New York: Three Rivers Press, 1993), 233–236.
6. Stephen W. Baskerville and Ralph Willett, introduction to *Nothing Else to Fear: New Perspectives on America in the Thirties*, ed. Stephen W. Baskerville and Ralph Willett (Manchester: Manchester University Press, 1985), 7–8.
7. Schlesinger, *Age of Roosevelt*, 3.
8. Ibid., 484–487.
9. Mary E. Stuckey, *The Good Neighbor: Franklin D. Roosevelt and the Rhetoric of American Power* (East Lansing: Michigan State University Press, 2013), chap. 1.
10. Terry Golway, *Together We Cannot Fail: FDR and the American Presidency in Time of Crisis* (Napierville, IL: Sourcebooks, 2009), 59; McElvaine, *Great Depression*, 225.
11. Amity Shlaes, *The Forgotten Man: A New History of the Great Depression* (New York: Random House, 2009), 299.
12. Interlocutors attempting to change social hierarchies often rely for their authority on existing ones; they thus become complicit in reinscribing the hierarchies they seek to challenge or other, cognate hierarchies. See Ryan Skinnell, "Elizabeth Cady Stanton's 1854 'Address to the Legislature of New York' and the Paradox of Social Reform Rhetoric," *Rhetoric Review* 29 (2010): 129.
13. Debra Hawhee, "Looking into Aristotle's Eyes: Toward a Theory of Rhetorical

Vision," *Advances in the History of Rhetoric* 14 (2011): 139–165; Michele Kennerly, "Getting Carried Away: How Rhetorical Transport Gets Judgment Going," *Rhetoric Society Quarterly* 40 (2010): 269–291.

14. Hawhee, "Looking into Aristotle's Eyes," 150.
15. Kenneth Burke, "Terministic Screens," in *Language as Symbolic Action: Essays on Life, Literature, and Method* (Berkeley: University of California Press, 1966), 45.
16. See Paul Stob, "'Terministic Screens,' Social Constructionism, and the Language of Experience: Kenneth Burke's Utilization of William James," *Philosophy and Rhetoric* 41 (2008): 130–152.
17. See Eric King Watts, "'Voice' and 'Voicelessness' in Rhetorical Studies," *Quarterly Journal of Speech* 87 (2001): 179–196.
18. For an extended discussion of the importance of visibility and place in the national hierarchy, see Mary E. Stuckey, *Defining Americans: The Presidency and National Identity* (Lawrence: University Press of Kansas, 2004).
19. Robert Hariman, "Status, Marginality, and Rhetorical Theory," *Quarterly Journal of Speech* 72 (1986): 38–54.
20. Ibid., 41.
21. Burke, *Rhetoric of Motives*, 141.
22. Selsus E. Tull, Middlesboro. Kentucky, October 8, 1935.
23. D. Earl Daniel, Charleroi, Pennsylvania, October 23, 1935.
24. Charles C. Harris, Wilmington, Delaware, September 30, 1935; Frank E. Wilke, Groton, South Dakota, September 27, 1935.
25. Joseph E. Beal, New Albany, Indiana, October 21, 1935; William Hood, Sylacauga, Alabama, October 14, 1935. See also, among many others, R. F. Hallford, Slocomb, Alabama, September 28, 1935.
26. Frank F. Walters, Wionita, Kansas, October 29, 1935.
27. C. M. Grall, Freeport, Illinois, October 1, 1935.
28. Victor H. Offermann, Fort Smith, Arkansas, October 25, 1935.
29. C. L. Noss, Greenville, Pennsylvania, October 3, 1935.
30. L. L. Tucker, Stockton, Missouri, October 7, 1935.
31. Augustine Batten, New York City, New York, October 11, 1935.
32. Edward Williams, Rock Island, Illinois, September 27, 1935.
33. Thomas W. Barbour, Ramona, California, October 4, 1935.
34. Howard A. Gibbs, Fort Defiance, Arizona, no date.
35. Charles Wesley Adams, Tampa, Florida, December 2, 1935.
36. James G. Widdlifield, Detroit, Michigan, October 1, 1935.

37. Lloyd C. Glisson, New York, New York, Thanksgiving Day, 1935.
38. D. Z. Jackson, Chicago, Illinois, October 2, 1935.
39. Allan Duncan, Moberly, Missouri, September 26, 1935.
40. Alvah D. Griff, Milan, Missouri, September 26, 1935.
41. J. W. Hairston, Asheville, North Carolina, October 14, 1935.
42. Peter W. Lambert Jr., Penland, North Carolina, October 5, 1935.
43. Raymond B. Blakney, Williamstown, Massachusetts, October 6, 1935.
44. C. L. Munsun, Bloomington, Illinois, September 27, 1935.
45. Henry Barnson, Houston, Texas, October 7, 1935.
46. D. S. Smith, Brookline, Massachusetts, October 19, 1935.
47. Although Walter J. Jerge was more committed to consistency than to a particular theory of government. He wrote, "As I see it, either we should put everyone on the public pay-roll or take practically everyone off; i.e. Socialism or old-fashioned Democracy. I do not care very much which it is. But I do not like this mongrel policy which we seem to be following now." Somerville, Massachusetts, October 22, 1935.
48. C. J. Carmichael, White Bluff, Mississippi, September 30, 1935.
49. Myron W. Adams, Mason, New Hampshire, October 14, 1935.
50. John C. Blommestein, Onamia, Minnesota, October 2, 1935.
51. R. W. McEwan, Hanover, Indiana, October 29, 1935.
52. J. Lawrence Connolly, Roscommon, Michigan, September 27, 1935.
53. Joseph F. Fitzgerald, St. Louis, Missouri, September 30, 1935.
54. George C. Lee, Brady, Montana, November 26, 1935.
55. D. W. Hawkins, Andulasia, Alabama, September 25, 1935.
56. John B. Reese, Mitchell, South Dakota, October 7, 1935.
57. Loyal Y. Graham, Newark, New Jersey, October 1, 1935.
58. Will A. Kelley, Oakland, Maine, September 26, 1935.
59. Arthur L. Duncan, Indianapolis, Indiana, October 2, 1935.
60. This is probably related to FDR's tendency, also on display among his supporters, to refer to his opponents as "Tories." See, for example, E. R. Rorem, Slater, Iowa, October 18, 1935.
61. R. R. Diggs, New Iberia, Louisiana, October 22, 1935.
62. Fred L. Hainer, Arlington, New Jersey, September 27, 1935.
63. Arthur B. Papineau, Vineyard Haven, Massachusetts, October 23, 1935.
64. Leroy G. Allen, Taunton, Massachusetts, October 28, 1935.
65. Don J. Kraemer, "Identification and Property: Burke's and Lincoln's Ratio of Act

and Purpose," *Advances in the History of Rhetoric* 11–12 (2008): 39.

66. Kristy Maddux, "Finding Comedy in Theology: A Hopeful Supplement to Kenneth Burke's Logology," *Philosophy and Rhetoric* 39 (2006): 208–232.
67. Joan Faber MacAlister, "Good Neighbors: Covenantal Rhetoric, Moral Aesthetics, and the Resurfacing of Identity Politics," *Howard Journal of Communication* 21 (2010): 276–277. On covenants, see Denise M. Bostdorff, "George W. Bush's Post–September 11 Rhetoric of Covenant Renewal: Upholding the Faith of the Greatest Generation," *Quarterly Journal of Speech* 89 (2003): 293–319.
68. David P. Gaines, Hartford, Connecticut, October 4, 1935.
69. John Bailey Kelley, Emporia, Kansas, October 4, 1935.
70. A. MacAllister, Trenton, New Jersey, September 30, 1935.
71. Thomas Tyack, Highstown, New Jersey, September 26, 1935.
72. Paul E. Nelson, Sterling, Illinois, November 23, 1935.
73. Ben R. Stripling, Zegler, Illinois, October 5, 1935.
74. Howard S. Frazer, Medford, New Jersey, October 19, 1935.
75. J. S. Hawkins, Elizabethtown, Kentucky, October 4, 1935. See also, among many others, A. A. Morton, Talpa, Texas, September 27, 1935; William A. Young, Peoria, Illinois, October 3, 1935.
76. John H. Nolan, Springfield, Massachusetts, October 3, 1935.
77. R. R. Detweiler, North Hollywood, California, October 10, 1935.
78. Harry Noble Wilson, St. Paul, Minnesota, October 14, 1935.
79. W. Ernest Collins, Box 12 (no city or state given), September 26, 1935.
80. Charles M. Prugh, Decatur, Indiana, November 20, 1935.
81. Skinnell, "Elizabeth Cady Stanton's 1854 'Address to the Legislature of New York,'" 139.
82. Ibid., 141.
83. Carroll Hamilton, Skene, Mississippi, September 25, 1935.
84. Richard D. Hatch, Brooklyn, Connecticut, October 1, 1935.
85. Edgar Lucas, Augusta, Georgia, October 10, 1935.
86. S. S. Pike, Bolivar, Missouri, September 30, 1935.
87. Harry Evan Owings, Santa Ana, California, November 13, 1935.
88. Robert Fred Mosley, Alhambra, California, November 1, 1935.
89. Shlaes, *Forgotten Man*.
90. J. W. Coleman, Maywood, Illinois, no date, wrote, "There was a good deal of comment on the administration's lack of support for the anti-lynching bill": Coleman represented much of this commentary, writing, "We, the fifteen million

negro population of these United States had faithfully hoped, that among your Social Security Legislation would have been an Anti Lynching Bill, which might guarantee us justice, full equal rights, freedom, and protection as citizens against the mob rule of the South and per the Constitution of this nation."

91. On the Indian Reorganization Act, see Brian W. Dippie, *The Vanishing American: White Attitudes and U.S. Indian Policy* (Lawrence: University Press of Kansas, 1982); Graham D. Taylor, *The New Deal and American Indian Tribalism: The Administration of the Indian Reorganization Act, 1934–45* (Omaha: University of Nebraska Press, 1980).
92. W. H. Rourcer, Oxford, Mississippi, October 3, 1935.
93. See Eric King Watts, *Hearing the Hurt: Rhetoric, Aesthetics, and Politics in the New Negro Movement* (Tuscaloosa: University of Alabama Press, 2012), 36.
94. A. A. Graham, Corona, New York, October 3, 1935.
95. H. Leonard Clark, Bunker, Louisiana, October 22, 1935.
96. Barnabas Meyer, Oames, New Mexico, October 18, 1935.
97. Neil E. Ambrose, Dayton, Kentucky, October 2, 1935.
98. A. C. Smith, Greenfield, Missouri, September 30, 1935.
99. Constant M. Klein, Carlsbad, New Mexico, October 4, 1935.
100. R. M. Hunter, Mobile, Alabama, September 28, 1935. For a strikingly similar argument, see Samuel James Garner, Arkadelphia, Arkansas, October 22, 1935.
101. Russell K. Smith, Atlanta, Georgia, September 25, 1935.
102. Arthur B. Dimmick, Key West, Florida, October 19, 1935.
103. Roy L. Osborne, Tennessee, October 13, 1935.
104. Clayton Grover, Phalanx Station, Ohio, September 25, 1935.
105. Winfrid Stauble, Keams Canyon, Arizona, October 7, 1935.
106. For a similar view, expressed by a self-identified American Indian, see Ben Brave, Mission, South Dakota, November 15, 1935.
107. See, for example, Harry W. Miller, Ada, Oklahoma, September 27, 1935.
108. Arthur D. Gray, Box 5 (no location given), October 24, 1935.
109. J. L. Horace, Chicago, Illinois, September 28, 1935.
110. Charles A. Ward, Toledo, Ohio, October 21, 1935.
111. Daniel Iverson, Miami, Florida, October 4, 1935.
112. Macon Interdenominational Ministerial Alliance, Macon, Georgia, November 1, 1935.
113. Alice Kessler-Harris, *Out to Work: A History of Wage-Earning Women in the United States*, 20th anniversary ed. (New York: Oxford University Press, 2003),

251. Married women workers remained in the minority, even among very low-income families. See Winifred D. Wandersee, *Women's Work and Family Values, 1920–1940* (Cambridge, MA: Harvard University Press, 1981), 2.

114. On ER's symbolic importance, see Maurine Hoffman Beasley, *Eleanor Roosevelt and the Media: A Public Quest for Self-Fulfillment* (Champaign: University of Illinois Press, 1987); Allida Mae Black, *Casting Her Own Shadow: Eleanor Roosevelt and the Shaping of Postwar Liberalism* (New York: Columbia University Press, 1996); Robin Gerber, *Leadership the Eleanor Roosevelt Way: Timeless Strategies from the First Lady of Courage* (New York: Penguin, 2003).
115. On Perkins, see Kirstin Downey, *The Woman behind the New Deal: The Life and Legacy of Frances Perkins—Social Security, Unemployment Insurance, and the Minimum Wage* (New York: Anchor, 2009).
116. Raymond E. Brock, Riverdale-on-Hudson, New York, October 20, 1935.
117. Walter W. Pippin Jr., Eutaw, Alabama, October 5, 1935.
118. G. M. Brassharro, Wichita, Kansas, October 16, 1935. See also, among many others, Theo Andree, New Kensington, Pennsylvania, September 27, 1935; Michael S. Roach, Lead, South Carolina, October 1, 1935; George W. Bell, Whiteville, Tennessee, September 28, 1935; Fred O. Base, Rupert, Idaho, November 12, 1935.
119. Francis Jerome, Balto, Maine, September 25, 1935.
120. Bernard Sinne, Omaha, Nebraska, October 10, 1935.
121. M. J. Clare, Portland, Oregon, October 3, 1035.
122. A. S. Rachal, Low Moor, Virginia, September 26, 1935.
123. Walter Henry MacPherson, Joliet, Illinois, October 9, 1935.

Chapter 4. The American Eden: Mythic Elements of Political Vocabularies

1. These labels are Walter Fisher's and are a bit unfortunate, as both versions of the myth have materialistic and moralistic aspects, and the distinction is more one of degree than of kind. See Walter Fisher, "Reaffirmation and Subversion of the American Dream," *Quarterly Journal of Speech* 59 (1973): 160–167.
2. V. William Balthrop, "Culture, Myth, and Ideology as Public Argument: An Interpretation of the Ascent and Demise of 'Southern Culture,'" *Communication Monographs* 51 (1984): 350.
3. For more on the links between ideology and myth, see Kenneth Burke, *A Rhetoric of Motives* (Berkeley: University of California Press, 1969), 103–104.

4. See James Jasinski, *Sourcebook on Rhetoric: Key Concepts in Contemporary Rhetorical Studies* (Thousand Oaks, CA: Sage, 2001), 383.
5. On myth in general, see Mircea Eliade, *Myth and Reality* (New York: Harper and Row, 1963). Farrell says that they "detail our figurative origins." Thomas B. Farrell, *Norms of Rhetorical Culture* (New Haven, CT: Yale University Press, 1993), 56.
6. Chiara Bottici, *A Philosophy of Political Myth* (New York: Cambridge University Press, 2010).
7. James O. Robertson, *American Myth, American Reality* (New York: Hill and Wang, 1980), xv.
8. Robert C. Rowland and David A. Frank, "Mythic Rhetoric and Rectification in the Israeli-Palestinian Conflict," *Communication Studies* 62 (2011): 42.
9. Jasinski, *Sourcebook on Rhetoric*, 383.
10. Chiara Bottici and Benoit Challard, *The Myth of the Clash of Civilizations* (New York: Routledge, 2010) chaps. 2 and 4.
11. Leroy G. Dorsey, "Sailing into the 'Wondrous Now': The Myth of the American Navy's World Cruise," *Quarterly Journal of Speech* 83 (1997): 447–465; Zoe Hess Carney and Mary E. Stuckey, "The World as the American Frontier: Racialized Presidential War Rhetoric," *Southern Communication Journal* 80 (2015): 163–188.
12. J. H. Bently, "Myths, Wagers, and Some Implications of World History," *Journal of World History* 16 (2005): 51–82; Robert C. Rowland and Kirsten Theye, "The Symbolic DNA of Terrorism," *Communication Monographs* 75 (2008): 52–85.
13. Michael C. McGee, "In Search of 'the People': A Rhetorical Alternative," *Quarterly Journal of Speech* 61 (1975): 235–249.
14. Maurice Charland, "Constitutive Rhetoric: The Case of the 'Peuple Quebecois,'" *Quarterly Journal of Speech* 73 (1987): 137.
15. Ibid., 138.
16. Larry Williamson stresses the nonrational component of myth. See Larry A. Williamson, "Bush's Mythic America: A Critique of the Rhetoric of War," *Southern Communication Journal* 75 (2010): 217.
17. Leroy G. Dorsey, "The Frontier Myth and Presidential Rhetoric: Theodore Roosevelt's Campaign for Conservation," *Western Journal of Communication* 59 (1995): 3–4.
18. Alan DeSantis, "Selling the American Dream Myth to Black Southerners: The Chicago *Defender* and the Great Migration of 1915–1919," *Western Journal of Communication* 62 (1998): 479.
19. Dorsey, "The Frontier Myth and Presidential Rhetoric," 4; Leroy Dorsey and

Rachel M. Harlow, "'We Want Americans Pure and Simple': Theodore Roosevelt and the Myth of Americanism," *Rhetoric & Public Affairs* 6 (2003): 62.

20. See, for example, Mary E. Stuckey, *Defining Americans: The Presidency and National Identity* (Lawrence: University Press of Kansas, 2004).
21. Although it is also important to note that for René Girard, myths derive from a founding violence that is specifically attentive to such distinctions. See René Girard, *The Scapegoat* (Baltimore: Johns Hopkins University Press, 1989), chap. 3.
22. Farrell, *Norms of Rhetorical Culture*, 234.
23. Kurt W. Ritter, "The Myth-Making Function of the Rhetoric of the American Revolution: Francis Hopkinson as a Case Study," *Communication Quarterly* 23 (1975): 25–31.
24. Balthrop, "Culture, Myth, and Ideology as Public Argument"; Ritter, "The Myth-Making Function of the Rhetoric of the American Revolution."
25. Roland Boer, *Myth: On the Use and Abuse of Biblical Themes* (Durham, NC: Duke University Press, 2009).
26. Charland, "Constitutive Rhetoric," 140.
27. Dorsey, "The Frontier Myth and Presidential Rhetoric," 3.
28. See also, Janice Hocker Rushing, "Mythic Evolution of the 'New Frontier' in Mass Mediated Rhetoric," *Critical Studies in Mass Communication* 3 (1986): 265–296; Mike Milford, "The Rhetorical Evolution of the Alamo," *Communication Quarterly* 61 (2013): 114; and Eric W. Rothenbuhler, "Myth and Collective Memory in the Case of Robert Johnson," *Critical Studies in Media Communication* 24(2001): 189–205.
29. Milford, "The Rhetorical Evolution of the Alamo," 126.
30. Balthrop, "Culture, Myth, and Ideology as Public Argument."
31. Dorsey, "Sailing into the 'Wondrous Now,'" 447.
32. Rowland and Frank, "Mythic Rhetoric," 43.
33. Williamson, "Bush's Mythic America," 215.
34. Bottici and Challard, *Myth of the Clash of Civilizations*, chap. 4.
35. Williamson, "Bush's Mythic America," 218. Others, who are less hostile to myth, also see it as a narrative that authorizes transformation. See, for example, Ritter, "The Myth-Making Function of the Rhetoric of the American Revolution"; Thomas Rosteck and Thomas S. Frentz, "Myth and Metaphoric Readings in Environmental Rhetoric," *Quarterly Journal of Speech* 95 (2009): 1–19; Janice Rushing and Thomas S. Frentz, "The Frankenstein Myth in Contemporary Cinema," *Critical Studies in Mass Communication* 6 (1989): 61–80.

36. There are other important myths—the melting pot myth comes most immediately to mind. But immigration was minimal during these years, and thus so were the anxieties produced by it. On the melting pot myth, though, see David Michael Smith, "The American Melting Pot: A National Myth in Public and Popular Discourse," *National Identities* 4 (2012): 387–402.
37. Eugene Spiess, St. Meinrad, Indiana, October 30, 1935. See also Mary E. Stuckey, "The Donner Party and the Rhetoric of Westward Expansion," *Rhetoric & Public Affairs* 14 (2011): 229–260.
38. On the frontier myth in general, see, among many others, M. J. Heale, "The Role of the Frontier in Jacksonian Politics: David Crockett and the Myth of the Self-Made Man," *Western Historical Quarterly* 4 (1973): 405–423; Frederick J. Turner, *The Significance of the Frontier in American History* (London: Penguin, 2008). On its centrality to American nationalism, see Milford, "The Rhetorical Evolution of the Alamo," 118–130.
39. Sacvan Bercovitch, *The Rites of Assent: Transformation in the Symbolic Construction of America* (Madison: University of Wisconsin Press, 1978); Miller, *Errand into the Wilderness*.
40. Richard Slotkin, *The Fatal Environment: The Myth of the Frontier in the Age of Industrialism, 1880–1890* (Norman: University of Oklahoma Press, 1998); Richard Slotkin, *Regeneration through Violence: The Mythology of the American Frontier, 1600–1880* (Norman: University of Oklahoma Press, 2000); Richard Slotkin, *Gunfighter Nation: The Myth of the Frontier in Twentieth-Century America* (Norman: University of Oklahoma Press, 1992).
41. Milford, "The Rhetorical Evolution of the Alamo," 114.
42. On the significance of the frontier myth to American national identity, see, among many others, Richard Drinnon, *Facing West: The Metaphysics of Indian Hating and Empire Building* (Norman: University of Oklahoma Press, 1997); Perry Miller, *Errand into the Wilderness* (Cambridge, MA: Harvard University Press, 1956); Robertson, *American Myth, American Reality*; Ronald Takaki, "*The Tempest* in the Wilderness: The Racialization of Savagery," *Journal of American History* 79 (1992): 892–912; John Tirman, "The Future of the American Frontier," *American Scholar* 78 (2009): 30–40.
43. See Robert Kagan, *Dangerous Nation: America's Foreign Policy from Its Earliest Days to the Dawn of the Twentieth Century* (New York: Vintage, 2006), 3–4; Richard Kluger, *Seizing Destiny: The Relentless Expansion of American Territory* (New York: Vintage, 2007); Walter Nugent, *Habits of Empire: A History of*

American Expansion (New York: Alfred A. Knopf, 2008).

44. Drinnon, *Facing West*.
45. Janice Hocker Rushing, "The Rhetoric of the American Western Myth," *Communication Monographs* 50 (1983): 14–32.
46. Dorsey, "The Frontier Myth and Presidential Rhetoric," 16.
47. See, for example, Ronald H. Carpenter, "America's Tragic Metaphor: Our Twentieth-Century Combatants as Frontiersmen," *Quarterly Journal of Speech* 76 (1990): 1–22; Greg Dickenson, Brian L. Ott, and Eric Ioki, "Memory and Myth at the Buffalo Bill Museum," *Western Journal of Communication* 69 (2005): 85–108; Brian W. Dippie, *Custer's Last Stand: The Anatomy of an American Myth* (Lincoln: University of Nebraska Press, 1976); Janice Hocker Rushing, "Evolution of the 'New Frontier' in *Alien* and *Aliens*: Patriarchal Co-Option of the Feminine Archetype," *Quarterly Journal of Speech* 75 (1989): 1–24; Slotkin, *Fatal Environment*; Slotkin, *Regeneration through Violence*; Henry N. Smith, *Virgin Land: The American West as Symbol and Myth* (Lincoln: University of Nebraska Press, 1978); Mark West and Chris Carey, "(Re)Enacting Frontier Justice: The Bush Administration's Tactical Narration of the Old West Fantasy after September 11," *Quarterly Journal of Speech* 92 (2006): 379–412.
48. On Kennedy's use of the frontier myth, see J. Justin Gustainis, "John F. Kennedy and the Green Berets: The Rhetorical Use of the Hero Myth," *Communication Studies* 40 (1989): 41–53. On Reagan's use of it, see William F. Lewis, "Telling America's Story: Narrative Form and the Reagan Presidency," *Quarterly Journal of Speech* 73 (1987): 280–302.
49. On TR's use of the myth, see Dorsey, "The Frontier Myth and Presidential Rhetoric"; Leroy G. Dorsey, "Managing Women's Equality: Theodore Roosevelt, the Frontier Myth, and the Modern Woman," *Rhetoric & Public Affairs* 16 (2013): 423–456; Dorsey and Harlow, "'We Want Americans Pure and Simple.'"
50. See, for example, Dorsey and Harlow, "'We Want Americans Pure and Simple,'" 55.
51. Milford, "The Rhetorical Evolution of the Alamo," 114.
52. A. R. Beck, Dubuque, Iowa, October 7, 1935.
53. J. O. Johnson, Little Rock, Arkansas, September 30, 1935.
54. Russell H. McConnell, Charlotte, Michigan, October 10, 1935.
55. Charles W. Neill, Placerville, California, October 15, 1935.
56. See J. Edwin Dale, Oregon, Illinois, October 4, 1935.
57. Richard Greeley Preston, Worcester, Massachusetts, October 2, 1935.

58. Arthur S. Lewis, Lakewood, Ohio, November 26, 1935.
59. DeSantis, "Selling the American Dream Myth to Black Southerners," 480.
60. For a discussion of cultural fictions, see Stephen John Hartnett, *Democratic Dissent and the Cultural Fictions of Antebellum America* (Urbana: University of Illinois Press, 2002), 2.
61. Fisher, "Reaffirmation and Subversion of the American Dream."
62. Ibid., 161.
63. Ibid.
64. Ibid., 161–162.
65. Ibid., 162.
66. Ernest M. Whitesmith, Pomona, California, October 23, 1935.
67. Daniel W. Fielder, Purcell, Oklahoma, October 31, 1935.
68. Charles C. Wilkerson, Camden, Alabama, October 12, 1935.
69. D. W. Hawkins, Andulasia, Alabama, September 25, 1935.
70. E. J. Lemine, R. E. Sullivan, and James R. Flynn, Redlake Falls, Minnesota, October 12, 1935.
71. Claude R. Cook, Carroll, Iowa, October 8, 1935.
72. Manning M. Patillo, Interlaken, New York, September 30, 1935.
73. E. Herrington, Chicago, Illinois, September 27, 1935.
74. S. H. Markowitz, Fort Wayne, Indiana, October 4, 1935.
75. G. Robert Forrester, Del Rio, Texas, October 14, 1935.
76. John W. Starie, Amherst, New Hampshire, October 25, 1935.
77. Gus Dattilo, Louisville, Kentucky, September 27, 1935.
78. George Long, Philosophy and Religion, University of Alabama, November 3, 1935.
79. William Tober, Baltimore, Maryland, September 26, 1935.
80. Phillip W. Sarles, Chicago, Illinois, October 14, 1935.
81. Charles J. Allen, Sheffield, Alabama, October 21, 1935.
82. C. Robert Ardry, Madison, Indiana, September 28, 1935.
83. John S. Johnson, Rex, North Carolina, September 27, 1935.
84. Norman Joseph Kilbourne, Los Angeles, California, October 1, 1935. See also Arthur Rablen, Valley Stream, New York, October 14, 1935.
85. Arthur B. Patten, Claremont, California, October 4, 1935.
86. W. A. Settlag, St. Louis, Missouri, October 8, 1935.
87. Warren E. Mosley, Morrill, Maine, October 10, 1935.
88. W. H. Ezell, Lawson, Missouri, October 23, 1935.
89. John E. Rees, Iowa State Penitentiary, Fort Madison, Iowa, November 13, 1935.

90. Orlo J. Price, Rochester, New York, September 27, 1935.
91. Sidney H. Babcock, Holdenville, Oklahoma, September 30, 1935.
92. Gaston W. Duncan, Kennett, Missouri, September 26, 1935.
93. William B. Heagerty, Gilroy, California, September 20, 1935.
94. C. S. Newsom, Erie, Pennsylvania, September 27, 1935. The Brain Trust took a fair amount of criticism. See, for example, Elmer E. Voelkel, Beloit, Wisconsin, October 15, 1935; William Kerr McKinney, Westfield, New Jersey, September 30, 1935; H. E. R. Reck, Baltimore, Maryland, October 3, 1935. My favorite example comes from Herbert R. Whitelock, who wrote, "I suggest that you rid the Government of the Brain Trust at once. Take these muddle-minded misfits, who have so confused government and business that nobody knows who's who, what's what, where we are at, or where we may end up, and lead them out of the city limits." Chelsea, Massachusetts, September 23, 1935.
95. Walter P. Hill, Mackinac Island, Michigan, September 26, 1935.
96. J. T. Michael, Hooker, Oklahoma, September 30, 1935.
97. Fred Anderson, Scobey, Montana, no date.
98. H. Spencer Edmunds, Roanoke, Virginia, October 2, 1935.
99. Robert T. Craig, Jersey City, New Jersey, September 26, 1935.
100. Robert L. Ivie and Oscar Giner, "More and Less Evil: Contesting the Mythos of National Security in the 2008 Presidential Primaries," *Rhetoric & Public Affairs* 12 (2008): 280–281.
101. Paul Tanner, Milwaukee, Wisconsin, September 26, 1935.
102. S. C. Cornell, Chazy, New York, September 27, 1935.
103. H. F. Crim, Townley, Alabama, September 27, 1935.
104. Hugh H. Ellis, Andulasia, Alabama, September 25, 1935.
105. See Stuckey, "Donner Party."
106. Howard A. Gibbs, Fort Defiance, Arizona, no date.
107. Gregory A. Sheradon, Winchester, Massachusetts, October 22, 1935.
108. Paul L. Rider, Syracuse, New York, September 29, 1935.
109. C. Arthur Sadofsky, Sparrows Point, Maryland, September 26, 1935.
110. H. O. Pritchard, Indianapolis, Indiana, October 1, 1935.
111. Isidor B. Hoffman, New York, New York, October 31, 1935.
112. E. H. H. Holmes, St. Paul, Minnesota, September 27, 1935.
113. George W. Pendes, Newburgh, New York, April 16, 1936.
114. Raymond O. Hall, Charlotte, Vermont, no date.
115. DeSantis, "Selling the American Dream Myth to Black Southerners," 479.

Chapter 5. Making a City on a Hill: Political Vocabularies and National Policy

1. See Mary E. Stuckey, *The Good Neighbor: Franklin D. Roosevelt and the Rhetoric of American Power* (East Lansing: Michigan State University Press, 2013).
2. Gerard A. Hauser, *Vernacular Voices: The Rhetoric of Politics and Public Spheres* (Columbia: University of South Carolina Press, 1999), 1.
3. J. Michael Hogan, "George Gallup and the Rhetoric of Scientific Democracy," *Communication Monographs* 64 (1987): 173.
4. Darrin Hicks, "The Promise(s) of Deliberative Democracy," *Rhetoric & Public Affairs* 5 (2002): 223–260.
5. On the problematic role of polling in a democracy, see John Brehm, *The Phantom Respondents: Opinion Surveys and Political Representation* (Ann Arbor: University of Michigan Press, 1993); J. Michael Hogan, *The Nuclear Freeze Campaign: Rhetoric and Foreign Policy in the Telepolitical Age* (East Lansing: Michigan State University Press, 1994); Hogan, "George Gallup"; J. Michael Hogan et al., "Report of the National Task Force on the Presidency and Public Opinion," in *The Prospect of Presidential Rhetoric*, ed. Martin J. Medhurst and James Arnt Aune (College Station: Texas A&M University Press, 2008), 293–316.
6. See Mary E. Stuckey, *Voting Deliberatively: FDR and the 1936 Presidential Election* (University Park: Penn State University Press, 2015).
7. Susan Herbst lists this as among the important elements in deliberation. See *Numbered Voices: How Opinion Polling Has Shaped American Politics* (Chicago: University of Chicago Press, 1993), 165.
8. For a fuller discussion of this point, see Stuckey, *Voting Deliberatively*.
9. Scott Welsh, *The Rhetorical Surface of Democracy: How Deliberative Ideals Undermine Democratic Politics* (Lanham, MD: Lexington Books, 2013), 101.
10. For a discussion of the pros and cons of pluralism, see William Kelso, *American Political Theory: Pluralism and Its Critics* (New York: Praeger, 1978).
11. Gerard A. Hauser and Chantal Benoit-Barne, "Reflections on Rhetoric, Deliberative Democracy, Civil Society, and Trust," *Rhetoric & Public Affairs* 5 (2002): 261–275.
12. Walter Lippmann, *The Phantom Public* (Piscataway, NJ: Transaction Publishers, 1927).
13. John Dewey, *The Public and Its Problems: An Essay in Political Inquiry* (New York: Henry Holt, 1927).
14. Hauser, *Vernacular Voices*, 31.

15. For a discussion of the importance of these elements, see Kendall R. Phillips, "Spheres of Public Dissension: Reconsidering the Public Sphere," *Communication Monographs* 63 (1996): 231–248.
16. Calvin L. Troup, "Civic Engagement from Religious Grounds," *Journal of Communication and Religion* 32 (2009): 240–267.
17. James Jasinski, *Sourcebook on Rhetoric: Key Concepts in Contemporary Rhetorical Studies* (Thousand Oaks, CA: Sage, 2001), 160.
18. Thomas B. Farrell, *Norms of Rhetorical Culture* (New Haven, CT: Yale University Press, 1993), 77.
19. Jasinski, *Sourcebook on Rhetoric*, 161.
20. Ibid., 160.
21. Jeanne Fahnestock, *Rhetorical Style: The Uses of Language in Persuasion* (New York: Oxford University Press, 2011), 330.
22. Simone Chambers, "Behind Closed Doors: Publicity, Secrecy, and the Quality of Deliberation," *Journal of Political Philosophy* 12 (2004): 389–410.
23. Robert Asen, "A Discourse Theory of Citizenship," *Quarterly Journal of Speech* 90 (2004): 189–211.
24. Christian Erik J. Kock and Lisa Storm Villasden, "Introduction: Citizenship as Rhetorical Practice," *Rhetoric and Democratic Deliberation* 3 (2012): 1–10.
25. Don Waisanen, "Toward Robust Public Engagement: The Value of Deliberative Discourse for *Civil* Communication," *Rhetoric & Public Affairs* 17 (2014): 287–322.
26. Farrell, *Norms of Rhetorical Culture*, 145; Ronald Walter Greene, "Another Materialist Rhetoric," *Critical Studies in Mass Communication* 15 (1998): 21.
27. Farrell, *Norms of Rhetorical Culture*, 76.
28. Hauser, *Vernacular Voices*, 64.
29. Robert E. Goodin, "How Can Deliberative Democracy Get a Grip?" *Political Quarterly* 83 (2012): 806–813.
30. Hauser, *Vernacular Voices*, 12.
31. Ibid., 57.
32. Janet M. Atwill, "Rhetoric and Civic Virtue," in *The Viability of the Rhetorical Tradition*, ed. Richard Graff, Arthur E. Walzer, and Janet M. Atwill (Albany: SUNY Press, 2005), 84–85.
33. Hauser, *Vernacular Voices*, 96.
34. Jasinski, *Sourcebook on Rhetoric*, 162.
35. James Bohman, *Public Deliberation: Pluralism, Complexity, and Democracy* (Cambridge, MA: MIT Press, 2000).

36. John W. Jeffries, Lebanon, Missouri, November 2, 1935. See also J. F. Lawrence, Hornbeck, Louisiana, October 1, 1935; Earle A. Brooks, Northern (illegible) Highlands, Massachusetts, October 18, 1935.
37. L. J. Pederson, Boston, Massachusetts, September 30, 1935.
38. Don M. Case, San Francisco, California, October 10, 1935.
39. C. Arlin Heydon, Phoenix, Arizona, October 8, 1935.
40. Helen M. Heligman, Jefferson, Missouri, November 16, 1935.
41. Edward B. Lund, San Diego, California, October 15, 1935.
42. W. H. Brightmire, Indianapolis, Indiana, September 25, 1935.
43. Theodore C. Williams, Maricopa, California, March 30, 1936.
44. J. J. Sharpness, Thompson, Iowa, October 15, 1935. The idea of returning people to the land was fairly common. See also Milton H. Lyon, Daytona Beach, Florida, October 9, 1935.
45. Samuel Jefferson Hood, Matthews, North Carolina, October 2, 1935.
46. Paul Little, Chico, California, October 3, 1935.
47. Samuel M. Zwemer, Princeton, New Jersey, September 25, 1935.
48. General Lee Phelps, Indian Department, Wetumka, Oklahoma, October 18, 1935.
49. Charles R. Bell Jr., Anniston, Alabama, October 3, 1935.
50. "Report on Clergy Letters," Samuel I. Rosenman papers, The Public Papers and Addresses, Memos to Be Used for Annotation: China and Japan, Transportation of Munitions to Cotton, Box 34, File: Clergy Letters, Franklin D. Roosevelt Presidential Library, Hyde Park, NY, 13.
51. Harold Francis Branch, Tuscaloosa, Alabama, September 25, 1935. See also Albert C. Monkman, Gresham, Nebraska, October 22, 1935; Jesse C. Wilson, Palmdale, California, October 9, 1935.
52. W. H. Whitlock, Springfield, Illinois, October 1, 1935.
53. Hugh N. Ronald, Portland, Indiana, October 29, 1935. See also David M. Boggs, Anamosa, Iowa, November 25, 1935.
54. Lorenz I. Hansen, Andover, Massachusetts, November 7, 1935.
55. L. J. Powell, Washington, Illinois, November 6, 1935. See also J. M. Stambaugh, Charleston, West Virginia, October 7, 1935.
56. Frank H. Haydenfork, Chicago, Illinois, October 3, 1935.
57. Theodore Bauer, Des Moines, Iowa, October 24, 1935.
58. Perry F. Webb, Pine Bluff, Arkansas, October 20, 1935.
59. A. M. Harrington, Camden, Arkansas, October 1, 1935. See also Fred H. Wright, Long Beach, California, October 1, 1935.

60. J. W. Storer, Tulsa, Oklahoma, October 23, 1935.
61. Martin B. Quill, Waco, Texas, October 7, 1935.
62. Reginald Shepley, Princeton, Illinois, October 2, 1935.
63. Holden H. Clements, Brooksburg, Indiana, October 15, 1935.
64. "Report on Clergy Letters," 10.
65. James W. Hailwood, Grand Rapids, Michigan, October 14, 1935.
66. Kenneth Danskin, Lindsay, California, October 15, 1935.
67. Robert Ray, Arkadelphia, Arkansas, October 16, 1935.
68. William Hart, Dalhart, Texas, September 30, 1935.
69. Alan Brinkley, *The Unfinished Nation: A Concise History of the American People* (New York: McGraw Hill, 1993), 694–695; George McJimsey, *The Presidency of Franklin Delano Roosevelt* (Lawrence: University Press of Kansas, 2000), 139.
70. G. W. Austin, Lindsey, Wisconsin, October 1, 1935.
71. Walter L. Thompson, *U.S.S. Chaumont*, San Diego, California, November 5, 1935. He was not alone in finding support for the Townsend Plan in California. See also B. M. Collins, Ventura, California, October 9, 1935.
72. Jesse Marhoff, Los Angeles, California, October 3, 1935. See also Martin Luther Price, Dayton, Ohio, September 30, 1935.
73. O. M. Showalter, Emporia, Kansas, September 26, 1935.
74. A. Quello, Minneapolis, Minnesota, October 10, 1935.
75. Carl J. Nolstad, LeMoure, North Carolina, no date.
76. H. L. Thomas, Tampa, Florida, October 24, 1935.
77. "Report on Clergy Letters," 17.
78. See, for example, E. Albert Cook, Chicago, Illinois, September 27, 1935. See also Theo Andree, New Kensington, Pennsylvania, September 27, 1935; James V. Claypot, East Providence, Rhode Island, September 27, 1935 (letter located in "Church Leaders" file).
79. Clifford E. Hay, Philadelphia, Pennsylvania, October 12, 1935.
80. W. C. Cranston, Nashville, Tennessee, October 16, 1935.
81. R. B. Lee, Beaumont, Mississippi, October 1, 1935.
82. Kiddoro P. Simons, Pikesville, Kentucky, October 5, 1935.
83. George A. Percival, Menominee, Michigan, November 13, 1935.
84. Ernest E. Ventres, Rockport, Massachusetts, October 8, 1935.
85. Kenneth W. Moore, Trenton, New Jersey, September 27, 1935.
86. W. S. Thornton, Birmingham, Alabama, October 17, 1935.
87. Alexander Hood, North Fork, California, October 1, 1935.

88. Frederick W. Hatch, Santa Monica, California, October 2, 1935.
89. Harry N. Young, Medford, Oregon, November 9, 1935.
90. J. R. Griffith, Birmingham, Alabama, November 6, 1935.
91. See, among many others, Wayne S. Cole, *Roosevelt and the Isolationists, 1932–1945* (Lincoln: University of Nebraska Press, 1983); William E. Kinsella Jr., *Leadership in Isolation: FDR and the Origins of the Second World War* (Cambridge, MA: Schenkman, 1978).
92. Walter F. Troeger, Santa Monica, California, September 27, 1935.
93. J. E. Flew, Davidson, North Carolina, October 17, 1935.
94. William Lasley, Mt. Pleasant, Iowa, October 11, 1935.
95. Robert S. Sidebotham, Tiffin, Ohio, October 8, 1935.
96. Harold F. Shimeall, Topeka, Kansas, October 8, 1935.
97. Rolla Earl Brown, Akron, Iowa, October 21, 1935.
98. Winfred H. Johnson, Lewistown, Illinois, October 13, 1935.
99. Llewelyn A. Owen, University of Iowa, October 1, 1935.
100. F. L. Raney, Petaluma, California, October 12, 1935.
101. See Manfred Jonas, *Isolationism in America, 1935–1941* (Ithaca, NY: Cornell University Press, 1966), 141.
102. Charles S. Owen, Lockport, New York, October 15, 1935. See also Phillips Elliot, Brooklyn, New York, November 4, 1935; W. J. Briggs, Economy, Indiana, October 2, 1935.
103. Lester R. Minion, Polo, Illinois, November 9, 1935.
104. Ernest Baker, Elmwood, Nebraska, November 11, 1935.
105. Francis E. Stifer, East Orange, New Jersey, October 1, 1935.
106. Franklin D. Southworth, Little Compton, Rhode Island, October 31, 1935.
107. Father Bonaventure, Parnell, Missouri, October 19, 1935.
108. Paul E. Meyer, Baltimore, Maryland, October 14, 1935.
109. Charles T. McKay, Brooklyn, New York, October 6, 1935.
110. Basil Maniosky, Baltimore, Maryland, October 1, 1935.

Conclusion

1. Celeste Michelle Condit and John Louis Lucaites, *Crafting Equality: America's Anglo-African Word* (Chicago: University of Chicago Press, 1993).
2. Stephen Skowronek, *The Politics Presidents Make: Leadership from John Adams to Bill Clinton* (Cambridge, MA: Harvard University Press, 1993), 3–33.
3. See, for example, Warren E. Miller, "Party Identification, Realignment, and Party

Voting: Back to the Basics," *American Political Science Review* 85 (1991): 557–568; Paul Allen Beck, "Incomplete Realignment: The Reagan Legacy for Parties and Elections," in *The Reagan Legacy: Promise and Performance*, ed. Charles O. Jones (New York: Seven Bridges Press, 1988), 145–171.

4. Skowronek, *Politics Presidents Make*.
5. Obama is frequently compared to FDR. See, as one among numerous examples, Mark Hendrickson, "Obama Is the Second FDR, Not the Second Carter," *Forbes*, November 8, 2012, http://www.forbes.com/sites/markhendrickson/2012/11/08/president-obama-is-the-second-fdr-not-the-second-carter/. *Time* famously associated the two on its September 14, 2010, cover.
6. See Robert Asen, "Women, Work, Welfare: A Rhetorical History of Images of Poor Women in Welfare Policy Debates," *Rhetoric & Public Affairs* 6 (2003): 285–312.
7. The nonpartisan Pew Research Center, for instance, found that Trump's supporters were concerned with issues of diversity, especially immigration. See Bradley Jones and Jocelyn Kiley, "More 'Warmth' for Trump among GOP Voters Concerned by Immigrants, Diversity," Pew Research Center, June 2, 2016, http://www.pewresearch.org/fact-tank/2016/06/02/more-warmth-for-trump-among-gop-voters-concerned-by-immigrants-diversity/.
8. Robert L. Ivie and Oscar Giner, "More and Less Evil: Contesting the Mythos of National Security in the 2008 Presidential Primaries," *Rhetoric & Public Affairs* 12 (2008): 279–301.
9. See H. A. Goodman, "On Foreign Policy, Bernie Sanders Is the Democrat and Hillary Clinton Is a Republican," *Huffington Post*, October 30, 2015, http://www.huffingtonpost.com/h-a-goodman/on-foreign-policy-bernie-sanders-is-the-democrat-_b_8430036.html.
10. On the complexities of the Sanders coalition, see Jeff Stein, "Bernie Sanders' Base Isn't the Working Class. It's Young People," May 19, 2016, *Vox.com*, http://www.vox.com/2016/5/19/11649054/bernie-sanders-working-class-base; on the Trump campaign, see Jamelle Bouie, "What Pundits Keep Getting Wrong about Donald Trump and the Working Class," *Slate*, May 5, 2016, http://www.slate.com/articles/news_and_politics/politics/2016/05/what_pundits_keep_getting_wrong_about_donald_trump_and_the_working_class.html.

Bibliography

Ahlstrom, Sidney E., and David D. Hall. *A Religious History of the American People*. New Haven, CT: Yale University Press, 2004.

Albanese, Catherine L. *A Republic of Mind and Spirit: A Cultural History of American Metaphysical Religion*. New Haven, CT: Yale University Press, 2006.

Alter, Jonathan. *The Defining Moment: FDR's Hundred Days and the Triumph of Hope*. New York: Simon and Schuster, 2006.

Altman, Janet Gurkin. *Epistolarity: Approaches to a Form*. Columbus: Ohio State University Press, 1982.

Anderson, Benedict. *Imagined Communities: Reflections on the Origin and Spread of Nationalism*. Rev. ed. New York: Verso, 2006.

Andrews, James R. "The Imperial Style: Rhetorical Depiction and Queen Victoria's Diamond Jubilee." *Western Journal of Communication* 64 (2000): 53–77.

Arnold, Peri. *Making the Managerial Presidency: Comprehensive Reorganization Planning, 1905–1996*. Lawrence: University Press of Kansas, 1998.

Asen, Robert. "A Discourse Theory of Citizenship." *Quarterly Journal of Speech* 90 (2004): 189–211.

———. "Women, Work, Welfare: A Rhetorical History of Images of Poor Women in Welfare Policy Debates." *Rhetoric & Public Affairs* 6 (2003): 285–312.

Atwill, Janet M. "Rhetoric and Civic Virtue." In *The Viability of the Rhetorical Tradition*, edited by Richard Graff, Arthur E. Walzer, and Janet M. Atwill, 75–94. Albany: SUNY Press, 2005.

Aune, James Arnt. "The Argument from Evil in the Rhetoric of Reaction." *Rhetoric & Public Affairs* 6 (2003): 518–522.

———. "Reinhold Niebuhr and the Rhetoric of Christian Realism." In *Post-Realism: The Rhetorical Turn in International Relations*, edited by Francis A. Beer and Robert Hariman, 75–93. East Lansing: Michigan State University Press, 1996.

Balthrop, V. William. "Culture, Myth, and Ideology as Public Argument: An Interpretation of the Ascent and Demise of 'Southern Culture.'" *Communication Monographs* 51 (1984): 339–352.

Baskerville, Stephen W., and Ralph Willett, eds. *Nothing Else to Fear: New Perspectives on America in the Thirties*. Manchester: Manchester University Press, 1985.

Beasley, Maurine Hoffman. *Eleanor Roosevelt and the Media: A Public Quest for Self-Fulfillment*. Champaign: University of Illinois Press, 1987.

Beasley, Vanessa. *You, the People: American National Identity in Presidential Rhetoric*. College Station: Texas A&M University Press, 2003.

Beck, Paul Allen. "Incomplete Realignment: The Reagan Legacy for Parties and Elections." In *The Reagan Legacy: Promise and Performance*, edited by Charles O. Jones, 145–171. New York: Seven Bridges Press, 1988.

Béland, Daniel. *Social Security: History and Politics from the New Deal to the Privatization Debate*. Lawrence: University Press of Kansas, 2005.

Bellah, Robert Neeley. *The Broken Covenant: American Civil Religion in Time of Trial*. Chicago: University of Chicago Press, 1992.

Bently, J. H. "Myths, Wagers, and Some Implications of World History." *Journal of World History* 16 (2005): 51–82.

Bercovitch, Sacvan. *The American Jeremiad*. Madison: University of Wisconsin Press, 1978.

———. *The Rites of Assent: Transformation in the Symbolic Construction of America*. Madison: University of Wisconsin Press, 1978.

Best, Gary Dean. *The Critical Press and the New Deal: The Press versus Presidential Power, 1933–1938*. Westport, CT: Praeger, 1993.

Black, Allida Mae. *Casting Her Own Shadow: Eleanor Roosevelt and the Shaping of Postwar Liberalism*. New York: Columbia University Press, 1996.

Boer, Roland. *Myth: On the Use and Abuse of Biblical Themes*. Durham, NC: Duke University Press, 2009.

Bohman, James. *Public Deliberation: Pluralism, Complexity, and Democracy*. Cambridge, MA: MIT Press, 2000.

Bonom, Patricia U. *Under the Cope of Heaven: Religion, Society, and Politics in Colonial America*. New York: Oxford University Press, 2003.

Bordo, Michael D., Claudia Goldin, and Eugene N. White, eds. *The Defining Moment: The Great Depression and the American Economy in the Twentieth Century*. Chicago: University of Chicago Press, 2007.

Bosmajian, Haig A. "The Rhetoric of Martin Luther King's Letter from Birmingham Jail." *Midwestern Quarterly* 8 (1967): 127–143.

Bostdorff, Denise M. "George W. Bush's Post–September 11 Rhetoric of Covenant Renewal: Upholding the Faith of the Greatest Generation." *Quarterly Journal of Speech* 89 (2003): 293–319.

Bottici, Chiara. *A Philosophy of Political Myth*. New York: Cambridge University Press, 2010.

Bottici, Chiara, and Benoit Challard. *The Myth of the Clash of Civilizations*. New York: Routledge, 2010.

Brehm, John. *The Phantom Respondents: Opinion Surveys and Political Representation*. Ann Arbor: University of Michigan Press, 1993.

Brinkley, Alan. *The Unfinished Nation: A Concise History of the American People*. New York: McGraw Hill, 1993.

———. *Voices of Protest: Huey Long, Father Coughlin, and the Great Depression*. New York: Vintage, 1981.

Browne, Stephen H. "Edmund Burke's Letter to a Noble Lord: A Textual Study in Political Philosophy and Rhetorical Action." *Communication Monographs* 55 (1988): 215–229.

———. "The Pastoral Voice in John Dickinson's First Letter from a Farmer in Pennsylvania." *Quarterly Journal of Speech* 76 (1990): 46–57.

Bruner, David. *Herbert Hoover: A Public Life*. New York: Alfred A. Knopf, 1979.

Burke, Kenneth. *A Grammar of Motives*. Berkeley: University of California Press, 1969.

———. *Language as Symbolic Action: Essays on Life, Literature, and Method*. Berkeley: University of California Press, 1966.

———. *A Rhetoric of Motives*. Berkeley: University of California Press, 1969.

Burnham, Walter Dean. *Critical Elections and the Mainsprings of American Politics*. New York: Norton, 1970.

Burns, James MacGregor. *Roosevelt: The Lion and the Fox, 1882–1940*. New York: Harcourt, Brace, Jovanovich, 1956.

Camargo, Martin. "Epistolary Rhetoric." In *Encyclopedia of Rhetoric*, edited by Thomas O. Sloane, 257–261. New York: Oxford University Press, 2001.

Carey, Brycchan. *From Peace to Freedom: Quaker Rhetoric and the Birth of American Antislavery, 1657–1761*. New Haven, CT: Yale University Press, 2012.

Carlson, A. C. "Character Invention in the Letters of Maimie Pinzer." *Communication Quarterly* 43 (1995): 408–419.

Carney, Zoe Hess, and Mary E. Stuckey. "The World as the American Frontier: Racialized Presidential War Rhetoric." *Southern Communication Journal* 80 (2015): 163–188.

Carpenter, Daniel P. *The Forging of Bureaucratic Autonomy: Reputations, Networks, and Policy Innovation in Executive Agencies, 1862–1928*. Princeton, NJ: Princeton University Press, 2001.

Carpenter, Ronald C. "The Historical Jeremiad as Rhetorical Genre." In *Form and Genre: Shaping Rhetorical Action*, edited by Karlyn Kohrs Campbell and Kathleen Hall Jamieson, 103–117. Falls Church, VA: Speech Communication Association, 1981.

———. "Frederick Jackson Turner and the Rhetorical Impact of the Frontier Thesis." *Quarterly Journal of Speech* 63, no. 2 (1977): 117–129.

Carpenter, Ronald H. "America's Tragic Metaphor: Our Twentieth-Century Combatants as Frontiersmen." *Quarterly Journal of Speech* 76 (1990): 1–22.

Cashman, Sean David. *America Ascendant: From Theodore Roosevelt to FDR in the Century of American Power*. New York: NYU Press, 1998.

Ceccarelli, Leah. *On the Frontier of Science: An American Rhetoric of Exploration and Exploitation*. East Lansing: Michigan State University Press, 2013.

Chambers, Simone. "Behind Closed Doors: Publicity, Secrecy, and the Quality of Deliberation." *Journal of Political Philosophy* 12 (2004): 389–410.

Charland, Maurice. "Constitutive Rhetoric: The Case of the 'Peuple Quebecois.'" *Quarterly Journal of Speech* 73 (1987): 135–150.

Chubb, Jerome M., William H. Flanigan, and Nancy H. Zingate. *Partisan Realignment: Voters, Parties, and Government in American History*. Beverly Hills, CA: Sage, 1980.

Clarke, Lynn. "Contesting Definitional Authority in the Collective." *Quarterly Journal of*

Speech 91 (2005): 1–36.

Classen, C. Joachim. "St. Paul's Epistles and Ancient Greek and Roman Rhetoric." *Rhetorica* 10 (1992): 319–344.

Cohen, Adam Seth. *Nothing to Fear: FDR's Inner Circle and the Hundred Days That Created Modern America.* New York: Penguin, 2009.

Cole, Wayne S. *Roosevelt and the Isolationists, 1932–1945.* Lincoln: University of Nebraska Press, 1983.

Condit, Celeste Michelle, and John Louis Lucaites. *Crafting Equality: America's Anglo-African Word.* Chicago: University of Chicago Press, 1993.

Crick, Nathan. *Democracy and Rhetoric: John Dewey on the Arts of Becoming.* Columbia: University of South Carolina Press, 2012.

Cronin, Thomas E., and Michael A. Genovese. *The Paradoxes of the American Presidency.* New York: Oxford University Press, 1998.

Darsey, James. *The Prophetic Tradition and Radical Rhetoric in America.* Albany: SUNY Press, 1999.

Daughton, Suzanne M. "Metaphorical Transcendence: Images of the Holy War in Franklin D. Roosevelt's First Inaugural." *Quarterly Journal of Speech* 79 (1993): 427–446.

Day, Robert Adams. *Told in Letters: Epistolary Fiction before Richardson.* Ann Arbor: University of Michigan Press, 1966.

Delgado, Fernando. "Rigoberta Menchú and Testimonial Discourse: Collectivist Rhetoric and Rhetorical Criticism." *World Communication* 28 (1999): 17–29.

Deneen, Patrick J. *Democratic Faith.* Princeton, NJ: Princeton University Press, 2005.

DeSantis, Alan. "Selling the American Dream Myth to Black Southerners: The Chicago *Defender* and the Great Migration of 1915–1919." *Western Journal of Communication* 62 (1998): 474–511.

Dewey, John. *A Common Faith.* New Haven, CT: Yale University Press, 1934.

———. *The Public and Its Problems: An Essay in Political Inquiry.* New York: Henry Holt, 1927.

Dickenson, Greg, Brian L. Ott, and Eric Ioki. "Memory and Myth at the Buffalo Bill Museum." *Western Journal of Communication* 69 (2005): 85–108.

Dippie, Brian W. *Custer's Last Stand: The Anatomy of an American Myth.* Lincoln: University of Nebraska Press, 1976.

———. *The Vanishing American: White Attitudes and U.S. Indian Policy.* Lawrence: University Press of Kansas, 1982.

Dorsey, Leroy G. "The Frontier Myth and Presidential Rhetoric: Theodore Roosevelt's

Campaign for Conservation." *Western Journal of Communication* 59 (1995): 1–19.

———. "Managing Women's Equality: Theodore Roosevelt, the Frontier Myth, and the Modern Woman." *Rhetoric & Public Affairs* 16 (2013): 423–456.

———. "Sailing into the 'Wondrous Now': The Myth of the American Navy's World Cruise." *Quarterly Journal of Speech* 83 (1997): 447–465.

Dorsey, Leroy, and Rachel M. Harlow. "'We Want Americans Pure and Simple': Theodore Roosevelt and the Myth of Americanism." *Rhetoric & Public Affairs* 6 (2003): 55–78.

Downey, Kirstin. *The Woman behind the New Deal: The Life and Legacy of Frances Perkins—Social Security, Unemployment Insurance, and the Minimum Wage*. New York: Anchor, 2009.

Drinnon, Richard. *Facing West: The Metaphysics of Indian Hating and Empire Building*. Norman: University of Oklahoma Press, 1997.

Drury, Jeffrey P. Mehltretter. *Speaking with the People's Voice: How Presidents Invoke Public Opinion*. College Station: Texas A&M University Press, 2014.

Earle, Rebecca, ed. *Epistolary Selves: Letters and Letter-Writers, 1600–1945*. Burlington, VT: Ashgate, 1999.

Edwards, Janis L., and Carol K. Winkler. "Representative Form and the Visual Ideograph: The Iwo Jima Image in Editorial Cartoons." *Quarterly Journal of Speech* 83 (1997): 289–310.

Eisensach, Eldon. *Sacred Discourse and American Nationality*. Lanham, MD: Rowman and Littlefield, 2013.

Eliade, Mircea. *Myth and Reality*. New York: Harper and Row, 1963.

Fahnestock, Jeanne. *Rhetorical Style: The Uses of Language in Persuasion*. New York: Oxford University Press, 2011.

Farrell, Thomas B. *Norms of Rhetorical Culture*. New Haven, CT: Yale University Press, 1993.

Fineman, Ronald L. *Twilight of Progressivism: The Western Republican Senators and the New Deal*. Baltimore: Johns Hopkins University Press, 1981.

Finnegan, Cara. "FSA Photography and the New Deal Visual Culture." In *American Rhetoric in the New Deal Era, 1932–1945*, edited by Thomas W. Benson, 115–155. East Lansing: Michigan State University Press, 2006.

———. *Picturing Poverty: Print Culture and FSA Photography*. Washington, DC: Smithsonian, 2003.

Fisher, Walter R. *Human Communication as Narration: Toward a Philosophy of Reason, Value, and Action*. Columbia: University of South Carolina Press, 1989.

———. "Narration as a Human Communication Paradigm: The Case of Public Moral Argument." *Communications Monographs* 51 (1984): 1–22.

———. "Reaffirmation and Subversion of the American Dream." *Quarterly Journal of Speech* 59 (1973): 160–167.

Flynn, John T. *Country Squire in the White House.* New York: Doubleday, 1940.

Frank, David A. "The Prophetic Voice and the Face of the Other in Barack Obama's 'A More Perfect Union' Address, March 18, 2008." *Rhetoric & Public Affairs* 12 (2009): 167–194.

Fried, Albert. *FDR and His Enemies.* New York: St. Martin's Press, 1999.

Fulkerson, Richard P. "The Public Letter as a Rhetorical Form: Structure, Logic, and Style in King's 'Letter from Birmingham Jail.'" *Quarterly Journal of Speech* 65 (1979): 121–136.

Gans, Herbert J. "Positive Functions of the Undeserving Poor: Uses of the Underclass in America." *Politics & Society* 22 (1994): 269–283.

Gastil, John, Don Braman, Dan Kahan, and Paul Slovic. "The Cultural Orientation of Mass Political Opinion." *PS* 44, no. 4 (October 2011): 711–714.

Gerber, Robin. *Leadership the Eleanor Roosevelt Way: Timeless Strategies from the First Lady of Courage.* New York: Penguin, 2003.

Gerring, John. *Party Ideologies in America, 1828–1996.* New York: Cambridge University Press, 1998.

Girard, René. *The Scapegoat.* Baltimore: Johns Hopkins University Press, 1989.

Golway, Terry. *Together We Cannot Fail: FDR and the American Presidency in Time of Crisis.* Napierville, IL: Sourcebooks, 2009.

Goodin, Robert E. "How Can Deliberative Democracy Get a Grip?" *Political Quarterly* 83 (2012): 806–813.

Gould, Lewis L. *The Modern American Presidency.* Lawrence: University Press of Kansas, 2009.

Greene, Ronald Walter. "Another Materialist Rhetoric." *Critical Studies in Mass Communication* 15 (1998): 21–40.

Greer, Thomas A. *What Roosevelt Thought: The Social and Political Ideas of Franklin D. Roosevelt.* East Lansing: Michigan State University Press, 1958.

Gring-Pemble, Lisa M. "'Are We Going to Now Govern by Anecdote?': Rhetorical Constructions of Welfare Recipients in Congressional Hearings, Debates, and Legislation, 1992–1996." *Quarterly Journal of Speech* 87 (2001): 341–365.

———. "Writing Themselves into Consciousness: Creating a Rhetorical Bridge between the Public and Private Spheres." *Quarterly Journal of Speech* 84 (1998): 41–61.

Guinsburg, Thomas N. *The Pursuit of Isolationism in the United States Senate from Versailles to Pearl Harbor*. New York: Garland, 1982.

Gustafson, Merlin. "Franklin D. Roosevelt and His Protestant Constituency." *Journal of Church and State* 35 (1993): 285–297.

———, "The President's Mail," *Presidential Studies Quarterly* 8 (1978): 36–44.

Gustafson, Merlin, and Jerry Rosenberg. "The Faith of Franklin D. Roosevelt." *Presidential Studies Quarterly* 19 (1989): 559–566.

Gustainis, J. Justin. "John F. Kennedy and the Green Berets: The Rhetorical Use of the Hero Myth." *Communication Studies* 40 (1989): 41–53.

Hammerback, John C., and Richard J. Jensen. "History and Culture as Rhetorical Constraints: Cesar Chavez's Letters from Delano." In *Doing Rhetorical History: Concepts and Cases,* edited by Kathleen J. Turner, 207–220. Tuscaloosa: University of Alabama Press, 1998.

Hanson, Russell L. *The Democratic Imagination in America: Conversations with Our Past.* Princeton, NJ: Princeton University Press, 1985.

Haran, Barnaby. "Machine, Montage, and Myth: *Experimental Cinema* and Politics of American Modernism during the Great Depression." *Textual Practice* 25 (2011): 563–584.

Hariman, Robert. "Status, Marginality, and Rhetorical Theory." *Quarterly Journal of Speech* 72 (1986): 38–54.

Hartnett, Stephen John. *Democratic Dissent and the Cultural Fictions of Antebellum America.* Urbana: University of Illinois Press, 2002.

Hauser, Gerard A. *Vernacular Voices: The Rhetoric of Politics and Public Spheres.* Columbia: University of South Carolina Press, 1999.

Hauser, Gerard A., and Chantal Benoit-Barne. "Reflections on Rhetoric, Deliberative Democracy, Civil Society, and Trust." *Rhetoric & Public Affairs* 5 (2002): 261–275.

Hawhee, Debra. "Looking into Aristotle's Eyes: Toward a Theory of Rhetorical Vision." *Advances in the History of Rhetoric* 14 (2011): 139–165.

Heale, M. J. "The Role of the Frontier in Jacksonian Politics: David Crockett and the Myth of the Self-Made Man." *Western Historical Quarterly* 4 (1973): 405–423.

Heimert, Alan. *Religion and the American Mind: From the Great Awakening to the Revolution.* Eugene, OR: Wipf and Stock Publishers, 2006.

Herbst, Susan. *Numbered Voices: How Opinion Polling Has Shaped American Politics.* Chicago: University of Chicago Press, 1993.

Hicks, Darrin. "The Promise(s) of Deliberative Democracy." *Rhetoric & Public Affairs* 5 (2002): 223–260.

Hofstadter, Richard. *The Age of Reform: From Bryan to FDR*. New York: Vintage, 1955.

Hogan, J. Michael. "George Gallup and the Rhetoric of Scientific Democracy." *Communication Monographs* 64 (1987): 161–179.

———. *The Nuclear Freeze Campaign: Rhetoric and Foreign Policy in the Telepolitical Age*. East Lansing: Michigan State University Press, 1994.

Hogan, J. Michael, George C. Edwards III, Wynton C. Hall, Christine L. Harold, Gerard A. Hauser, Susan Herbst, Robert Y. Shapiro, and Ted J. Smith. "Report of the National Task Force on the Presidency and Public Opinion." In *The Prospect of Presidential Rhetoric*, edited by Martin J. Medhurst and James Arnt Aune, 293–316. College Station: Texas A&M University Press, 2008.

Houck, Davis W., and Amos Kiewe. *FDR's Body Politics: The Rhetoric of Disability*. College Station: Texas A&M University Press, 2003.

Houck, Davis W., and Mihaela Nocasian. "FDR's First Inaugural Address: Text, Context, and Reception." *Rhetoric & Public Affairs* 5 (2002): 649–678.

Howard, Victor B. *Religion and the Radical Republican Movement, 1860–1870*. Lexington: University Press of Kentucky, 1990.

Hurd, Charles. *When the New Deal Was Young and Gay*. New York: Hawthorn Books, 1965.

Inabinet, Brandon Michael. "When Pastors Go Public: Richard Furman's Public Letter on Slavery." *Southern Communication Journal* 76 (2011): 169–190.

Isetti, Ronald. "The Moneychangers of the Temple: FDR, American Civil Religion, and the New Deal." *Presidential Studies Quarterly* 26 (1996): 678–693.

Ivie, Robert L. "Metaphor and the Rhetorical Invention of Cold War 'Idealists.'" *Communication Monographs* 54 (1987): 165–182.

Ivie, Robert L., and Oscar Giner. "More and Less Evil: Contesting the Mythos of National Security in the 2008 Presidential Primaries." *Rhetoric & Public Affairs* 12 (2008): 279–301.

Jackson, Robert H. *That Man: An Insider's Portrait of Franklin D. Roosevelt*. New York: Oxford University Press, 2003.

James, David R. "The Transformation of the Southern Racial State: Class and Race Determinants of Local-State Structures." *American Sociological Review* 53 (1988): 191–208.

Jasinski, James. *Sourcebook on Rhetoric: Key Concepts in Contemporary Rhetorical Studies*. Thousand Oaks, CA: Sage, 2001.

Johnson, James Turner, ed. *The Bible in American Law, Politics, and Political Rhetoric*. Philadelphia: Fortress Press, 1985.

Jonas, Manfred. *Isolationism in America, 1935–1941*. Ithaca, NY: Cornell University Press, 1966.

Josephson, Matthew. *Infidel in the Temple: A Memoir of the Nineteen-Thirties*. New York: Knopf, 1967.

Kagan, Robert. *Dangerous Nation: America's Foreign Policy from Its Earliest Days to the Dawn of the Twentieth Century*. New York: Vintage, 2006.

Kantowicz, Edward R. "Cardinal Mundelein of Chicago and the Shaping of Twentieth-Century American Catholicism." *Journal of American History* 68 (1981): 52–68.

Katznelson, Ira. *Fear Itself: The New Deal and the Origins of Our Time*. New York: Liveright Publishing, 2013.

Kelso, William. *American Political Theory: Pluralism and Its Critics*. New York: Praeger, 1978.

Kennedy, David M. *Freedom from Fear: The American People in Depression and War, 1929–1945*. Oxford: Oxford University Press, 1999.

Kennerly, Michele. "Getting Carried Away: How Rhetorical Transport Gets Judgment Going." *Rhetoric Society Quarterly* 40 (2010): 269–291.

Kessler-Harris, Alice. *Out to Work: A History of Wage-Earning Women in the United States*. 20th anniversary ed. New York: Oxford University Press, 2003.

Kinsella, William E., Jr. *Leadership in Isolation: FDR and the Origins of the Second World War*. Cambridge, MA: Schenkman, 1978.

Kluger, Richard. *Seizing Destiny: The Relentless Expansion of American Territory*. New York: Vintage, 2007.

Kock, Christian Erik, and Lisa Storm Villadsen. "Introduction: Citizenship as a Rhetorical Practice." *Rhetoric and Democratic Deliberation* 3 (2012): 1–10.

———, eds. *Rhetorical Citizenship and Public Deliberation*. University Park: Penn State University Press, 2012.

Kovel, Joel. *Red Hunting in the Promised Land: Anticommunism and the Making of America*. New York: Basic Books, 1994.

Kraemer, Don J. "Identification and Property: Burke's and Lincoln's Ratio of Act and Purpose." *Advances in the History of Rhetoric* 11–12 (2008): 35–57.

Kuhn, Thomas S. *The Structure of Scientific Revolutions*. 4th ed. Chicago: University of Chicago Press, 2012.

Ladd, Everett Carll, Jr., with Charles D. Hadley. *Transformations of the American Party System: Political Coalitions from the New Deal to the 1970s*. 2nd ed. New York: W. W. Norton, 1978.

Lakoff, George. *Don't Think of an Elephant: Know Your Values and Frame the Debate*.

White River Junction, VT: Chelsea Green Publishers, 2004.

———. *Moral Politics: How Liberals and Conservatives Think.* Chicago: University of Chicago Press, 2002.

Lakoff, George, and Mark Johnson. *Metaphors We Live By.* 2nd ed. Chicago: University of Chicago Press, 2003.

Leeman, Richard W. "Speaking as Jeremiah: Henry McNeal Turner's 'I Claim the Rights of a Man.'" *Howard Journal of Communications* 17 (2006): 223–243.

Leff, Michael, and Andrew Sachs. "Words the Most Like Things: Iconicity and the Rhetorical Text." *Western Journal of Speech Communication* 54 (1990): 252–273.

Leff, Michael, and Ebony A. Utley. "Instrumental and Constitutive Rhetoric in Martin Luther King, Jr.'s, 'Letter from Birmingham Jail.'" *Rhetoric & Public Affairs* 7 (2004): 37–51.

Leuchtenburg, William E. *Franklin D. Roosevelt and the New Deal, 1932–1940.* New York: Harper, 2009.

Lewis, William F. "Telling America's Story: Narrative Form and the Reagan Presidency." *Quarterly Journal of Speech* 73 (1987): 280–302.

Lippmann, Walter. *The Phantom Public.* Piscataway, NJ: Transaction Publishers, 1927.

Lucaites, John Louis, and Celeste Michelle Condit. "Re-constructing Narrative Theory: A Functional Perspective." *Journal of Communication* 35, no. 4 (1985): 90–108.

Lyon, Arabella. "Rhetorical Authority in Athenian Democracy and the Chinese Legalism of Han Fei." *Philosophy and Rhetoric* 41 (2008): 51–71.

Lyon, Arabella, and Lester C. Olson. "Special Issue on Human Rights Rhetoric: Traditions of Testifying and Witnessing." *Rhetoric Society Quarterly* 41 (2011): 203–212.

MacAlister, Joan Faber. "Good Neighbors: Covenantal Rhetoric, Moral Aesthetics, and the Resurfacing of Identity Politics." *Howard Journal of Communication* 21 (2010): 273–293.

Maddux, Kristy. "Finding Comedy in Theology: A Hopeful Supplement to Kenneth Burke's Logology." *Philosophy and Rhetoric* 39 (2006): 208–232.

Maney, Patrick J. *The Roosevelt Presence: The Life and Legacy of FDR.* New York: Twayne, 1992.

Marback, Richard. "The Rhetorical Space of Robbin Island." *Rhetoric Society Quarterly* 34 (2004): 7–27.

Mayhew, David R. *Electoral Realignments: A Critique of an American Genre.* New Haven, CT: Yale University Press, 2002.

McCormick, Samuel. *Letters to Power: Public Advocacy without Public Intellectuals.*

University Park: Penn State University Press, 2011.

McElvaine, Robert S. *The Great Depression: America, 1929–1941*. New York: Three Rivers Press, 1993.

McGee, Michael C. "In Search of 'the People': A Rhetorical Alternative." *Quarterly Journal of Speech* 61 (1975): 235–249.

McJimsey, George. *The Presidency of Franklin Delano Roosevelt*. Lawrence: University Press of Kansas, 2000.

McKann, Dan. *Prophetic Encounters: Religion and the American Radical Tradition*. Boston: Beacon Press, 2011.

Medhurst, Martin J. "Argument and Role: Monsignor John A. Ryan on Social Justice." *Western Journal of Speech Communication* 52 (1988): 75–90.

———. "From Duche to Provost: The Birth of the Inaugural Prayer." *Journal of Church and State* 24 (1982): 573–588.

———. "Religious Rhetoric and the Ethos of Democracy: A Case Study of the 2000 Presidential Campaign." In *The Ethos of Rhetoric*, edited by Michael J. Hyde, 114–135. Columbia: University of South Carolina Press, 2004.

Milford, Mike. "The Rhetorical Evolution of the Alamo." *Communication Quarterly* 61 (2013): 113–130.

Milkis, Sidney M. *Political Parties and Constitutional Government: Remaking American Democracy*. Baltimore: Johns Hopkins University Press, 1999.

Miller, Gary, and Norman Schofield. "Activists and Partisan Realignment in the United States." *American Political Science Review* 98 (2003): 245–260.

Miller, Perry. *Errand into the Wilderness*. Cambridge, MA: Harvard University Press, 1956.

Miller, Warren E. "Party Identification, Realignment, and Party Voting: Back to the Basics." *American Political Science Review* 85 (1991): 557–568.

Murphy, John M. "Barack Obama, the Exodus Tradition, and the Joshua Generation." *Quarterly Journal of Speech* 97 (2011): 387–410.

———. "Inventing Authority: Bill Clinton, Martin Luther King, Jr., and the Orchestration of Rhetorical Traditions." *Quarterly Journal of Speech* 83 (1997): 71–89.

———. "No End Save Victory: FDR and the End of Isolationism, 1936–1941." In *Making the Case: Advocacy and Judgment in Public Argument*, edited by Kathryn M. Olson, Michael William Pfau, Benjamin Ponder, and Kirt H. Wilson, 127–160. East Lansing: Michigan State University Press, 2012.

———. "'A Time of Shame and Sorrow': Robert F. Kennedy and the American

Jeremiad." *Quarterly Journal of Speech* 76 (1990): 410–414.

Niebuhr, H. Richard. *The Kingdom of God in America*. New York: Harper, 1937.

Niebuhr, Reinhold. "The Christian Witness in the Social and National Order." In *The Essential Reinhold Niebuhr: Selected Essays and Addresses*, edited by Robert Macafee Brown, 93–101. New Haven, CT: Yale University Press, 1986.

Nugent, Walter. *Habits of Empire: A History of American Expansion*. New York: Alfred A. Knopf, 2008.

Osborn, Michael M. "Rhetorical Depiction." In *Form, Genre, and the Study of Political Discourse*, edited by H. W. Simons and A. A. Aghazarian, 79–107. Columbia: University of South Carolina Press, 1986.

———. "The Trajectory of My Work with Metaphor." *Southern Communication Journal* 74 (2009): 79–87.

Palczewski, Catherine H. "Bodies, Borders, and Letters: Gloria Anzaldúa's 'Speaking in Tongues: A Letter to Third World Women.'" *Southern Communication Journal* 62 (1996): 1–16.

Perelman, Chaim, and Lucie Olbrechts-Tyteca. *The New Rhetoric*. Translated by John Wilkinson and Purcell Weaver. Notre Dame, IN: University of Notre Dame Press, 1969.

Perkins, Frances. *The Roosevelt I Knew*. New York: Viking, 1946.

Peters, John Durham. "Witnessing." *Media, Culture & Society* 23 (2001): 707–723.

Peterson, Tarla Rai. "The Rhetorical Construction of Institutional Authority in a Senate Subcommittee Hearing on Wilderness Legislation." *Western Journal of Speech Communication* 52 (1988): 259–276.

Phillips, Kendall R. "Spheres of Public Dissension: Reconsidering the Public Sphere." *Communication Monographs* 63 (1996): 231–248.

Polk, Andrew. "'Unnecessary and Artificial Divisions': Franklin Roosevelt's Quest for Religious and National Unity Leading up to the Second World War." *Church History* 82 (2013): 667–677.

Rentschler, Carrie A. "Witnessing: U.S. Citizenship and the Vicarious Experience of Suffering." *Media, Culture & Society* 26 (2004): 296–304.

Rhodes, Joseph E. "Reinhold Niebuhr's Ethics of Rhetoric." PhD diss., Eastern Michigan University, 2012.

Ribuffo, Leo P. *The Old Christian Right: The Protestant Far Right from the Great Depression to the Cold War*. Philadelphia: Temple University Press, 1983.

Richardson, Malcolm. "The *Ars Dictaminis*, the Formulary, and Medieval Epistolary Practice." In *Letter-Writing Manuals and Instruction from Antiquity to the*

Present: Historical and Bibliographic Studies, edited by Carol Poster and Linda C. Mitchell, 52–66. Columbia: University of South Carolina Press, 2007.

Ritter, Kurt W. "American Political Rhetoric and the Jeremiad Tradition: Presidential Nomination Addresses, 1960–1975." *Communication Studies* 31 (1980): 153–171.

———. "The Myth-Making Function of the Rhetoric of the American Revolution: Francis Hopkinson as a Case Study." *Communication Quarterly* 23 (1975): 25–31.

Robertson, James O. *American Myth, American Reality.* New York: Hill and Wang, 1980.

Rosenman, Samuel I., ed. *The Public Papers and Addresses of Franklin D. Roosevelt*. New York: Random House, 1950.

Rosteck, Thomas, and Thomas S. Frentz. "Myth and Metaphoric Readings in Environmental Rhetoric." *Quarterly Journal of Speech* 95 (2009): 1–19.

Rothenbuhler, Eric W. "Myth and Collective Memory in the Case of Robert Johnson." *Critical Studies in Media Communication* 24 (2007): 189–205.

Rowland, Robert C. "On Mythic Criticism." *Communication Studies* 41 (1990): 101–116.

Rowland, Robert C., and David A. Frank. "Mythic Rhetoric and Rectification in the Israeli-Palestinian Conflict." *Communication Studies* 62 (2011): 41–57.

Rowland, Robert C., and John M. Jones. "A Covenant-Affirming Jeremiad: The Post-Presidential Ideological Appeals of Ronald Wilson Reagan." *Communication Studies* 56 (2005): 157–174.

Rowland, Robert C., and Kirsten Theye. "The Symbolic DNA of Terrorism." *Communication Monographs* 75 (2008): 52–85.

Rushing, Janice Hocker. "Evolution of the 'New Frontier' in *Alien* and *Aliens*: Patriarchal Co-Option of the Feminine Archetype." *Quarterly Journal of Speech* 75 (1989): 1–24.

———. "Mythic Evolution of the 'New Frontier' in Mass Mediated Rhetoric." *Critical Studies in Mass Communication* 3 (1986): 265–296.

———. "The Rhetoric of the American Western Myth." *Communication Monographs* 50 (1983): 14–32.

Rushing, Janice, and Thomas S. Frentz. "The Frankenstein Myth in Contemporary Cinema." *Critical Studies in Mass Communication* 6 (1989): 61–80.

Schattschneider, Elmer E. *The Semi-Sovereign People: A Realist's View of Democracy in America*. New York: Wadsworth, 1975.

Schiappa, Edward. *Defining Reality: Definitions and the Politics of Meaning.* Carbondale: Southern Illinois University Press, 2003.

Schlesinger, Arthur M., Jr. *The Age of Roosevelt: The Coming of the New Deal*. Boston: Houghton Mifflin, 1959.

Scott, James C. *Seeing Like a State: How Certain Schemes to Improve the Human Condition Have Failed*. New Haven, CT: Yale University Press, 1998.

Shesol, Jeffrey. *Supreme Power: Franklin Roosevelt vs. the Supreme Court*. New York: W. W. Norton, 2010.

Shlaes, Amity. *The Forgotten Man: A New History of the Great Depression*. New York: Random House, 2009.

Simons, Herbert W. "From Post-9/11 Melodrama to Quagmire in Iraq: A Rhetorical History." *Rhetoric & Public Affairs* 10 (2007): 183–193.

Skinnell, Ryan. "Elizabeth Cady Stanton's 1854 'Address to the Legislature of New York' and the Paradox of Social Reform Rhetoric." *Rhetoric Review* 29 (2010): 129–144.

Skowronek, Stephen. *The Politics Presidents Make: Leadership from John Adams to Bill Clinton*. Cambridge, MA: Harvard University Press, 1993.

Slotkin, Richard. *The Fatal Environment: The Myth of the Frontier in the Age of Industrialism, 1880–1890*. Norman: University of Oklahoma Press, 1998.

———. *Gunfighter Nation: The Myth of the Frontier in Twentieth-Century America*. Norman: University of Oklahoma Press, 1992.

———. *Regeneration through Violence: The Mythology of the American Frontier, 1600–1880*. Norman: University of Oklahoma Press, 2000.

Smith, David Michael. "The American Melting Pot: A National Myth in Public and Popular Discourse." *National Identities* 4 (2012): 387–402.

Smith, Gary Scott. *Faith and the Presidency: From George Washington to George W. Bush*. New York: Oxford University Press, 2006.

———. *Religion in the Oval Office: The Religious Lives of American Presidents*. New York: Oxford University Press, 2015.

Smith, Henry N. *Virgin Land: The American West as Symbol and Myth*. Lincoln: University of Nebraska Press, 1978.

Smith, Jean Edward. *FDR*. New York: Random House, 2008.

Snow, Malinda. "Martin Luther King's 'Letter from Birmingham Jail' as Pauline Epistle." *Quarterly Journal of Speech* 71 (1985): 318–334.

Sowards, Stacey K. "Rhetorical Functions of Letter Writing: Dialogic Collaboration, Affirmation, and Catharsis in Dolores Huerta's Letters." *Communication Quarterly* 60 (2012): 295–315.

Steedman, Carolyn. "A Woman Writing a Letter." In *Epistolary Selves: Letters and Letter-Writers, 1600–1945*, edited by Rebecca Earle, 111–133. Burlington, VT: Ashgate, 1999.

Stob, Paul. "Louis Brandeis and the Rhetoric of Transactional Morality." *Rhetoric &*

Public Affairs 14 (2011): 261–290.

———. "'Terministic Screens,' Social Constructionism, and the Language of Experience: Kenneth Burke's Utilization of William James." *Philosophy and Rhetoric* 41 (2008): 130–152.

Stuckey, Mary E. *Defining Americans: The Presidency and National Identity*. Lawrence: University Press of Kansas, 2004.

———. "The Donner Party and the Rhetoric of Westward Expansion." *Rhetoric & Public Affairs* 14 (2011): 229–260.

———. "FDR, the Rhetoric of Vision, and the Creation of a National Synoptic State." *Quarterly Journal of Speech* 98 (2012): 297–319.

———. *The Good Neighbor: Franklin D. Roosevelt and the Rhetoric of American Power*. East Lansing: Michigan State University Press, 2013.

———. *Voting Deliberatively: FDR and the 1936 Presidential Election*. University Park: Penn State University Press, 2015.

Sullivan, R. "'Classical Epistolary Theory and the Letters of Isocrates." In *Letter-Writing Manuals and Instruction from Antiquity to the Present: Historical and Bibliographic Studies*, edited by Carol Poster and Linda C. Mitchell, 7–20. Columbia: University of South Carolina Press, 2007.

Sundquist, James L. *Dynamics of the Party System: Alignment and Realignment of Political Parties in the United States*. Washington, DC: Brookings, 2011.

Taillon, Paul Michael. "'All Men Are Entitled to Justice by the Government': Black Workers, Citizenship, Letter Writing and the World War I State." *Journal of Social History* 4 (2014): 88–111.

Takaki, Ronald. "*The Tempest* in the Wilderness: The Racialization of Savagery." *Journal of American History* 79 (1992): 892–912.

Taylor, Charles. "Modern Social Imaginaries." *Public Culture* 14 (2002): 91–124.

Taylor, Charles Alan. "Of Audience, Expertise, and Authority: The Evolving Creationism Debate." *Quarterly Journal of Speech* 78 (1992): 277–295.

Taylor, Graham D. *The New Deal and American Indian Tribalism: The Administration of the Indian Reorganization Act, 1934–45*. Omaha: University of Nebraska Press, 1980.

Tirman, John. "The Future of the American Frontier." *American Scholar* 78 (2009): 30–40.

Trattner, Walter I. *From Poor Law to Welfare State: A History of Social Welfare in America*. New York: Simon and Schuster, 2007.

Troup, Calvin L. "Civic Engagement from Religious Grounds." *Journal of*

Communication and Religion 32 (2009): 240–267.

Tulis, Jeffrey. *The Rhetorical Presidency.* Princeton, NJ: Princeton University Press, 1987.

Turner, Frederick J. *The Significance of the Frontier in American History*. London: Penguin, 2008.

Vail, Mark. "The 'Integrative' Rhetoric of Martin Luther King Jr.'s 'I Have a Dream' Speech." *Rhetoric & Public Affairs* 9 (2006): 51–78.

Vatz, Richard E. "The Myth of the Rhetorical Situation." *Philosophy and Rhetoric* 6 (1973): 154–161.

Venn, Fiona. *The New Deal*. Edinburgh: Edinburgh University Press, 1998.

Vivian, Bradford. "Witnessing Time: Rhetorical Form, Public Culture, and Popular Historical Education." *Rhetoric Society Quarterly* 44 (2014): 204–219.

Waisanen, Don. "Toward Robust Public Engagement: The Value of Deliberative Discourse for *Civil* Communication." *Rhetoric & Public Affairs* 17 (2014): 287–322.

Wallace, Max. *The American Axis: Henry Ford, Charles Lindbergh, and the Rise of the Third Reich*. New York: Macmillan, 2004.

Wandersee, Winifred D. *Women's Work and Family Values, 1920–1940*. Cambridge, MA: Harvard University Press, 1981.

Watts, Eric King. *Hearing the Hurt: Rhetoric, Aesthetics, and Politics in the New Negro Movement*. Tuscaloosa: University of Alabama Press, 2012.

———. "'Voice' and 'Voicelessness' in Rhetorical Studies." *Quarterly Journal of Speech* 87 (2001): 179–196.

Weaver, Richard Mervin, Richard L. Johannesen, and Renard Strickland. *Language Is Sermonic*. Baton Rouge: Louisiana State University Press, 1970.

Weiss, Nancy. *Farewell to the Party of Lincoln: Black Politics in the Age of FDR*. Princeton, NJ: Princeton University Press, 1983.

Welsh, Scott. *The Rhetorical Surface of Democracy: How Deliberative Ideals Undermine Democratic Politics*. Lanham, MD: Lexington Books, 2013.

West, Mark, and Chris Carey. "(Re)Enacting Frontier Justice: The Bush Administration's Tactical Narration of the Old West Fantasy after September 11." *Quarterly Journal of Speech* 92 (2006): 379–412.

White, Graham J. *FDR and the Press*. Chicago: University of Chicago Press, 1979.

Williams, Mark T. "Ordering Rhetorical Contexts with Burke's Terms of Order." *Rhetoric Review* 24 (2005): 170–187.

Williams, Raymond. *Marxism and Literature*. New York: Oxford University Press, 1977.

Williamson, Larry A. "Bush's Mythic America: A Critique of the Rhetoric of War." *Southern Communication Journal* 75 (2010): 215–223.

Wilson, Joan Hoff. *Herbert Hoover: Forgotten Progressive*. Boston: Houghton Mifflin, 1975.

Wimbush, Vincent L., ed. *The Bible and the American Myth: A Symposium on the Bible and Constructions of Meaning*. Macon, GA: Mercer University Press, 1999.

Wolfskill, George. "New Deal Critics: Did They Miss the Point?" In *Essays on the New Deal*, edited by Wilmon H. Droze, George Wolfskill, and William E. Leuchtenburg, 49–68. Austin: University of Texas Press, 1969.

Wolfskill, George, and John Allen Hudson. *All but the People: Franklin D. Roosevelt and His Critics, 1933–39*. London: Macmillan, 1969.

Yarsinske, Amy Waters. *Rendezvous with Destiny: The FDR Legacy*. Virginia Beach, VA: Dunning, 2009.

Zarefsky, David. *President Johnson's War on Poverty: Rhetoric and History*. Tuscaloosa: University of Alabama Press, 2005.

Zelizer, Barbie. "Finding Aids to the Past: Bearing Personal Witness to Traumatic Public Events." *Media, Culture & Society* 24 (2002): 687–714.

Index

F

G

H

I

J